W9-CRK-646

OF UNCOMMON BIRTH

OF UNCOMMON BIRTH

Dakota Sons in Vietnam

MARK ST. PIERRE

UNIVERSITY OF OKLAHOMA PRESS : NORMAN

ALSO BY MARK ST. PIERRE

Madonna Swan: A Lakota Woman's Story (Norman, 1991)

(with Tilda Long Soldier) *Walking in the Sacred Manner: Healers, Dreamers, and Pipe Carriers—Medicine Women of the Plains Indians* (New York, 1995)

The characters depicted in this narrative bear a strong resemblance to their historical namesakes. While many of their actions and statements are carefully reported, their motivations can only be a matter of conjecture.

Lyrics from the song "Mule Skinner Blues" are used by permission. Copyright © 1931 by Peer International Corporation. Copyright © renewed. International rights secured. All rights reserved.

LIBRARY OF CONGRESS CATALOGING-IN-PUBLICATION DATA
St. Pierre, Mark, 1950–
Of uncommon birth : Dakota sons in Vietnam / Mark St. Pierre
p. cm.
ISBN 0-8061-3517-4 (hc : alk. paper)
1. Vietnamese Conflict, 1961–1975—United States—South Dakota.
2. Vietnamese Conflict, 1961–1975—Participation, Indian.
3. South Dakota—Race relations.   I. Title.
DS558.2 .S68 2003
959.704′3′0922783—dc21
2002035883

The paper in this book meets the guidelines for permanence and durability of the Committee on Production Guidelines for Book Longevity of the Council on Library Resources, Inc. ∞

1 2 3 4 5 6 7 8 9 10

To my wife, Tilda, in honor of
all her tribal brothers and sisters
who have fought and died in service
to the United States

CONTENTS

ILLUSTRATIONS

OF UNCOMMON BIRTH

PROLOGUE

AT FIFTY-FOUR, BEING ON CALL ALL NIGHT AT THE HOSPITAL WAS TORTURE. Two deliveries had left him exhausted, so it was later than usual when Dale got up. He showered and now stood before the mirror, staring at himself, wondering if he would do what had been on his mind for some time.

He'd looked for Connie in the other room, but she'd evidently left for town, taking the baby with her. He frowned at the face in the mirror. His hair was still thick enough, but gray; God he was getting gray. And these creases were getting to be canyons.

He tried to recall what he looked like when he'd last seen Frank—the angular, boyish face as it was thirty-five years earlier, before the war had permanently furrowed it. But then he realized, I don't have to worry whether Frank will recognize me. The thought pricked his heart.

Back by ten from checking his cattle, he threw a light backpack in the cab and settled in behind the wheel. His blue and gray pickup rolled slowly down a narrow dirt road that wound from the bluff where their small house sat past acres of rich bottomland he irrigated along the Belle Fourche River. On the valley floor he drove slowly past rows of irrigated feed corn; on either side they stretched straight and orderly into the distance. Their orderliness, the predictability of their growth, was reassuring, and in some way was what had brought him to this life.

He hated being indoors, despised the antiseptic smells of the hospital and clinic. At times he even resented the sick people who forced him there. He had sometimes followed the hatred back in his mind, back to some distant fear of the place where there is no light, no more day, no glorious sunshine like today's.

Water from a rainy spring lay in ditches and low spots of his perfect fields. Through an open window came a strong smell of slough grass, so strong and sweet that it caused him to stop his truck, close his eyes, and drink it in. In the darkness he could see Frank's face, and the Indian was smiling as he had thirty-five years earlier.

As he neared Bear Butte, his thoughts came fast, pulsing through his consciousness. He acknowledged, as he had hundreds of times, that solitary Bear Butte, rising tall against the green, shortgrass prairie, was a fine holy place for the tribes who had used it for thousands of years.

St. Pierre told him it's where the Cheyenne people were born. It is where their hero, Sweet Medicine, emerging from the womb of mother earth, brought them out of the darkness. Now it's crawling with tourists. . . . He wondered if any white person could understand what this place really means, that this is the most sacred of churches where Indian people come to speak with their creator.

Soon the spruce-topped "Bear" loomed high above the truck. Tied to shrubs and pines along her flanks were tattered cotton prayer flags, red, yellow, blue, and white, snapping in the prairie wind.

Damn that St. Pierre anyway, always talking! Always remembering some obscure historical or cultural fact and passing it along. When he's not doing that, he's asking questions. . . . It's really all his fault that I'm even on this road today; couldn't let sleeping dogs lie, had to stay on me . . . for eight years pursuing me with his tape recorder.

He was glad the work was over. St. Pierre would edit the book now and try to sell it. . . . After today he wouldn't have to think about "it" anymore.

The truck swung west, and the Black Hills filled the horizon to a hazy terminus north and south. In the west rose Terry Peak. Even from this distance he could see its once-proud shoulders were pockmarked from open-pit mining.

He remembered the summers when he'd worked deep underground in the Black Hills. He recalled suffocating darkness and thousands of miles of track, spreading like veins in every direction through the blackness, down ten thousand feet and more. Gold and money too often seem the white man's obsession, and the red man's curse.

The Sioux loved these hills for their beauty, their spirits, not even knowing what gold was. "They still love the hills because that is where they believe the rain-bringing thunder beings live," St. Pierre said. In some people's eyes it was their ultimate mistake; they'd never valued money enough.

It was gold that brought Grandpa, and his father before him. Immigrants from Norway. First at home, then in New York City, the gaunt face of unemployment drove them on, brought them here and molded them into hard-rock miners.

His grandfather had worked up from "mucker" all the way to night-shift boss, deep in the Homestake mines under the town of Lead. As a boy, Dale had seen how his grandfather died, coughing his life away. Dale thought of his own lungs and his own nagging cough—it was the only health problem he had—wondering, never out loud, about the two summers he'd spent in the mines before the war, breathing silica particles and radon gas.

In his mind's eye he could see the narrow streets of Lead, South Dakota as it was before he left for Vietnam. Drastically inclining upward on the narrow canyon walls were rows of shanties and run-down Victorians. Grime. A dusty narrow main street. But still, it had been a town. Now, mournfully little was left. The biggest mining pit of all had slowly swallowed most of the town—a pit so big that locals had always just called it "the Open Cut." In the years since the war the pit had grown monstrous, devouring forest, mountains, and whole villages.

Once on I-90, his horizon narrowed to the canyon formed by the Black Hills on one side and the "Race Track" buttes on the other. Ahead lay a burgeoning corridor of civilization, sprawling northward from Rapid City.

Amazing how people build . . . how every day Rapid gets a little closer to Newell, he thought. He'd always wondered about the red-walled rims of the pine-studded canyon, now filled with three-bedroom homes. He'd often imagined what it might have looked like in the old days, even before the whites came, before the Fort Laramie Treaty had ceded it to the Lakota "forever." A grim smile crossed his face.

Heading into Rapid, east of the highway, he could see the pastel blandness of the perfect rows of little HUD houses that formed Sioux Addition. He thought of apartheid and South Africa. An old ambivalence welled up in him, as real and powerful as a solid object. It was the misgiving he always felt about his own people and their treatment of the Sioux. How peculiar, he thought, that this little village of poverty sits here isolated, with no shops, no center, just a nonannexed neighborhood of Rapid, born of the deadly flood in 1972. Sioux Addition was no prettier than it sounded—just a place to move the poor Indians flooded out along Rapid Creek. Relocated here where they're not a part of Rapid City, not part of anything but the grinding flow of Indian/white history.

When the Sioux were no longer seen as a threat, whites had poured into the hills lured by Colonel Custer's exaggerated reports of "gold and silver in the grass roots." It had always struck Dale as odd, how white folks despite their extreme sense of propriety couldn't understand or recognize ownership feelings or property rights in others.

Of course he knew the answer; the explanation was as old as humankind. In South Dakota Indians simply were not always perceived as human in the same way that whites were. As a physician, Dale Nielsen knew the truth, and felt ashamed for those who did not. He got off I-90 and drove up the Lafayette Street exit into Rapid.

Passing Kmart, Family Thrift, and Wal-Mart, he noticed that the parking lots teemed with poor ranchers, and poorer Indians, all in Mecca this weekend, to shop and break up the monotony of their unshared existence.

As he turned south onto Highway 44, he felt a slight tightening in his chest. A part of him was wondering why he was doing this and another part was chastising him for not doing it sooner. He'd always let others pursue or acknowledge that friendship exists. If it was up to him, he'd have no friends. He guessed he couldn't blame anyone or anything for that, except maybe the war.

As his truck roared south he felt the heaviness grow, at times fighting with himself to turn back. Something put off for thirty-five years could certainly be put off longer . . .

Another recollection came to him as the yellow, pink, and gray Badlands rose to dot the horizon. As they were watching Al Pacino in *Revolution*, Tilda, St. Pierre's full-blood wife, had innocently asked him, "Who's fighting who?"

He had answered, "The British are fighting the Americans."

When she had asked, "Aren't the Americans British?" some small yet building insight had opened for him. Despite mission, public, and government schools, Tilda and her people had not been impressed with any white history. For her and her full-blood relatives, as for those of Frank Jealous Of Him, white American history was largely irrelevant. In their view white people came like a huge flock of camp-robber jays and took everything. Tilda had once told him the Lakota word for white man, *wasicu,* means "They take the fat." Beyond that, the rest of white history was not important or interesting. His recent acceptance of this reality had made memories of Frank more strangely poignant.

At the decaying reservation border town of Scenic, five Indians leaned bleary-eyed against the blue metal walls of Merrill's Trading Post. They held paper bags tightly in gnarled brown hands. Ravaged faces showed the slow death they were drinking.

The Badlands now spread out under a sky as blue as Dale's eyes. Jagged striped towers of ancient, fossil-rich mud surrounded tables of emerald grass. Brilliant red and yellow flowers of the prickly pear cactus dotted the land. Yucca with their spires of white blossoms lined the road's shoulders.

St. Pierre had told him how, in the days before the Wounded Knee massacre, whites had hunted and killed Indians with impunity, using deadly guns freely supplied to the Dakota Militia by Governor Mellette. Somewhere, back further into the jagged walls, was the plateau the Lakota call the "Stronghold," where frightened and enraged hostiles had gathered to dance the Ghost Dance and resist the white man's promise of extinction.

The Lakota spiritual resistance in 1890 had been short-lived, ending in violence and massacre. Yet in some ways it had never ended. Tilda's quiet question about the Revolution was proof of that.

Ahead, a large faded wooden sign said simply, "Welcome to the Pine Ridge Indian Reservation, Land of Chief Red Cloud: Please follow our laws." He fumbled in his pocket for the crumpled paper on which St. Pierre had drawn a map. Sadness filled him. A duty long ignored would be fulfilled, and it would hurt.

These people produced Crazy Horse, he thought. Now poverty and isolation were their perennial punishments for defying America's value system.

He knew the history too well. In 1868 the Lakota agreed to boundaries they thought the whites would respect because they had smoked and touched the pen and accepted a place where they could live the way they wanted to. But gold had brought thousands of miners. And cattle barons saw the unfenced prairie as another gold mine. In the 1870s immigrants were crowding Chicago and New York. Congress saw Indian lands as a way of turning these "huddled masses" into productive citizens. It was simply national destiny that the Indians would lose most of their designated lands.

He drove on, recalling the bleached sign's humble request: "Please follow our laws." He had never heard of a white person hurt while traveling on a reservation, although many whites still considered Indians a danger. Most whites simply avoided these roads. He knew few white men who gave a damn about Indian laws. He'd grown up with stories about white pastimes—like running down Indians with their trucks, beating them to death, or convicting them in numbers that crowded the state penitentiary. He thought about the request on that old weathered plywood and shook his head.

The rough-drawn map indicated Sharp's Corner, then Porcupine Butte. When he'd gone that far he stopped, studied the map again, then turned east up a narrow dirt track. The journey he'd avoided for thirty-five years would soon end. In these last few miles his memories of the army, Frank, and Vietnam took on physical form, became hard as the steering wheel in his sweaty hands. A spiral of tan dust ascended into the blue sky behind his pickup.

1

THE BATON SLICED CRISPLY THROUGH AIR THICK WITH SIXTY VOICES. ON three tiers stood the varsity choir, male and female, from baritone to soprano. All eyes were to the front, watching the balding, boyish-faced man's every subtle gesture. Some faces strained for control; others seemed serene. But their voices were united in common effort, to attempt perfection, to create that flawless blend, to see the choir director smile in shut-eyed ecstasy.

These students were the grandchildren of Swedish, Norwegian, German, and Russian immigrants, determined men and women who had followed on the heels of the military, wrestling with the stubborn land to create farms and industry on the great midwestern prairies. These early sodbusters, barely literate, united to build colleges like the campus of Iowa State University at Ames, proud enough to embrace the nickname "Moo U."

The varsity choir sang softly now, slowly building to a crescendo, cautiously, so as not to leave a voice behind. The alto built, then the vibrato swelled, until the vibration actually shook the glass doors of the recital hall and the floor until it traveled through the feet of the choirmaster. He smiled broadly at the sea of faces before him, nodding his head softly, blissfully, with the music. Then a serious look, a warning of impending change, crossed his round face, and Handel's *Messiah* was done.

The man beamed at his students. All had felt that brief moment of exquisite harmony. It was the reward that held their youthful energy captive for two hours every day.

"All right, so you've improved a tad," he chuckled. "But this is no time to let up. The Christmas Concert Series is fast approaching and there are a lot of people who expect to hear . . . ," he paused smiling, "what I experienced today." A cheer rose from the choir as they scrambled for their books and jackets.

"Don't get too excited: I've got two sonatas you haven't seen yet." A low groan rose from the choir. "One more thing. I need to have a final Spring Tour list to turn in to the department chairman; so if you cannot make the Spring Tour to Europe, please see me immediately. And take care of those voices!"

After the choirmaster neatly stacked his sheet music, he tied it into a package between leather binders, then tapped the thick bundle. When the plump man turned to descend from the podium, he jumped. "God, you scared me, Nielsen! I thought all my little cherubs had flown."

The six-foot slat of a boy said nothing until they reached the teacher's cluttered office. "Yes, Mr. Nielsen, can I help you?" Dr. Douglas Pritchard asked without looking up.

"You told us to see you after practice," the teenager said with a reticent smile.

"I did?" Caught off guard, the choir director sat nervously scratching at what remained of his curly hair, feeling the hot, middle-aged sense of embarrassment at the growing holes in his short-term memory.

"Yes, Dr. Pritchard. You said if we weren't going to make the Spring Tour to tell you, so I'm telling you." He grinned nervously, whirled on his heel, and headed for the exit.

"Oh!" The teacher took a deep breath. "Just a moment. Not one step further, Mr. Nielsen!" Pritchard jumped to his feet. "You've got to be putting me on. I'm counting on you, Dale. All I heard last year was how much you wanted to be on varsity . . . Now here you are telling me you can't go." Pritchard studied the boy. There was little to distinguish the face of this awkward teenager from the thousands of other undergraduate men who walked this campus. It seemed to Pritchard that most of the boys at the university arrived with the same large freckles burned onto their cheeks and noses by the same relentless prairie sun, and that this sepia band behaved as a gauge, fading away with childhood innocence just in time for graduation.

Dale looked across the room at his teacher. "It's not that I can't go; I could go, I guess; it's just that, I, ah, don't think I'll be in school next spring." He took a deep breath, relieved he had finally told somebody.

Pritchard now remembered that Dale was not in fact a child of the flat grasslands, but a South Dakota mountain boy, almost as rare in these parts as mountains themselves. The professor took another hard look. If there was anything that distinguished this boy's soul from the others it was the eyes, blue and cold. "Dale, I think you had better go straight to the infirmary. There's a war on! Or haven't you heard? You'll lose your student deferment and be drafted! Come on, my good man, you've become quite a tenor. With Kritzer graduating midyear, you're critical." Pritchard looked down, searching nervously with his chubby fingers for a string. "Don't make me beg."

After he tied the gold string around the bundle, he looked up. The boy's forehead was prematurely creased, and it appeared to Pritchard that his brain was just too large, the cranium extending slightly beyond the intelligent eyes. The earnest eyes reflected a brilliance and determination that humbled the professor.

"Begging won't do you any good." Dale smiled. Then his gaze dropped. "And I know there's a war on."

Again Pritchard studied the boy, noting his straight nose, thin lips, the strong, square chin, a thick shock of woolly, Scandinavian hair. "You're not going to tell me this leaving college rubbish has to do with the war. I thought you told me your dad was a school superintendent, not a farmer."

Dale thought for a moment. "He's not. It's not that I'm needed at home. It's just me . . . I haven't told my folks . . . you're the first."

Pritchard slapped the bundle of music onto his cluttered desk. "Spare me the favoritism, this is not exactly what I wanted to hear today." But when they had stepped out the door, Pritchard asked, "Do you have a few minutes?"

"Yeah, I don't need to be anywhere till dinner." Dale relished any opportunity to shoot the breeze with the "profs." So far that was the only thing he liked about college.

It was an early fall evening. The oaks, elms, and maples lining the five-acre commons were at the height of their color. Pritchard picked a grassy spot, pulled a handkerchief from his breast pocket, unfolded it, and sat with it in front of him. Then he reached into his jacket pocket and took out some green grapes, placing them on the cloth. Noticing Dale grinning, Pritchard said, "Don't worry, Mr. Nielsen, the handkerchief is quite clean." He motioned for Dale to take some.

The gangly boy sat, then pulled a single grape from the bunch, popped it in his mouth, and said, "You know it's strange: when I look at this campus today with all the trees changing, I get excited. It looks like the picture in the catalogue. I used to look at those pictures and try to imagine what college would be like . . . and now I'm thinking of leaving."

"College not what you thought it would be?" was all Pritchard could think to ask.

"Either college isn't what I expected it to be, or I'm not what college expected me to be; either way I've got a decision to make." He reached for another grape.

"And, of course, that means you would lose your student deferment and be eligible for the draft. Is that where the war part comes in?"

"Yes and no. It's not that simple. I think maybe some guys hide out in college just screwing off. They don't know why they're here; they just know that student status will keep them out of Vietnam and that their folks will pay for them to be screw-offs, to keep them safe. Sir, I don't respect guys who are like that. Maybe I'm old fashioned."

Pritchard held his tongue.

"Well, I figure if I'm not going to be in school becoming a veterinarian, I might as well serve my country."

"For Christ's sake, Nielsen, I'm a choir director, not an army recruiter." Dr. Pritchard stared at his wide-eyed tenor. "I'm not as out of it as you might think; I listen to all kinds of music. I've heard John Fogerty's song about "senator's sons" and "fortunate ones." I hear what you're saying, but to die in that illegal war . . . Do you really believe all that idealistic stuff?" Pritchard already knew Dale's answer.

Dale's voice was tense. "It's not 'stuff.' Do you think it's fair that rich kids who can afford to go to college should be hiding over here when poor kids go and fight our wars for us? Do you think that the Constitution provides special rights for the wealthy?"

Pritchard's expression changed. "No, I don't, but I'll tell you something. That's the way it is, and that is the way it always will be. Your going to Vietnam and getting yourself killed is not going to alter human behavior one iota. Oh, I hear what you're saying. I can, with a mental stretch, even understand what you're saying. But you're wrong. What good does it do this country, or any other, for the sake of objectivity, to have its best and brightest killed in war? Like ancient Rome, we have a powerful society fighting a small-scale, police action in a remote land. It doesn't require an all-out effort, so we send in the most replaceable element of our society. Wake up, my boy . . . We simply turn the poor and working class into gun fodder, the factory orders go up for the production of more death machines, and in the end there are big profits for the upper class. That's what you'll really be participating in."

Dale sat for a moment staring at the picked-over grape stems. "I don't agree with you, sir. Maybe I haven't thought or read about it as much as you have, but I am an American; I live in a pretty decent country. I like the idea of freedom, whether it's to be a Republican or a Marxist. Our allies deserve the same help whether they are white or Asian." He nodded toward the professor. "I happen to think the Constitution is worth defending, and our country is at war whether we like it or not."

Pritchard's face was red. "I'm not a communist; I like the freedoms we have . . . I'm not unenlightened either, and to set you straight, I don't know when anyone was 'free' to be a Marxist in America. I don't believe in the war. I am a teacher. I've dedicated my life to that. If just one of my kids comes home in a body bag . . . well, Congress, the president, and the military lobbyists can screw their self-serving interpretation of the Constitution!"

2

IN THE GLARING SUNLIGHT STOOD A FADED BLUE QUONSET HUT. BEFORE IT, facing the dusty gravel road, was a homemade plywood sign. Its hand-painted surface, faded by sun and wind after only a year, read "Head Start Center: Wounded Knee District, Pine Ridge Indian Reservation."

Off to one side of the metal building sat a small yellow school bus. In the distance were patches of ponderosa pine climbing the large hills, as much a part of the landscape as the yellow-brown prairie grass and the creek bottoms lined with cottonwood and ash.

Inside the fluorescent-lit rooms the teacher's aide, an eighteen-year-old Indian man, moved comfortably amid the laughter and glistening black eyes of two dozen Oglala Lakota children. He did not have the high cheekbones so identified with this western South Dakota tribe the U.S. government had mistakenly called Sioux. The young man's face was softer, almost oval, its color a light brown. These were the people of Red Cloud and Crazy Horse, and like them this young man's eyes were Mongolian, piercing black, and spirited. As he moved through the room, he would stop at a table, pat a child on the head, straighten a piece of their construction paper puzzles, speak a few words in the native Lakota language to the children he knew would understand or in English to the others. He was slender, of medium height, his movements athletic and graceful. His arms and upper body were sinewy with the kind of toned, young muscles that require little attention.

As if to spite the worn walls of the classroom, bright-colored papers hung everywhere. The young Indian man moved from student to student, his eyes occasionally glancing up at the clock as if something urgent awaited.

At three o'clock the man quietly signaled the children to get their coats. Some groaned; others squealed in delight. An older Indian woman came into the room. "Billy, I thought you might want this." She held out an envelope. The man tore it open and glanced at the check stub. "Pay Period September 15–September 30, 1967—Frank William Jealous Of Him, $180." He folded it and shoved it into his pocket.

"Thanks" was all he said.

As they climbed aboard the bus, a little girl in red-ribbon-bound braids turned to him, studying his face. "You goin' home Billy?"

Her teacher's faraway look broke for a moment. He gently dropped his eyes and said, "No, not right away, Ella, but I'm going to ride the bus with you anyway!" He reached out and tickled the child, sending her scurrying back to her seat.

The old Blue Bird bus roared to life, then haltingly rolled onto the main road. Ella sat fidgeting with the end of a long braid of hair while she studied her teacher, wondering why he had been so quiet lately and why he now stared blankly across the landscape of broken prairie. In the distance Billy saw small houses scattered among groves of pine and thickets of chokecherry and wild plum.

The bus stopped at weathered cottonwood log cabins, some of which, despite it being October, still sprouted green grass from their sod roofs. A few homes had been covered with chicken wire and stuccoed, giving their exteriors a wrinkled effect like flesh over ribs; others were one- and two-room framed shacks, covered with rolled asphalt roofing material or tar paper. Some homes had a hand pump outside. All had an outhouse behind; some had two. Many of these toilets were cabled to the ground to protect the occupant from the awful surprise of being blown over by a wind, so constant in South Dakota that only its absence was commented on. Here and there a chicken pecked at the hard ground.

One by one the children were dropped off, yet neither the barked greetings of dogs nor the scurrying of noisy chickens distracted the teacher from his far-off thoughts.

As the bus approached a lonely dirt track that stretched into the hilly distance, Billy stood and made his way to the front. "Let me out here, Ted," he spoke in Lakota.

The older man looked a little surprised. "What for Billy? You're a long way from home."

Billy beamed and for the first time since he had gotten on the bus, a look of mischief wrinkled his brow. "Oh, I've got something to do. I've got a ride back."

The rusting yellow bus, children waving madly from the windows, left the young teacher standing near the cattle guard and its sagging barbed-wire gate.

Ten minutes later Billy walked down a hill, thick with pine, toward a small reservation farmstead. The old log house and tin-covered outbuildings sat on the rolling prairie surrounded by trees and yellow sandstone outcroppings.

As he approached, Billy could see a familiar broad-chested Lakota man bent over in the tiny corral struggling to trim the hooves of a reluctant mare. "*Hou Leksi!* Hello Uncle!" Billy called out.

"*Hou Tonksi!* Hello Nephew! You come for that horse?" the gray-haired man asked without looking up.

"Sure did. Which one is it?"

"Well, I'd loan you Mickey here, but she's been having some foot problems and besides I kind of need her around the place. How 'bout that gelding over there." The man pointed with his chin toward a small shed in which a pinto gelding was standing. "He's cut proud and I haven't worked him much, but you're welcome to him. Keep him as long as you want."

Two hours later and six miles away, in a part of the Pine Ridge Reservation locals called Grass Creek, a tall, heavy-boned Oglala Lakota girl with a pretty face noisily bounced a volleyball against a small, rectangular two-room house. The clapboard structure sat at the base of a small grass- and sagebrush-covered hill. Behind the house was an ancient aluminum Gruman trailer. Only yards from it was a white Body of Christ Church no more than twenty-five feet front to back.

It was here that Billy's father, an Oglala Sioux full-blood, preached Pentecostal Christianity. The building lacked a steeple or stained windows and was poorly constructed. Its doors were old hollow cores salvaged from a demolished house.

Outsiders might think it barely a chapel, but like most things to the Lakota, it served the purpose and there was little need and even less money to make more of it. Barbed-wire fencing surrounded all of the buildings, creating a sort of compound.

In the center of the enclosure stood a square, brush arbor made from upright ash poles whose crotched tops held up rafters of smaller peeled pine poles. These were covered with a thick layer of yellowing pine boughs. A wood-burning cook stove sent its rusty pipe up through the fading needles.

Whap! Whap! Whap! the ball sprung off the palms of the girl's large hands, then off her fingertips, and again off her palms. She smiled contentedly.

From down the lane, toward the main road, Billy Jealous Of Him led the spotted gelding. He studied his fourteen-year-old half sister as he walked toward her, amused by the fact that despite the clopping sound of the approaching hooves, she never noticed, until an accidental glance in his direction startled her.

"Why do you have that horse, Billy?" she asked in Lakota.

"For you, Clynda," was all he said, keeping a straight face.

"I'll bet it's for me . . . Really, Billy, why'd you bring it?" Her high forehead wrinkled.

"Well, there are some things that Indian girls are supposed to know and one of them is how to ride a horse." Billy looked sure of himself.

Clynda grinned. "And what are the others?"

"The others . . . well, most of them should be left to other teachers," he laughed. "I borrowed this horse for a few weeks so I can teach you how to ride."

"Why do I have to learn that now?" Clynda first eyed the horse, then her brother.

"There are some things for a brother to teach a sister if our Indian ways are to go on. I mean, I've got to teach you things while I can."

The "while I can," sounded foreboding to Clynda, but she passed on it without comment. Just then the rounded door of the old trailer opened and a muscular boy, older than Clynda but younger than Billy, walked out.

"Hey, Congo! Clynda is going to learn to ride."

The stockier boy moved toward the spotted pony and patted its withers. He looked at the horse, then at his half sister and back at the horse, shaking his head. "He's really bony. Are you sure it will hold her up?" he asked in mock concern for the horse.

The young woman stared at the boy. "Well, it won't matter if the horse is too bony, 'cause I'm not riding that horse. I don't even like horses. Women today learn how to drive cars, not ride horses!" she said, stomping her foot on the dry ground.

"Oh, come on. You can climb on behind me and hang on. Then you can try it on your own! I'll teach you to drive next week." Laughing, Billy took the rope hackamore and swung up onto the horse's bare back. "Climb up or I'll come get you!" he said to the girl, who was now backing up.

Congo stood near the horse making a stirrup of his hands. "Climb up!" he said.

Losing the battle, the girl slipped into place behind her brother. Billy nudged the gelding in the flank with his heels, and the small, spotted horse sprang forward and up the sagebrush-covered hill.

Clynda, half-laughing, half-screaming, had barely fastened her hands around Billy. The horse dropped its head, and with its first violent and unexpected crow-hop her fingers pulled apart. Losing her grip on her brother, with each jerk Clynda slid further down the horse's backside. The little horse bucked and crow-hopped until Clynda landed with a jarring thud on the hard prairie. Her knees and palms ground into the dirt and cactus. She stood up examining herself and then yelled, "Billy! You did that!"

Congo's big frame shook with laughter. Billy's own shoulders shuddered with silent giggling. "You have to hold on Clynda. I can't do that for you!

"Well, come on, you can't give up that easily," he said before she could interrupt. "This time hang on! Sometimes horses don't know enough to stand still, and this is one of them."

"I'll bet!" Clynda stammered as she stepped cautiously toward the bug-eyed pony.

This time the pinto stood still, and Clynda hung on for dear life. It was while coming back down the hill that a slow motion slide off to the left took her down, ending in an uncontrolled roll.

Clynda's jeans were torn, and her left knee bled slightly. Billy was still laughing nervously when he jumped off. "I think you are meant to ride by yourself," he said, handing her the single rein. Sobbing gently but not willing to be humiliated, Clynda grabbed the horse's mane and used her considerable strength to pull herself up.

"Try to balance yourself and use your legs to hold on," Congo called out in English.

"Aggh!" Clynda groaned as the spirited horse galloped up the hill. She made it almost to the top before the horse won the battle and she landed in a tall clump of sagebrush.

"Go catch it, Congo!" Billy yelled, frowning while he shook his head. He noticed Clynda glaring at him.

Moments later Clynda reached her oldest brother. "I hate you, Billy!" she yelled.

He tried to calm her. "Oh come on, Sis, you'll get it. Uncle Ted told me this horse was tame. So at least there is one important lesson you learned today: Never believe anything you hear about any horse!" He put his arm around her and hugged her. "Seriously, by the end of the week you'll be a good rider."

"Or I'll be dead!" she said, finally managing a smile.

• • •

It was true. Every day of that week in October they practiced. Each day the riding was easier than the day before, and as the big girl became one with the horse, Billy's response changed from laughter to nodding approval. Clynda loved that week but continued wondering what her brother meant about teaching her things while he still could.

3

A BONE-CHILLING, LATE AUTUMN PRAIRIE WIND SWEPT ACROSS THE IOWA State campus. Dale pulled his collar up in a futile attempt to fend off the cold. The Student Union loomed ahead, its entrance and hallway crowded with longhaired kids in brightly patched bell bottoms protesting the Vietnam War. The mood was one of loud humor, more like a frat party than a protest. They held cardboard placards whose crudely rendered letters read, "Screw McNamara, Burn Your Draft Card!" or "Moo U ROTC Supports Murder in Nam! Out of Vietnam Now!" Dale had trouble understanding how or why so many of them were so damned sure they were right.

"Excuse me, I need to get at my mail box!" Dale said after waiting for the longhaired kid sitting on the floor to notice him.

"Oh, yeah, sure," the fuzzy-faced blond said with no apparent emotion, and moved only enough to avoid being stepped on.

"Some day!" Dale muttered as he twisted the tumblers on his mailbox. A smile spread over his face as he slid the first military envelope from the box. The sight of the next letter, in a familiar handwriting, removed the smile.

"Bad news?" A sunny voice called from behind him. Almost tripping over a pimply-faced protester, Dale turned to a pretty, fair-skinned girl, her blue eyes framed by a simple pageboy of blond hair. He blushed, quickly shoving one of the letters into his pocket.

"Ah, hello, Elaine," he managed.

"Did you get a letter from an old girlfriend?" her face screwed up in a teasing pout.

"Ah, no, I, ah . . ." Dale's voice cracked. Damn! he thought, Why can't I even tell a simple lie without making an ass of myself?

Noticing the discomfort on his face, the girl pushed her hand into his. "Come on, let's get something to drink!"

As they walked, Elaine looked up at Dale. No other boy she had known was so mysterious, so hidden; yet no other had a face that made his feelings so apparent.

The large cafeteria hummed with a thousand voices as the couple moved to the counter. "A Coke, and a . . ." Elaine nudged him playfully.

"And, ah, a milk shake." Dale snapped back from his reverie and the troublesome letter in his pocket. "Elaine, I'm not sure I have enough on me to . . ." He dug into the tight pockets of his jeans.

"That's OK, I've got it," she said, pulling her purse from her shoulder. "Let's sit near the heat duct." She pointed to the far side of the cafeteria. "It's cold in here!"

After threading his way through the crush of students, Dale placed the cups down on a cafeteria table. "God, it's crowded in here!" he said with irritation. Elaine didn't notice the crowd or the noise. She was thinking about the letter Dale had shoved into his pocket.

He pulled out the military envelope from his pocket, tore at it, then began reading it to himself. Long moments passed before Elaine interrupted him. "Hey! I buy you a milk shake, and then you sit here and ignore me! You're not that handsome!"

"Oh, it's, ah, from my cousin," Dale said matter-of-factly while the skin on his face blushed pink.

"I can see that from the envelope. Is it anything I can't hear?"

"No, so long as you don't mind hearing a lot of foul language!" He grinned.

"I've probably heard worse from the guys on the feedlot at home!" Elaine said, teasing him.

Dale began to read out loud.

> September 24, 1968. Cam Ranh Bay, Republic of Vietnam
> Dear Cuz,
>
> How the fuck are you? I'll bet the women on your campus keep you too busy to even think about biology!

Dale looked up grinning.

> That's certainly not a problem over here! There's nothing to take our minds off anything unless it's the damned dive-bomber mosquitoes! It's been a month since I've even seen a young lovely; at least a white one! All we have to entertain ourselves with is a pair of Kurt Gowdy water skis. This sixteen foot aluminum patrol boat with its Mercury engine makes one hell of a fuckin water ski boat.

The blush once more invaded Dale's cheeks as he paused to catch Elaine's reaction. She was grinning. "Go on. I've heard worse."

Dale laughed and continued reading.

> Things haven't improved much since my last letter. The rains let up enough two days ago to finally go up the river on patrol. We were on a routine night mission twenty miles up river when all hell broke

loose! We were still supposed to be well within our own area! But what the fuck.

Charlie opened up on us as we rounded the bend. We never expected it, although I don't know why the hell not, that seems to be the calling card to hell. I didn't have anything on but my shorts. Did you ever think about getting blown away with nothing on but your fuckin shorts?

The damn jungle was so fuckin black I couldn't see anything, just machine gun tracers flying toward us. McCarthy, that huge black man I wrote you about, grabbed the 50 on the bow, but he never even fired a shot. The fuckin bullet passed right through his neck!

Jesse was the biggest, blackest son of a bitch I ever met, but damn it, Dale, he was one of the best friends I ever had. Damn it, he just laid there, in the bilgewater, his eyes wild, the blood just frothing out that bullet hole. Fuckin McCarthy's eyes just glazed over and he was gone!

Dale paused, realizing a group of black students sat not twenty feet away. How odd it was, he thought, that his cousin had never even met a black before the army; now he was mourning one.

Lt. Salway grabbed the outboard, then I called in an air strike. It's as if they send this silly aluminum rowboat up the Mekong just to pull fire so the Air Force bastards can have something to shoot at.

The show was fuckin incredible though, palm trees and bushes blown sky high, the smell of burning napalm.

Yesterday I tried to write a letter to Jesse's mom, but as of yet I can't think of anything to say. It's fucked over here! Young kids no sooner come on patrol when their American blood gets spilled all over the deck. Some of them don't even shave yet!

Dale absently stroked at his chin and felt reassured by the prickly roughness of his own late puberty. He read on.

In your last letter you said something about how boring college is and how it must be exciting over here. Well, Cuz, I can't wait to get home and slide my ass into a college class. In fact, I'd like to be home, period. The kind of excitement we have here is the kind that fries your brain; makes you look and feel old.

Keep your ass out of here. Don't even THINK of putting your fuzzy little buns in a situation like this! Things I've seen, you don't want to see!

Dale looked briefly out the window to the drizzly campus. How does he know what I should see and what I shouldn't? he wondered.

> You stay right there in Ames, Iowa and get that degree. And keep writing. It's like getting letters from home is the only thing that keeps me sane. Keep in touch.
>
> As Ever,
> Jim

Dale carefully folded the thin paper, and, as if it were sacred, slid it back in the envelope.

Elaine quietly extended her hand, touching Dale's. His hand was damp. There was a faraway look on his thin face.

4

MOONLIGHT ILLUMINATED THE FLAT PRAIRIE BELOW THE LITTLE HILL AT Grass Creek. Except for the wind whistling in the barbed wire and against the eaves of the house and little church, all was quiet. Then between howling gales of wind, the sound of yelling filled the night air.

The shouts were in Lakota. "I don't care if you are hungry! I won't have you talking back. Now just get out!"

Billy and Congo ran from the cabin, around the back, past the outhouse to the tiny aluminum trailer. It was obvious to the panting boys, standing in the frosty dark of their little house trailer, that no matter what they did, it would upset their stepmother, Bernice.

Congo grinned sheepishly as the last of the screaming filtered in through the wind. ". . . and if you don't like it, Billy, you can leave too! We don't need your damned paycheck!"

The boys stood close. Each put a small piece of wood in the tiny stove while they shivered in the dim light of a kerosene lamp. "I'd just as soon kill her as look at her!" Congo's voice shook. "I've hated her since the first time Dad brought her home. And did you see Dad? Just like usual keeping his mouth shut."

Billy did not answer.

Early the next morning, while the prairie sky decided between gray and blue, Billy woke. The cold night air had invaded the old Gruman trailer through cracked windows and plywood patches. In the dim predawn light he stared at the frost stains on walls and ceiling, formed over the years by water and ice condensing on the blackened oak paneling along the aluminum ribs.

Outside, the earth was all grays and browns. Sparse prairie grass, coated with white frost, bent low before the endless wind. When the trailer stove was roaring, the teenager crawled back under his worn quilt and, with his empty stomach growling in protest, finally fell asleep.

At 7:00 A.M. Billy stood shivering in the old trailer while he added split pine to the fire in the woodstove. Slowly the fire built itself, sending a soft roar up the chimney stack. Like an army in stubborn retreat the cold air of late October began to give way. "Congo, you better get up." Billy reached over to shake his brother, now using his real name. "Matthew, you better get up, you'll be late for the bus."

"Jeeze, Billy, it's cold in here! I don't want to get up, and I don't want to go to school. It's too cold." Matthew spoke in Lakota as he rolled back onto his side, pulling the pile of frayed quilts with him.

"Well, you better get up anyway 'cause I'm not letting you skip classes." The older brother pulled the round cast-iron burner from the little barrel stove. He took a pan of ice water and placed it over the flaming opening.

"If you get up I'll make you a pan of U.S. Department of Agriculture Surplus Commodity mush, but I don't have anything to send with you for lunch. Unless you want some prunes." Billy pulled the covers off his brother, laughing at his own joke.

In the soft light of early day, Matthew rose from the swaybacked cot to tower over his brother.

He moved toward the stove, still in the clothes he had worn to bed. Carefully stirring USDA evaporated milk into his commodity wheat bulgur, he asked, "Well, if it's so important for me to go to school, why don't you go back, Billy? You could go to college and be a real teacher, like the ones at high school. Then maybe we could get our own place."

Billy hated the question, because it had no fine or easy answer. Quitting was something he hated in others and himself, and the truth was he had quit school for no reason different than most Lakota men—he saw no real purpose in it. Yet he did not want this for his brother.

As Matthew ate, Billy stared out a dusty window at his father's tiny Body of Christ Church that stood inside the cattle wire, thinking of an answer. Caught tight in the rusty barbs, faded cow-hair streamers snapped in the wind. "I told you before, I'm older than you. I didn't do as well in school. And," he smirked, "I didn't have a big brother to make me mush in the morning. Besides Dad needs someone to help out, and Bernice needs my Head Start check."

Matthew glanced up, surprised. Today's response had been weak, Billy's voice resigned.

Moments later the screen door of the main house slammed shut. Out stepped Clynda and a neatly dressed smaller girl, their black hair in perfect, ribbon-trimmed braids. Each carried a book bag and lunch box in gloved hands. "You'd better get going if you're going to walk with Clynda and Julie," Billy said, pointing to the road.

Matthew finished his cereal and then ran, coatless, to catch up with his half sisters. Watching the kids turn at the gate, Billy pulled a quilt over his shoulders. He shook the grates in the stove. As his brother and the girls went out of sight, Billy picked up an old guitar. "Gimme a ticket for an aeroplane . . ." He was still singing the Box Tops' hit when the little Blue Bird honked at the end of the narrow lane.

5

"GOD, I HATE MICROBIOLOGY . . ." DALE GROANED. FROM ACROSS THE BASE-ment bedroom, a towel snapped inches from the woolly tangle of hair on his head.

"What's the matter, Gail's letter give you the blues? Or is it massive attacks of puppy guilt?" his roommate asked while rewinding the towel.

Dale turned over to face his accuser. "For Christ's sake, Cliff, what the hell do you know about it? You try to act so cosmopolitan, but you don't even have a girl!"

"Ooh, you are in a snit!" Cliff taunted. "You've got two women that don't know about each other, one at home, and one here, and you're suffering over it!" *Snap!* The towel shot out again.

Eyes fixed on the cheap plastic light shade overhead, Dale lay on his side, silent for a long moment. "But it does bother me, Cliff. I know a lot of guys in my position would think it was great, but there must be something wrong with me. When I'm with Elaine everything is cool until I think of Gail. When I see Gail, or she calls, everything is all right until she asks me if she's still the only one.

"What the hell am I supposed to tell her? 'No, I've got this pretty farm girl I've been seeing.' I think it would kill her. I'm so tired of the games; some-times I feel like a shit."

"Well, for Christ's sake, don't shit in here. I'd probably get stuck cleaning up the mess!" Again Cliff's damp towel cracked by Dale's head.

Standing to protect himself, Dale changed the subject and asked, "Did you see all those hippies at the Student Union?"

"Yeah, what about them? They're just trying to express something they believe in . . ."

"Or think they believe in. They call the administration a bunch of fascists! I don't think they've even thought about that word. It's like the world and all the rhetoric in it is a playground for them. It's like crummy clothes and long hair give them some kind of special membership in a social club; a fraternity that allows them to know the truth about everything!" His anger built.

"God, Dale, you don't say much, but when you do it's like opening the door to a blast furnace." Cliff shook his head. "You may be right on about most of those guys, but that doesn't mean that they're entirely wrong. Two or three of those guys, those longhairs, are Vietnam vets!"

Dale turned toward Cliff with a look of intense irritation, shook his head, and shrugged. "You working the Football Banquet later, or just gonna practice popping that damned towel all day?"

"Oh, you can be such a bitch!" Cliff pouted.

6

THE RUSTED STATION WAGON SPED SOUTH FROM THE RESERVATION TOWARD Chadron, Nebraska. Behind the dented Mercury sank a blue-gray streak of greasy smoke. "I hope those other guys got there OK. Man, I can't believe you, Billy. You can't just tell the guys to find another singer. You *are* the band!" In the glow of the dash lights the older man poked the air forcefully with his index finger.

"Come on, Adolph!" Billy grew defensive. "I can do what I want. I don't have to answer to anybody." Billy pulled a small whiskey bottle from his coat and shook it toward the man. "As the Lord is my Shepherd I shall not want!" Billy shook the clear liquid, punching each word like a preacher. "Yea, though I walk through the valley of death I shall fear no evil, for soon, I'm going to kill Bernice." Adolph Hollow Horn could not help but laugh at the theatrics.

"Come on, Billy, slow down on that stuff. I'm still manager until you leave and you've got to sing tonight." The older man grabbed for the bottle.

"Relatives may give you a crust of bread and such but God bless the child who has his own!" Billy delivered in his best imitation of Billie Holiday. "And, Adolph Hollow Horn, I have some and you don't!"

The manager roared with laughter. "But Billy, I think the Lord has already given you enough!"

Screwing up his face like a preacher stuck for a quote, Billy said, "Well, my friend, the Lord giveth to each of us in our turn what we need . . ." He brandished the bottle. "Look at the birds of the air . . .," he pointed the mouth of the bottle skyward toward the stars, "and the lilies of the field . . .," Seagrams splashed on the window, "neither do they reap or sow and none are clothed as beautiful as that bitch Bernice!"

Adolph Hollow Horn knew better than to pursue Billy's last comment.

Even without encouragement the wild sermon went on into Chadron, Nebraska, clear up to the Chadron State College gymnasium. The manager's face hurt from laughing. "Let's go Reverend Ray, we're here!"

• • •

"Proud Mary" blared from the small speakers. The sound was tinny. Even the drum, emblazoned with "Sioux Playboys," rattled with a minor tear, but the band had rhythm and enthusiasm and the white kids gyrated to the tune.

On the floor close to Billy, two girls danced together. One was a tall, hawk-faced blond, the other a plump, sweet-faced brunette. Billy caught the eyes of the brunette and smiled to her as he sang and played simple chords on his electric guitar.

7

"DAMN IT, HE JUST LAID THERE, IN THE BILGEWATER, HIS EYES WILD, THE blood just frothing out that bullet hole."

"Dale, can you answer the question or not?"

Startled, Dale looked up from the letter toward the spectacled man at the front of the lab, then asked sheepishly, "What question, Dr. Cummins?"

"If you can tear your mind away from whatever it is that's more important to your future than this class, I want to see you later in my office."

Dr. Cummins had been one of his favorite instructors. Now Dale trudged up the long antiseptic hallway like some naughty sixth grader about to be expelled.

"Please have a seat, Mr. Nielsen," Cummins said softly, pointing toward the one chair that was free from the neat stack of papers and biology books. "You know, Dale, I've been teaching too long to think that my giving you a sermon is going to bring you back down to earth, so I'll come quickly to the point.

"Last year you showed me your potential. Maybe in some ways you were one of the best students I had. Your brains and talent are beyond question, yet this semester it's as if you send your body to class while the rest of you goes somewhere else!"

Heat began to crawl up Dale's back to form the dreaded blush. "I, ah, I am there, in class I mean, Dr. Cummins."

Cummins frowned. "That's bullshit, Mr. Nielsen, you are not there. I've seen that distant look on the faces of other students . . . What is it, son?"

"It's nothing . . ." Dale said to his paternal inquisitor. Then relenting, he reached into his pocket and withdrew the carefully folded letter and handed it to his professor. "This is what I was reading."

Putting on his bifocals, the middle-aged man pulled the letter from its envelope. He imitated the care Dale had shown the worn paper and read the letter with no outward response.

Finally he spoke. "So? What does this have to do with you?"

"Well, sir, it's just that, there's a lot of American boys over there being hurt and killed. I'm an American, just as much as those men or my cousin . . . We grew up together, he's not even a year older than I am . . . and here I am going to college."

"Because your parents think this is where you should be?" Cummins interjected.

Dale nodded. "Yeah, that's part of it. But my cousin Jim was always trying to protect me; I guess in a way it always made me feel younger and smaller than him. How does he or anyone else know what I should see or what I shouldn't? I'm just as brave, just as American as he is!"

"Dale, when you look at me you see an old man, but I was once just as young and idealistic as you are now. World War II changed all that. In it I had more than enough chance to grow up. If that's what you want to call what killing people does to a man. Certainly the ideology of World War II was much less fuzzy than this Vietnamese conflict, but all things being equal, they are both wars."

Cummins quickly finished the letter, then pulled his glasses off. "Dale, people really die. Dead patriots no longer care about the inherent right or wrong of war. Their mothers don't hug them anymore. They, as your cousin points out in this letter, are just dead."

Dale shifted uneasily in the hard chair. It was bad enough he had to hear this stuff from his cousin, but now from Dr. Cummins.

"I'll tell you one more thing, Dale, something you already know. If you don't get your head on straight, you're wasting your time here at Ames. We have one of the best pre-veterinary programs in the country, but C's are not going to get you into medical school, and you could pull B's in a walk! Even you have to pay the price, put in the hours, have your mind in the classroom, or you're wasting your time."

Dale looked into his teacher's eyes. "I appreciate your interest in me, Dr. Cummins, and your honesty. I only wish my dad could understand the way you do."

"Well, sir, you've taken the chance to be straightforward with me," the older man said quietly. "Try being honest with your folks." But Dale knew he had not been completely truthful. He thought of Gail and then of Elaine.

8

AT THE FIRST REDNESS OF DAWN IN THE EASTERN SKY, THE RUMBLE OF aged pickup trucks destroyed the perfect stillness. In the center of Porcupine Community stood a cluster of men and boys. Clynda stood there too; then she climbed into the cab of her uncle's truck.

Quietly they had slipped from their homes into the cool morning grayness. Some leaned against the idling trucks. Some of the younger boys carried only skillets and soup ladles; the older ones carried light rifles.

The conversations were subdued and efficient, mostly concerning the hunt and where the deer might be. This was not a sport hunt; on a reservation with eighty percent unemployment, it was a necessity.

Eventually, four trucks were ready to depart. In the headlights the boys could be seen climbing into the back of the pickup. Without speaking, in practiced precision, the hunters were loaded and gone. Their taillights soon faded to a formation of paired red fireflies over the brightening eastern horizon.

In the bouncing cab of the old GMC Apache, Billy nervously checked and rechecked the safety on the worn Remington. He seemed in no mood for easy conversation, so his uncle let him sit with his thoughts.

Ten minutes had passed when Uncle Sam finally broke the silence. "If that mixed-blood tribal council gets their way, we'll have their relatives as game wardens and we won't be able to hunt this way anymore!" The heavyset man's voice was tinged with resignation and anger.

"I suppose everything's gotta change some time," Billy answered in an extended sigh.

Clynda fidgeted between them. She spoke in Lakota. "Billy, why can't I ride in the back with Congo and Lloyd? They aren't much older than I am!"

Billy studied his sister's face. "Because I promised Dad I'd keep you up front. There's nothing more to it than that, Clynda, so I'm not going to talk about it."

Sam tried once more to get a conversation started, this time in English. "Don't you see, Frank, if we don't stand together, us full bloods are going to lose all our rights." It pleased the younger man that his uncle thought to use his real name. There was a growing part of him that no longer wanted to be Billy. Still, despite the older man's best effort, the dented cab again fell silent.

The tired truck rattled down a hillside. Occasionally, its bald tires would slide on a patch of frost or crusted snow. Ahead lay a narrow valley lined with leafless ash and cottonwoods, its bottom obscured in fog and darkness.

"So what you going to do with yourself now that you quit high school, Frank?" The graying man unnerved Billy with the question and the continued use of his first name.

"Oh, I'm staying out of trouble. Working at Head Start and helping Dad out with a few things, playin' some guitar and partying, I guess." He knew any attempt to fool the old man was futile.

"Hmm," his uncle sighed.

"It's just that I don't know what I should do. I'm tired of spending all day with little kids. I was thinking of going to Job Corps and learning heavy equipment like some of the other guys, but I'm just really not interested in driving trucks. Besides, Mike tells me he only works four months a year on that Bureau of Indian Affairs road crew, then they lay him off.

"He gets pretty discouraged. I think that's why he drinks." He ended the conversation with a squint toward a row of old cottonwood trees emerging from the mist.

At a wide creek bottom, alongside a grove of towering, gnarled cottonwood trees, Sam slowed the old truck, then pulled off the trail to the right making room for the trucks behind them.

Out of the open window Sam signaled with his left arm. Attempting to be quiet, the youngest boys grabbed their pots and jumped out of the trucks. For two hundred yards across the wooded bottom, they lined themselves out, until Sam was satisfied and signaled for the trucks to move ahead.

Like a row of short scarecrows, the younger boys were left standing in the cold creek bottom. The older boys with their rifles remained seated. Billy watched as the young boys quickly faded from view into the leafless trees. The metallic rumble of the trucks faded from the grove and was replaced by the excited whispers of the boys signaling each other to fan out before they started their beating. Clynda stood with them.

The four trucks soon split. Two forded the narrow creek bed, then headed up the pine-studded eastern slope. The old GMC Apache crawled back up the hill to the west. Billy turned toward Sam. "Uncle, I didn't want to say it in front of Clynda, but I've been thinking real hard about leaving Wounded Knee . . . soon."

The older man sat quietly, trying to pour Bull Durham onto a frail cigarette paper. Tobacco sprinkled toward the floor, blowing around in swirls, until it was sucked through rust holes. "Leaving to what, nephew?" the man asked, and licked the glue edge, sealed it, then popped the misshapen cigarette between his stubble-covered lips.

The two pickups on the eastern side of the valley now dropped out of sight over the ridge. "Oh, I thought about getting my GED and going on with my schooling, maybe playing ball for one of the state schools, . . . but to be truthful, the thought of going on to college scares me real bad. Don't tell anyone I'm leaving. I haven't told anyone but you."

He stared out the window. "I would like to have more education, even though I don't see much happening around here for the ones that do . . . I don't believe, like Mr. Emery used to tell us, that an education will lead to a job, at least not for us Indians!"

The valley dropped from sight as Sam's faded red GMC swung off the hilltop. One at a time the older teenagers, like Lloyd and Matthew, with their small-caliber rifles, jumped from the pickup boxes and made their way slowly back toward the ridge top.

"So what then, nephew, the army?"

"Or the navy," Billy completed the sentence. "I'm torn, I guess, because I'd like to be something someday . . . Maybe I'll learn something in the army that will help me make something better for myself when I come back. I have this feeling that sort of stays with me," he touched his chest, "that I was born for something, besides hanging around Wounded Knee and being a stepson."

The older man grinned at the boy's honesty. "I think you were, too, Frank. I know your dad feels the same way, but you must know folks around here are going to miss you."

Ten minutes after they had left the valley's rim, the lead truck pulled to a stop. Fifty yards later Sam stepped down on the emergency brake and set the shifter in first. The two men dropped to the hard ground that had recently been covered by a thin crust of snow, and began a careful crawl to the narrow crest.

This was the part of hunting Billy loved most, the slow meticulous movements, quietly stalking his prey. He always felt clearer when he hunted, like a warrior, or a cougar.

Even in the hunt Billy could not shake the thoughts that dogged him. "I'd have left sooner if it wasn't for being too young and for Congo. You know that woman Dad's married to makes it real hard on him. I'm almost afraid she'll starve him if I leave and she don't get my check. But something even worse is bothering me," Billy said in a half-whisper.

His uncle laid a blanket on the ground and slid onto it. "What's that, son?" he asked, indicating with his chin for Billy to take advantage of the blanket.

"I get these black thoughts, uncle, about killing Bernice and going to the state pen for a long time. I can even see the inside of the cell. What keeps me from doing it is Dad, the girls, and knowing that Matthew would have to go on alone living with the fact his brother murdered his stepmom." Sam's eyebrows rose, but he said nothing.

The rumble of the smaller boys banging on kettles grew in the distance.

Twenty minutes passed before the lead deer, driven by the younger boys' loud clanging, walked haltingly from the cottonwoods into the open. Soon there were three, then eight, and finally twelve. They moved warily. Conscious of their exposure, the deer sniffed loudly as they walked. Delicate legs moving slowly, brown eyes peering back. What was about to transpire was one of the oldest tricks in mankind's repertoire. A full minute passed while Billy studied the animals through his sight. He picked a four-point buck near the front, signaling to his uncle.

"Hold it, Frank, we'll give 'em a few more seconds to see if some stragglers come into the draw . . . give Congo and the other boys a chance." Soon, Sam held his arm up waving slowly to the boys on the eastern ridge, then dropped his arm, whispering, "ready, ready, now!"

Rifles sputtered in close staccato. Twelve deer dropped as if hit by one bullet. Some were still, others twisted and twitched, spewing warm crimson on the white snow.

9

DALE SNAPPED THE LEGS DOWN ON THE LAST TABLE. "JEEZE JENSEN, THIS isn't a vacation, you're supposed to be working." Cliff sat on another table in the Student Union banquet hall, finishing an apple.

Dale grabbed a stack of chairs and slammed them up against the table Cliff was perched on. "Here! I'll bring them to you! Is that good enough?"

Cliff climbed slowly off the table and began to spread the chairs out around it. "Okay! Okay! What's got you so upset?"

"Dr. Cummins agreed I should quit school!" Dale blurted out as he picked up a stack of six chairs.

The other boy stopped dead. "What?"

"Professor Cummins said if my mind wasn't here, I should wait to finish college until it is. I just wish my dad would see it that way."

Cliff unfolded a chair and set it down loudly. "Yeah, I'm sure Cummins told you to quit school!"

Dale squatted to set another stack down. "Fuck you, Cliff!"

"Hey, pal, I don't need this!" the other said in disgust, then started for the door.

"I'm sorry, Cliff. I guess I've just got a lot on my mind."

Cliff hesitated, and turned back toward his friend. "I don't need to know what's on your mind! I shouldn't even give a damn, but after four years of high school and rooming with your gloomy face all last year, I suppose some part of me must care."

He pulled two chairs from the stack, sat on one, and pointed to the other. "Dale, one time you told me you were raised Catholic; somehow, I don't think this patriotism stuff has much to do with the mood you're in! I think it has much more to do with your being Catholic."

Dale looked surprised, then sat down hard on the folding chair. "What mood? Why would you think that?" He tried to imagine what being Catholic had to do with leaving school or with patriotism.

Cliff smiled faintly. "Tell me this; what is your relationship with Elaine like?"

Squirming in discomfort, Dale answered, "Ah, it's great, she's a great girl, real fun to be with." Silence followed.

Cliff's look of amusement shifted to annoyance. "I mean do you sleep with her, have sex with her?"

"No, I haven't slept with her. So what's the point?"

Again Cliff showed annoyance. "You're getting ahead of me, pal. What is your relationship with Gail like?"

"Jeeze, Cliff, is this really important?" Dale balked.

Cliff slapped himself on the thigh. "Yeah! Just answer the question. What's your relationship with Gail like?"

"Well, pretty good, I guess. You know, I mean, I've been going with her since ninth grade." Dale held something back.

"Do you sleep with her?"

Dale grinned in embarrassment. "Yeah, I'm just a male slut!"

"Now you're getting ahead of me again. If Mr. Morality wants a lesson in logic, please answer the damn question!" Cliff cocked his head toward his friend and lowered his voice. "Was she the first?"

"Yeah, there's got to be a first." Dale did not offer more.

The irritating grin returned to Cliff's face, while Dale's cold blue eyes stared at the varnished floor. "Is Gail still the only one?"

"Oh for Christ's sake, Clifford, do I have to?" Dale looked anguished.

"Yes, you do! Now answer me, and spare me the gory details!"

Managing a weak smile, Dale paused. "Yeah. So what's the big deal."

A look of total triumph covered Cliff's face. "Well?!"

"Well what?" Dale grinned back.

"What? Sometimes you're so numb. G-U-I-L-T, guilt, you silly bastard. You think because you stuck it in Gail, and it fit, and you took away her virginity, that you love her . . . or you owe her something. But along comes Elaine to screw up God's plan. Man, I don't think you know what love is! And to deal with it and the fact that you're doing shitty in school, you run off and join the Foreign Legion and head off to Vietnam to be a patriot!"

Cheeks flushed red, Dale jumped to his feet. "That has got to be the dumbest damn thing I've ever heard! Do me a favor, Cliff, and go to hell." As he left the auditorium, he muttered, "There's a lot you don't have a clue about."

More relieved than angered, Cliff called after him, "I may be dumb, Dale, but I'm acing my classes, and you wouldn't know the truth if it lived in your BVDs with all those crabs!"

10

BILLY SLOUCHED ON THE BED IN THE DIM TRAILER. MARY HOLLOW HORN sat beside him as he spoke. "I can't deal with this any more. 'Cause of Bernice, Dad threw Congo out yesterday." He motioned toward the main house. "He's living with Grandma again. I guess Dad wasn't home yet, so she said something about feeding his face if there was something left. I guess he was late coming in.

"Well, there wasn't anything left, so Matt asked her if he could make something for himself. She said 'No! Dinner is over.' I guess he left after that. About three hours later he came home drunk. He almost hit her, so she fainted. Dad got so mad he told Matt to leave his house."

On a cheap transistor radio Marvin Gaye moaned, "I heard it through the grapevine, not much longer would you be mine."

Mary took Billy's hand into hers, looked into his eyes, and spoke in Lakota, *"Ohiniya sna ni te,* She's always fainting. Don't think about it too much, Billy, or something bad might happen, and I couldn't live without you."

Her perfect face turned toward him, dark eyes blazing. "In a few years we could have our own place . . . We'll, we'll have our own kids."

The darkness hid the deep blush in her sculptured cheeks. "I'll be sixteen soon. Mom wasn't much older than that when she had me."

Billy seemed lost in his thoughts, but finally said, "Oh Mary, you're such a crazy girl. You could do lots better than me. I didn't even finish high school. There's a lot of guys around here who could make you a better life than me."

"Billy, I don't want to hear about those other boys; you're the best man I know. I know you could be with whoever you want. I'm not worried about those things."

Pushing the hair away from her deep black eyes, he said in Lakota, "Mary, it's not you, or those other girls, I'm thinking about lately. I'm afraid if I don't leave this place, I'm going to do something awful to myself or Bernice. There's part of her that means well, but the pressure in my head is driving me crazy. She resents anything we eat, we get yelled at for things we have nothing to do with, and she calls us any ugly thing that comes to her mind. Most of the time it's like she just hates us. I can't remember the last time Matt got a new shirt or pants. What makes it even worse is that she treats her own kids with new clothes and nice coats, good food, whatever they want. We're just supposed to live out back and stay low. All the time she's treating Matt and me this way, she calls herself a Christian!

"If she knew you were here, she'd be out here screaming at me and you. She throws your age up to me all the time; she says you're my cousin and that you're . . . well, that you're only after one thing." Billy chuckled. "That's not true, is it?"

Mary smiled. "I am after one thing, and it's not what she thinks. I do want you and someday I want to have your baby, but right now I know that's no good. I don't know where she gets that cousin stuff.

"Even when I was in the third grade and you beat up Jim Yellow Dog for stealing my books, I've cared about you. I've never stopped loving you for a second."

Now it was the boy's turn to be embarrassed. "Oh, I only did that because you had the cutest smile in the third grade. What do you want, a man who looks at little girls?"

Mary laughed. "Billy! You were only in fifth grade!" She pulled herself closer.

The screen door slammed against the stuccoed logs. Both froze on the bed waiting. "Billy, get your lazy ass out of there and go over to the church; tell that father of yours dinner is ready!" The words were in Lakota, shrill. Her stepson did not answer.

Soon the little rounded door of the trailer flew open. Bernice peered in, glaring with anger. "Who is that, Billy?" she asked in loud English. "Who you whoring around with tonight?"

"It's me, Bernice, Mary. And I'm not a whore!"

"I know what you been doing with this little girl!" Her large fingers shook toward Billy. "I suppose you got a bottle in there, too. Two black devils! Cousins trying to make babies, and right near the house of God!"

Billy leaped up and lunged toward the leering face. "Damn you, Bernice, I'll . . ."

Mary caught him by his shirttail and yanked hard, unbalancing him long enough to allow Bernice to escape into the yard.

He stood his ground, shaking, quivering with anger. "I don't give a damn what she says to me, but if she ever says anything like that to you again, I'm going to kill her." Billy heard the wooden church door slam and then Bernice yelling at his dad.

11

REELING UNDER THE INFLUENCE OF DRUGS AND BOOZE, THE BOX TOPS, IN a poor rendition of their own hit, smashed out the last strains of "The Letter." Elaine turned to Dale. "Plan B?"

Grinning, Dale shouted, "Plan B!"

Sliding past rows of screaming fans, the two walked out into the crisp late November evening. "Frankly, I wasn't too thrilled with the performance!" Dale laughed.

"Me either. Those guys were wrecked! I'd be surprised if the university pays them. I heard they were pretty expensive."

As they walked arm in arm, Dale worked hard at keeping the conversation flowing, a conversation that was far away from his thoughts. He glanced at his watch, then put his arm around his date. "It's already ten-thirty . . . Are you warm enough?" His voice shook with a mixture of excitement and guilt. He was sure she noticed.

"I'm fine, but your arm feels pretty good anyway." She put her left arm across Dale's back and rested her small hand on his hip. They walked in silence off the campus toward Dale's apartment.

"Did you ask the guys not to come back after the concert?" Elaine asked shyly as they descended to the basement.

"Huh?"

"D-a-ale! Sometimes I can't believe how spaced out you are. What are you thinking about? And it better be me!" She sighed, poking him in the ribs.

"Of course it's you, Elaine!" Dale grinned in embarrassment. "The boys will be back in an hour."

"You sure know how to be romantic, don't you?" Elaine laughed.

"I guess," Dale answered, feeling a powerful guilt for what he wanted so badly to do.

Moments later he stood in the basement apartment beside a flickering candle while lighting a stick of vanilla incense. "See, I am romantic," he said grinning, then blew out the wooden match. By 10:45, undressed and visibly shaking, he lay on his side facing Elaine, his right hand resting on her soft arm and shoulder, feeling the smoothness of the skin while trying to hide how badly he wanted her. He marveled at her blondness, her pink nipples, the smell of her hair—so different from Gail's. His hands trembled with adolescent desire as he touched her. But his brow creased, betraying an ambivalence. Elaine lay with her left arm resting on his hip, a little frightened by his ceaseless shaking.

Wanting him, but new to this, Elaine's eyes moved like those of a nervous bird. Her body sensed an uneasiness in him. She tried to put it out of her mind, but couldn't.

Something across the bedroom caught her attention. Pulling from his grasp, she wrapped a loose blanket around her and stood. Her muscular, uncovered shoulders drew Dale's eyes as she moved gracefully across the small room. "Is something the matter?" he asked, guilt now palpable in his voice.

With incense and candlelight permeating the monastery-like room, Gail's body looked beautiful in the folds of the soft blanket. "I see you've gotten quite a few letters from that cousin of yours . . ." she said, lifting the stack. "Have you heard from him since the letter in October?"

"Yes, I have," Dale answered, relieved she hadn't instead seen a carelessly left letter from Gail.

"What has he been saying in all these?" she quizzed, setting the stack down on the bed next to him.

"Oh, not much," he said, trying to affect boredom. He reached up to bring the pale woman back into his arms. She ignored the effort, instead sitting on the bed next to him.

"Dale, sometimes you're so obvious. You tell me the letters are not important, but here they sit all thumb-worn in the middle of your desk. Has he been saying how dangerous it is? How many have been killed, or what an adventure it is for little boys who like guns?" She taunted him, pointing toward the hunting rifles in the corner.

A sense of entrapment instantly replaced Dale's sexual excitement.

"Elaine, there is something I've been meaning to tell you, that I've been putting off." He lapsed briefly into silence. "I don't think I'm coming back next semester. I mean, I just don't think school is the place for me right now."

The girl's blue eyes clouded with moisture, then flashed angrily as she grasped the stack of letters. "Sometimes men are so stupid! One man tells another how dangerous something is, and right away it becomes a matter of adventure, or some stupid macho game. You didn't even have to tell me! I knew when your grades started to drop that something inside you had changed. But you couldn't tell me about it. I knew, and I knew it wasn't good." Tears glistened in her eyes.

"But it's not masculinity or adventure I'm thinking about . . . It's because there are boys dying over there, because I'm no better than they are." Dale was convincing only himself as he spoke. "Do you think just 'cause my Dad can help me go to college that I'm better than the men who can't afford to go to college? They're dying over there and I'm no better than they are!" He was speaking in an angry tone Elaine had not heard before.

"Dale Nielsen, let me ask you something about this decision, since you want to be a damned patriot so bad! What about me? . . . And what about that girl at home? Are you going to ask one of us to marry you so you can go off to war with a wife back home like some old movie?"

Dale fell on his pillow, staring at the ceiling. "What do you know about the girl back home?" he finally asked.

"You men think women are so stupid! You think I don't notice you shoving letters into your pocket! That you're thinking of someone else when we're together. And when we study here . . . You think I actually believe that all those damned phone calls you don't answer are really from your folks?" Tears now flowed more freely. "Well, you can take your warrior fantasies and shove them. I don't think you love me or her! I never asked you if you loved me because I knew the answer." She was pulling furiously at her panty hose. "I never asked you to love me, just to be honest with me!"

She reached for her skirt. "You want to hear honesty?! It's a damn good thing we didn't go any further because you would have been the first, asshole, the first!

"I don't think you know what it feels like to be in love, or if you ever will! You're so goddamned brave—you want to go to Vietnam but you lie there next to me, shaking, you want me so bad. Or are you so guilty about that other woman that you can't make love to me?" Tears continued to flow. "You're really just scared. Scared to death that you might feel something for me, like I do for you!" She stood, forcing her feet into her loafers. "Well I haven't been completely honest with you! I hate that war over there, and I don't know what I think about someone who wants to go over there so damn bad he can't wait!

"It hurts, Dale, it hurts!" Elaine said over her shoulder as she pulled the door open. "It hurts so damned bad . . ." she sobbed, slamming the door. Behind her she heard a phone ring in the apartment.

Dale shook his head in disbelief at how quickly this most wonderful of evenings had turned on him. He sat up, picked up the phone, then lay back. "Hello . . . Gail?"

12

ON A GRAY NOVEMBER DAY, THE THREE BATTERED CARS CARRYING THE
Sioux Playboys drove north toward Rapid City. Patches of sunlight broke
through the clouds and grazed the tops of the jagged Badlands, creating saw-
toothed shadows on the scattered grassy mesas beyond. A light snow cover
lent a chilly strangeness to this familiar country. The dusty red Mercury
wagon slid north along the gravel highway, its carriage banging loudly against
the axles after each low spot. Billy was keeping his thoughts to himself.

Adolph Hollow Horn was excited, though. "I still can't believe you boys
did it! First place and you're playing on old equipment. If we could just get
you some real equipment, new guitars, new amps and speakers, maybe you
could get a recording contract!

"Billy, you hear me! This could be your break! You and the boys could be
headed for big things! People are going to see you on TV!

"Man, what's gotten into you, Billy? You used to get excited about stuff like
this. We worked hard to get this far."

Billy watched a distant coyote pursue a jackrabbit on a long plateau. Not
until he saw them tumble in death's final struggle did he respond. "It's not
that I don't appreciate all you've done for me, Adolph; all the miles and
putting up with us. It's just that I think you're taking all this a little too seriously. We may be the best Indian band in the state. We may even be one of
the best bands white or Indian; but it's still just a little TV station in Rapid
City, South Dakota!"

He shifted his haunting gaze toward the manager and said, "I don't need
to fool myself. Winning that contest was good for the band, good for the guys,
and I'm going to pretend it's a big deal, but just between us, it's not going to
lead anywhere for a lot of reasons.

"Do you think the record industry just hands out recording contracts? The
guys who get them are really great. I'm not Ritchie Valens playing original
music on something I built from junk! Adolph, I'm good enough to know
what we sound like compared to the big time, and we're lucky we got this far
... A few times this week I've even wondered if we won because we were just
a curiosity to those white judges."

The radio crackled to life, picking up Rapid. "Cry Like a Baby" by the Box
Tops vibrated through the car's old speaker. "I know now that you're not a

plaything" blared out, making Billy think of Mary, and about what she wanted from life.

By some miracle, the caravan made it to the TV station, and before airtime even Billy seemed to be genuinely excited. It was the closest to the big time he'd seen. There was a director, production crew, cameras, makeup, and stage lighting. Backstage, Adolph Hollow Horn tied small eagle feathers to the guitars and drums while he mouthed a silent prayer for the boys.

On the tiny set, James Hollow Horn leaned toward Billy. "I hear you and my sister are getting pretty serious." Torn between loyalty to his friend and to his family, James's voice was low. "I know you've got lots of women. Hell standing up there on stage and singing, you could probably have any girl you want. But Mary, she's got it bad for you . . . She says she knows you're supposed to be her man in this lifetime and she said you'll know that when you are ready. I tell her not to be a silly girl, that you're no saint. She says she doesn't care because one day soon you're going to realize who she is. She's a good girl, Billy, a hard worker. She does well in school and she's honest . . . I just felt I should say something."

Eyes diverted, as is the Lakota way, Billy listened to his friend, knowing in this speech, which must have been very hard on him, James did honor to his responsibility as a *tiblo,* Mary's oldest brother and the one who in the old days would have been bound to make sure his sister married a good man. Billy cleared his throat. "I'm real fond of your sister, Jimmy. Mary's a special girl, always has been. I guess there was something in the look on her face even the first time I saw her. In my dreams I often see the white man's devil . . . sometimes I am the devil. Those dreams are horrible. Because of those dreams I guess I used to wonder if there are Indian angels. One day I came around the corner at the school and a bigger boy was trying to take her books or just teasing her. He had knocked her down and was trying to punch and kick her, but she was hanging on to her books and giving that boy a hell of a time. I decided any girl that brave should have some help. I called that boy to fight me but that kid just ran. When I reached down to help her up, I noticed she had a face so *owang waste,* so good looking, that I knew from then till now that there are Indian angels. In the years that went by, I've watched her a lot. I came to know that her heart is the same as her face. She is the only girl I don't know what to do about." Billy laughed, then lowered his head again. "I just don't want to hurt her—that's one reason why I'm leaving soon . . ."

Jimmy's eyes grew large. "What do you mean you're leaving? You don't have to do that! Just be careful with her, that's all I'm trying to say, Billy. We got a good thing going here." He pointed with his chin toward the TV studio.

"Yeah, it's great, Jimmy," Billy said, slapping him on the back. "We're going to rock their socks off!"

· · ·

It was ten o'clock when the band hit the bootleggers in the ghost town of Scenic, and midnight when Adolph Hollow Horn slid to a stop in front of the tiny Body of Christ church. Billy pushed the door open. Frozen grass crunched under his feet. Above them the sky sparkled with a thousand crystalline lights. "You sounded great, Billy, the greatest!" the manager said, as his lead singer pulled three beers off a fresh six-pack.

"Yeah, we did. We sounded OK," Billy answered. "I'm thinking of getting my hair done like Mick Jagger!" He stuck out his lips, rocked his head side to side. Then his mood changed. "Adolph, when you get a chance, I want you to drive me to Hot Springs."

The manager's face screwed up like he wanted to ask the boy what was in Hot Springs that was so urgent. But he said only, "Sure thing, Billy."

Swaying a bit as he walked, Billy could see a faint light coming from the trailer. His thoughts went to Mary, and her brother's comments.

Inside the little trailer the air was warm. Matthew lay sleeping. The back room was lit with dim lantern light. Peeking from under the covers was a short-haired woman. Billy's eyes grew wide. "Darlene Ghost!?"

"Surprise! I always knew you'd be a star," she said, lifting the covers for him.

13

HIS FACE IN THE PILLOW, ELAINE SQUIRMED UNDER HIM AS IF SHE WAS THE one who was smothering. She resisted, and this confused him. He tried to lift his weight, but his arms wouldn't work. It was as if they had turned to mush. His neck burned as he tried to keep his weight off her. This all seemed so wrong to him, that he and Elaine should be here, doing this, in his parents' house. The bedroom door banged open. Dale jerked his head to the left. There stood Gail, her swollen stomach protruding over her jeans. Her distended belly button was horribly huge under her stretched T-shirt. Face contorted in desperate rage, she raised a small gun and fired at his forehead.

Eyes wild, Dale woke, banging his head on the frosted window of the bus as his head snapped up. Heart racing, head pounding with a slept-sitting-up headache, it took seconds to acknowledge the awful nightmare as only a dream.

The Greyhound swerved along the snow-packed road in the canyon between Spearfish and Deadwood. Dale's usual awe of the Black Hills in winter was disturbed by the fearful anticipation about seeing Gail. As the bus pulled up to the weathered wood and brick facade of the old Fairmont Hotel, a cold sweat began to form under his arms. Outside in the heavy snowfall stood Gail waving wildly toward the bus. Like an excited puppy, she grinned from ear to ear. His stomach churned with a noxious stew of emotions.

She hugged him until he gently pushed her back. Tears of joy wet her dark brown eyes. "Oh God, I've missed you!" she said. "Two months is such a long time!"

The slightly sweet, fruity smell of alcohol on her breath passed into the cold air. "Yes, it is a long time . . . I've missed you too, honey." The young couple walked quickly arm in arm up the crumbling Victorian main street toward a dented and rusting yellow Volkswagen Beetle.

"What's the matter, hon?" the boyish redhead asked, noticing the fleeting expression on Dale's brow.

"Oh, nothing." The awful dream in the bus had tumbled into his mind for an instant. "Has the ski area opened up?" he asked, resuming his casual air.

"Yeah! It's been real good," she said while reaching in her pocket for the car keys. "Mark and I both made the patrol, so when I'm not in class I can ski! I can't wait to show you my dorm room!" She offered Dale a cigarette.

Out of neglected habit, he took the cigarette, then chuckling at her excitement said, "It's sure good to see you."

• • •

The next morning, as Dale pushed open the front door he could see a Hallmark Cards sign suspended over the dining room table. It read "Welcome home!"

"Is that you, Mark?" a familiar voice called from the kitchen.

"No, it's just me!" Gail called, grinning at Dale.

"I guess the bus must have been . . ." The tall, handsome woman walked into the dining room. She stopped in midsentence, then ran into the dining room toward her son.

Embarrassed and pleased by his mother's emotion, Dale teased, "Jeeze, Mom, I just came home to get one of your famous peanut butter and cucumber sandwiches!"

She missed the joke. "Oh really! That's nice. I'll make you one tomorrow," she said, hugging him.

As he stepped back from his mom, Gail elbowed him gently and winked. "I'll see you after dinner!" She squeezed his waist and was out the door.

Later in the same dining room, now alive with the sound of clinking glasses and lively chatter, Grandma Rose Smith, with her kindly wrinkled face and cheerful blue eyes, faced her grandson and raised her glass. "I'd like to make a toast to my grandson!" The clamor hushed just long enough for the assembled room of cousins and nephews to raise their milk glasses at the "kids table." "As the matriarch of this clan, I'd like to welcome back a special grandson," she paused to wink at Dale, "and tell him how glad I am he's back . . . because he's getting awful skinny on that cafeteria food!" The room burst into laughter as Dale lifted his glass to return the salute.

That evening, as the family sat watching "A Bing Crosby Christmas," Dale tapped his grandmother on the shoulder. "Grandma Rose, I'd like to talk with you for a minute." The two moved quietly toward the kitchen.

Outside a soft snow fell in the glow of the yard light. The old woman sat as the young man gazed out at the drifting flakes.

"Grandma Rose, I've been thinking about quitting college. In fact, I haven't registered for next semester."

The silver-haired woman's voice was soft. "I guess that you haven't told your folks?"

Turning to face her, Dale blushed slightly. "Ah, no, I haven't; I just don't know what to say. They've been talking about college since I was in kindergarten . . . I don't want to hurt them; it's like they've been counting on it."

Grandma Rose looked with loving concern at her grandson. "You know, I had wondered if you weren't going for your folks, your grades being what they are and all . . . It's pretty hard to put anything past an old woman."

"It's not that I don't want to finish college someday. Just not right now."

Now it was his grandmother's turn to sit in silence. Finally, she added, "This will just about kill Jean. I wish there were an easy way to tell her." She sighed heavily. "I know you're not lazy, and I've never known you not to have a plan. That's what we'll have to remind your mother of when she finds out . . . So what's up?" she asked.

There was a long silence. Finally she nudged him gently. "Quit staring at that snow so hard—you're melting it before it hits the ground!" She laughed gently. "Are you that anxious to get out and away from all of us?"

Turning to face her, he struggled for the words. "Well, I've been thinking a lot. I've gotten a few letters from Jim. He says it's pretty rough on the men over there . . ." His grandmother's white eyebrows raised.

"Well, I'm no better than those boys over there, and I think . . . I think I should do my part." His chest sagged. He had finally said it.

Rose turned to face the boy straight on. "So, Jim makes it sound pretty exciting over there, does he?"

"No. I don't want anybody to blame him for what I'm doing. He's been real honest. In fact he's been adamant that I don't even think about it."

The white eyebrows raised again. "Come on now, son." The old lady's eyes narrowed as Dale turned to look outside. "All this talk about doing your share . . . Well, I know you pretty well, maybe better than you know yourself. I remember when that cousin of yours went backpacking for the first time; you practically drove your mother nuts begging her to let you go. And remember when he got his first hunting rifle? I think you were more excited than he was, if that's possible." The old woman chuckled softly. "You boys never appeared that close, but in a way, you were always peas in a pod!"

Outside, in the dim light of the alley, Dale could see that the snow had let up. Grandma Rose reached out to touch her grandson's hand, as if to bring him back into the room. Through gold-rimmed glasses the matron's eyes softened as she looked into his. "Jim will be coming back soon, so I'll at least have one big grandson at home."

A large lump formed in his throat. His grandma had seen inside him; she was the only one who always could.

Moisture formed in the wrinkled corners of the old eyes. Grandma Rose's throat narrowed with emotion as she grew serious. "You know, I don't think adventure is a good enough reason to do what you're talking about doing . . . and I don't think a boy your age can understand much about war, about shell-shocked and crippled young men who grew old in VA hospitals." She paused. "Well, maybe that's why there are always soldiers to fight our damned wars. But believe me, Dale, you didn't lose an ounce of my respect by what you just said." A tear stole down her cheek.

A subtle signal passed between them, and as he had done as a three-year-old, Dale moved toward the old woman. His cheek pressed against hers; the hug was long and hard.

The braying of a VW's horn ended the embrace. "That must be Gail!" He grabbed his parka. "Thanks, Grandma!" he called over his shoulder; then he was out the door.

It was freezing cold in Gail's air-cooled VW. "I can't wait to show you my dorm room," she winked. "It's pretty small, but at least I don't have to put up with Mom!" A familiar, devilish smile came to Gail's freckled face as she reached into the back seat and handed Dale a beer.

The familiar hummingbird chirp of the VW engine's valves and two cold beers made the college boy feel like he was back in high school—like maybe nothing had really changed very much. Remembering his grandmother's hug, though, he knew that everything had. He began to look more closely at the old familiar neighborhoods outside the frosted window as the moon broke through the clouds. The little car slid on the packed snow down Maitland Road past yellow-windowed shacks and cabins. Some were clapboard, others log or sided with tar paper. In almost every yard was the familiar collection of galvanized toolsheds and slowly collapsing garages. In dim yard lights sat old bulldozers, logging skidders, or tractor-trailer rigs sleeping beneath the new blanket of snow. This canyon was where many of the local loggers' families lived. Numerous children, job-related injuries, and low wages had long kept these houses small and their numerous additions improvised. Still, Dale had always liked them.

Soon the houses were behind them, and only the black shapes of the snow-covered spruce forest lined the road. Gail played with the radio, rolling the tuner from one station to the next in the irritating way she always did. Dale nervously rolled a half-empty beer can back and forth between his long fingers; he wanted to speak, to break the silence. When they reached the top, he could see the white ski slopes against the dark forest. He sipped his beer; he was home.

• • •

At midnight Gail drove into the campus of Black Hills State College, which even Dale acknowledged looked beautiful if deserted in the blowing and drifting snow. She parked the car in the empty lot near her dorm, and grabbed the remainder of a twelve-pack from the back seat. Dale looked nervously around. "Where's campus security? Isn't this Christmas break?"

"Yeah, but they figure we students have paid for our rooms, and if we want to stay it's fine. We won't even have to deal with co-ed hours; all the resident monitors are gone home for the holidays!" Gail took his hand, pulling him gently into the foyer. Soon they were standing in front of her door. Sneaking into a woman's dormitory only increased Dale's anxiety.

Gail switched on a single lamp on a nearby desk. Dale pushed the door closed while he glanced around the room. "I see you've been drawing again." In the dim light he could see the faint outlines of penciled flowers and detailed ink sketches of old barns push-pinned to the walls.

Gail pulled off her coat. "Yeah, when I'm not too lonely for you, I draw. Sometimes I'm so lonely I can't do anything." He had known her for years and now feared she suffered from what his psychology text had taught him was called depression. He smiled, but once more an ambivalence about their relationship welled up in him.

He was sure Gail could see through his reassuring smile, but if she did she didn't say anything. Instead she placed a record on the portable stereo, popped open a fresh can, then slipped off her clothes. Standing with her nude, freckled back to him she turned down the single bed on the west side of the room. He followed her lead.

. . .

Popping and hissing loudly, the old radiator disturbed their long moments of after-the-fact embracing. A small pile of beer cans rustled as Dale gently slid off. A thin film of guilty sweat covered his chest. As Gail rested next to him, he mechanically stroked her auburn hair, hoping she hadn't noticed anything different. He had.

He had struggled to put the thought of Elaine out of his mind, to feel aroused by Gail, but as usual, as he spent himself, Gail had laid there smiling adoringly up at him, as if the act of love was for her only a spectator sport. For a brief moment, he had wished, almost believed, Elaine was under him. He had smelled her perfume, almost called out her name.

14

THE OIL POT STOVE WARMED THE MAIN HOUSE WITH A DROWSY HEAT that, save for the company of Bernice, made Billy want to stay. After dinner, while his stepmother heated dishwater on the stove, he leaned toward his father and asked quietly in Lakota. "*Até,* I want to speak with you later, could you come by?"

"*O han.* Yes," the sharp-featured man answered in a whisper. As he did after supper every evening, Billy patted his two older half sisters on the head goodnight, first Clynda, then Julie. Even though little Carol smiled up her usual toothless grin, Billy could not smile back. He patted baby Verla on the head; then pulling the main door slowly closed, the teenager disappeared into the inky black. *Bang!* Caught in the biting wind the screen door smashed into the jamb behind him.

Fidgeting with her braids, Carol broke the silence. "What's the matter with Billy, Dad?"

"Oh he, ah, probably . . ."

His wife cut him off. "Probably everything! Probably thinks he's important enough to show us he's got problems. Folks been paying that boy too much attention since his damned TV show. And I'm sure that Adolph Hollow Horn has been filling his head with big ideas! There's something wrong with that boy all the time. Ever since that boy was little, he's been nothing but trouble." And she was off ranting about Billy and Matthew. As usual, Clayton only lowered his head.

• • •

It was nine o'clock when there came a gentle rapping on the aluminum door of the squat trailer. "Son?" The man poked his head into the dim kerosene light inside.

"Come on in, Dad. I'll turn up the lantern and poke up the fire." Billy's voice blew fog into the cold air.

For the next ten minutes as Billy put wood into the stove and adjusted the stove and flue dampers, there was only silence between them. When the place was warmer, Clayton Jealous Of Him took off his jacket, then reached into his shirt pocket for a tiny cotton sack of Bull Durham. Meticulously he rolled the tobacco into two perfect cigarettes. Handing the first to Billy, he placed the second between his own lips. With practiced speed he struck a stick match against his pants leg, and lit both.

When the smokes had been reduced to half their length, the old man spoke in his language, "Billy, otéhika slolwaye, I know it's been hard. I know Bernice comes down on you real hard, but you have got to know, son, I'm sorry about that. She does care." Emotion choked the older man, and his voice shook slightly. In the yellow light a thin, wet streak fell down his brown cheek.

"Billy, you and your brother mean so much to me, but I can't always control that woman." This was the part that always made the boy turn his head away in resentment.

"She's been fair with me, gave me four pretty daughters. I guess I knew there could be problems, but I always thought she'd do better, with you and your brother, that Jesus would heal her heart . . ." The older man lifted the stove burner and tossed in the remains of his cigarette. "Mi chinksi, My son, there's something I never told you, something you may already know, but I'm going to tell you anyway."

Turning to face his father, Billy said, "Dad, you don't have to say anymore. I . . ."

"But I do, son. I got to tell you something. A woman's jealousy is an awful thing. And well, I guess it's bad enough when she's jealous of a living, breathing woman, but when she's jealous of a dead woman, it's something different."

"How's that, Dad? How can Bernice be jealous of Mom, jealous of someone lying in her grave?" Anger colored the question.

"People can be jealous of the dead. Your mother was a good-looking woman; people still talk about her that way. And people liked her. Billy, it's like if Bernice was jealous of a living woman, she could beat her up. Or maybe just seeing that woman getting older, losing her shape, and wishing trouble on her would let it go, but Bernice can't do that. Bernice can't erase your mom from her mind and, she fears, from my mind either . . . She sees her every day in your face and Matthew's.

"In the photo Grandma has of your mom, she never gets older, she just stands there smiling, young and pretty." His voice again shook slightly.

"So, you see, she can't lash out at your mom. I think that's why she lashes out at you boys. And I blame myself, as a Christian man." He fingered the worn, pearl-inlaid crucifix on his hairless brown chest. "I blame myself . . . If I was more of a man I could bring myself to love Bernice as much as I loved your mom. I prayed that could happen, or maybe that we could have a boy together, but it never happened, and I think Bernice hates me for both failures, hers and mine."

Billy slid over to the stove and dropped three pieces of kindling into the top. He spoke in English. "I guess I never really thought about it quite that way. I guess I knew she was jealous of Mom, but not the part about Mom being dead. That's good that you told me that. Maybe you could have kept Bernice off our backs, maybe you didn't try hard enough, maybe you did, Dad, and Bernice will always be Bernice. But it don't make any difference now."

"What do you mean, son?"

Clearing his throat, Billy glanced at the floor. "Dad, you and Matthew, and the girls, you mean a lot to me. Most times I don't even care when Bernice puts me down. I've gotten pretty good at dealing with her. But when it comes to the way she treats Matthew, I can't deal with it. Even with what you just told me, I know that someday something's going to snap inside me and I'm going to do something awful. I've been getting these thoughts more and more and, so, I'm leaving."

Tears formed in the preacher's eyes, but he held his tongue. The teenager went on. "Ever since Matthew moved back to Grandma's, the last reason for staying around is gone. He doesn't need me to protect and feed him anymore. I made him promise me he would stay up there and stay in school."

The man's face slowly slumped toward his chest. He sat there shaking his head ever so slightly. "But I need you, son. I need you at the church. To sing and help me keep the place up . . ."

Billy looked out the frosted window toward the humble church building. "No, you don't, not really, Dad. You've got people from the church who can help you out around here."

"Where you going, son?" His father looked up.

"I joined the army, Dad. I had Adolph drive me over to Hot Springs the other day. I didn't tell him why I wanted to go. Man, was Adolph mad at me about that! He tried to tell me how I was throwin' away my music career. That man's really got bad hearing, never could hear what I been telling him . . . Never could tell the difference between a sharp and a flat either!" Billy laughed, then turned to catch his father's eye. "Dad, it's done. I leave in a month or so. I'll be here for Christmas and New Year's, and then I'm a soldier boy!" He stood and saluted his dad, trying as usual to lighten the mood.

Clayton also stood and moved toward his son, "Oh, God. Son, I'm so sorry it came to this. I should have done something. They'll send you to Vietnam, Billy, Vietnam!" His voice now openly shook as he held his son at arm's length so he could look into the boy's eyes. But it did no good.

Clayton lifted the small crucifix over his head, then lowered it over his son's. He fingered it on Billy's chest. "Then promise me one thing. Promise me you'll remember Jesus and that you'll wear this."

15

DALE STOOD BY THE FROSTY ROAD. NOTHING HAD HAPPENED OVER Christmas or New Year's to change his belief that joining the army was the way out of his problems with college, and his confusion about Elaine and Gail.

The hilly streets of Lead, South Dakota were slick with ice, the air raw with cold that January morning. Above, the sky was ominous. Tiny snowflakes fell from the gray heavens.

The first car sped by where the tall boy stood, its driver blind to the young man's thumb. The second car to approach belonged to Carl Finch, the high school's assistant basketball coach. He acknowledged Dale by touching his hat brim, and stopped to offer him a ride.

"So, where you going, son?" he asked as he pushed open the door.

Dale slid in. "I'm just heading toward Deadwood. Sure appreciate the ride though, it's cold this morning."

"How's college treating you? Still thinking about being a veterinarian?" The car moved slowly downhill past snow-laden spruce trees.

Dale glanced out the window. "Anything's still possible, sir, but I'm just not so sure about things like that anymore." He hedged, knowing how gossip traveled.

"Don't suppose you're playing any ball?" Finch asked, as he studied the icy road. When Dale did not respond, the coach said, "You could have been great if it wasn't for your asthma!"

"No, I'm not playing. It's just 'cause I'm not that good, but you're right, the asthma hasn't flared up since I stopped playing." He hadn't thought about his asthma for a long time.

"Dale, whatever you do with your college, whether you become a veterinarian or not, it's a whole lot safer than going off to Vietnam. My nephew Bob Reynolds . . . You might have known him?" Finch looked over to see if Dale recognized the name.

"I didn't know him very well," Dale answered.

"I think he was two years ahead of your class. Well, he just came back minus a leg . . . stepped on a land mine. Wished to hell he listened to me about college, but that's young folks I guess . . . tell them one thing they'll do another." He chuckled nervously. Slapping Dale on the leg, he said, "You just stay there in Ames, Iowa where it's safe and maybe play a little basketball for old time's sake!"

• • •

The car door slammed and Mr. Finch was off. Dale stood in the slush on Deadwood's narrow main street. He hesitated for a moment, staring at the polished gray and pink granite columns that lent a morbid formality to the old bank building. "My nephew just came back minus a leg. . . ." Mr. Finch's words echoed. "You just stay there in Ames, Iowa where it's safe." His cousin Jim's words blended with those of Finch: "where it's safe . . ."

Dale pushed open the bank's heavy oaken door, turned, then descended the stairs to find a stark office where a square, graying woman sat behind a desk. Above her on the wall were the traditional wartime posters of smiling young men and women in starched uniforms, whose slogans read, "Fly In The

Navy," "The Marines! We're looking a few good men." and "You Can Do It In The Army!" If the woman smiled, he never saw it.

"Can I help you?" she asked looking up.

"Yeah, I mean yes, ma'am. I want to join the army."

. . .

That evening Gail came by the Nielsens' for dinner; Dale greeted her at the door. Her first question could only have come from someone who knew him well enough to read his enigmatic face. "What's the matter, Dale? You look as if you've gotten some bad news."

He turned away. "No, it's nothing; I've just got something to tell the folks at dinner. I'm fine."

"Sounds more like something rather than nothing," Gail said suspiciously.

Somewhere between the mashed potatoes and the roast beef, Mr. Nielsen gave Dale the opportunity he needed. "You know your mother and I got your grades from Ames," he said without emotion. "If you're still thinking about veterinary school something's got to change. They've been getting worse each semester," he said flatly, not looking up from his food.

A long moment went by as Dale anguished over his response. "I know my grades aren't good, Dad. And I don't want you and Mom to think that I don't understand the sacrifices you make to help me go there. I'm just not sure anymore about being a veterinarian. I . . ."

His father cut in. "Son, we've had this conversation before. If your grades don't improve you might as well change majors, or come home and get a job."

"That's what I'm trying to tell the two of you. I know I'm not doing as well as you expected, or as well as I could. That's why I've made a decision." He paused. All eyes but his father's were now on him. "Dad, I don't want to waste any more of your money. I don't want to ruin my academic record with poor grades, so I'm quitting school, at least for now."

A dark cloud formed on his mother's brow. His father finally looked up from his potatoes: shock flickered on his face.

"I volunteered for the service today," Dale stated in the flat manner of his father. "I joined the army. I leave in February."

The fork slipped from his mother's hand, clanging to the floor. Tears formed in the corners of her eyes; she pushed herself from the table and stood near the kitchen door. "I wish you had said something to us, Dale. I've only got two boys. It's not like you're bringing home good news! How did you expect us to react to this little bombshell?" She was now screaming.

"Jean, calm down," her husband said.

"I can't calm down, Alan! I won't!" She pushed open the door to the kitchen.

Gail's only reaction was to reach under the table and angrily squeeze Dale's hand. Then she stood and followed Jean into the kitchen.

Dale glanced over at his brother, Mark, who sat looking stunned.

"I suppose you'll get a job? Six weeks is too long for you to be hanging around loafing." Neither his father's voice nor his face showed the slightest emotion.

"Actually, I wasn't. I was going to take some time for myself. I . . ."

Alan Nielsen looked up. "Get a job, son. I don't want you hanging around wasting your time." Dale could hear his mother crying in the kitchen. He felt like shit.

Later that night, standing alone in Dale's unlit bedroom, the street outside looked forever different to Alan Nielsen. No longer the safe quiet street he had raised his boys on. The outside world had suddenly invaded his own, leaving the view outside the window frozen, strange, foreboding. "What could I say?" he whispered to himself. "I would have done the same thing myself if I was his age."

16

BENEATH A BRIGHT BLUE JANUARY SKY, THE BASKETBALL SMACKED OFF THE frozen clay in a steady rhythm. Interrupting the rhythm was an occasional banging, as the ball bounced off the gray plywood backstop into the makeshift hoop, and the panting of the three players.

"Jeeze, Congo! Another year or two of practice and . . . I'll still beat the two of you!" Billy jeered at his brother. Clynda laughed as she knocked the ball from Billy's hands toward Matthew.

"And that's why the score is eighteen to twenty!" Matthew shot back, letting the ball fly. "Make that nineteen to twenty."

Billy took the ball in and tried to sweep past his sister. Clynda stood her ground, grabbed the ball, and passed it back to Matthew, who sank another one. "OK, OK, time out, little ones," Billy wheezed, as he leaned against his '53 Chevy, which had sat wheelless for months on blocks of split firewood.

The screen door slammed. "My turn to play!" Julie yelled at Billy as she ran toward them. Billy only winked at her as he caught his frosty breath.

"Clynda, go in and see if there's any Kool-Aid." The tall girl sauntered off toward the door, calling back, "Kool-Aid? It's the middle of winter! You're always trying to get rid of me." Julie followed her inside.

Once the girls had gone, Billy turned toward his brother. "I want to know if you'd like to come listen to the band this weekend? It's your big chance, a two-night gig in Gordon, Nebraska."

Matthew stood for a moment, mouth open, "Sure, Billy, I'd love to come! But what's the big deal? You never ask me. Why now?"

Billy just smiled, sank a shot, then threw his brother the ball. "Twenty-one!" he shouted.

. . .

On Tuesday, Billy was riding home from Head Start, east past Gildersleeve's store in Wounded Knee, when he saw a familiar blue Ford pickup parked in front of the store. He motioned for the bus driver to stop and then waving good-bye stepped off. Soon Mary Hollow Horn came out of the store with a bag of groceries and climbed into the driver's seat of the blue truck.

While she searched for her keys, Billy walked up to the driver's window. "Hey! When did they start giving driver's licenses to little girls?" He leaned against the truck door.

Her blush was like a crimson rose petal against deep bronze. "They don't! It's just that you still haven't noticed that I'm not a little girl." Intimidated once again by how beautiful she looked, Billy could not think of a smart remark.

In an instant she gunned the engine and popped the clutch. Nearly spun around by the force of the truck, Billy yelled, "Mary?!"

All he got was frozen dirt in his face.

Two days later when she came out of the trading post, Billy was sitting in the cab. Face tight, she glared at him, and then got into the truck. Eyebrows lowered, she turned toward him and said, "You looked so funny when I took off!" Sweet laughter tumbled from her.

Billy started to laugh with her. "Well, aren't you funny! I was going to tell you something important; now I'm not."

Mary sat up. "What? What were you going to tell me?"

His expression grew stony. "I was going to tell you about how I've been thinking a lot about things."

He paused for what seemed like a long time, then drew a deep breath. "I've made a decision. I ah . . ." The look on Mary's face was so expectant, so worried, Billy paused. "I, ah, want to invite you to hear us play this weekend.

The bar owner even got us Indians a motel room!" He smiled while hating himself for not telling her about enlisting.

"Is that all? You scared me, Billy. I thought you were going to tell me you were dumping me for that cow Darlene Ghost, or something."

"Come on, you know Darlene doesn't mean anything to me," Billy protested. His brow wrinkled. How did she find out?

"Darlene told the girls in school that your mom really likes her 'cause she's the only one of your girlfriends that's not lazy." A grin came to her perfect face. "She also told the girls that you were pretty good, except you get tired easy!"

Billy sat there thinking up a reply until a smile spread over his face. "It's not like that, not like that at all . . . I don't love Darlene, I did it for you; I didn't think you would make love to a man who had no experience. I was just trying to get some experience."

Mary frowned. "So that's what you call that, experience!" She had to stop herself from grinning at her squirming victim. "Is that what you're going to try and get from me this weekend? Some experience?"

Billy thought of the promise he had made Jimmy before the TV show. His head dropped. "You can trust me. I don't know what I even think about that, Mary. I mean, you're not like Darlene." Mary looked as if she might cry.

Billy tried to pull his foot from his mouth. "I mean for her it's nothing. With you . . ." the nature of his panic changed, feelings he'd had toward Mary for years welled up. "Well, it's like, I, ah, I'm inviting you to Gordon for the weekend and not Darlene."

"For the weekend? I'm not sure Dad would let me. I mean I know he won't, he's pretty old-fashioned." Mary tried to act calm as she backed the truck out onto the road. Her hands shook on the wheel. She had waited so long for Billy to give her some sign that she was special to him, and now it seemed he had. Her joy was short-lived.

• • •

Later, after jumping out of the truck cab, Billy pushed the door shut, then looked at Mary. Her eyes were red. Wet streaks ran from her oval black eyes down her high cheekbones and across her tight, quivering lips. "I haven't told Matt I'm leaving for the army yet, so please don't mention it to anyone."

Still crying, Mary said, "I still don't know why you didn't tell me before." She took a deep breath. "I'll talk to Dad, but even if he says no, I'm going with you to Gordon."

17

THE PRINTING WAS CAREFUL.

> Dear Mom and Dad,
>
> I love you and I know what kind of woman you want me to be and I've always tried to be that kind of girl. Billy Jealous is leaving for the army on Monday. He's taking the bus from Martin to Sioux Falls. You know how I've always thought about him. Now, he's leaving. I don't know what will happen but I want this chance to be with him.

She signed it simply "Mary," placed it on the table, and ran out the door.

• • •

The bar reeked of stale cigarette smoke and beer. The stage was a makeshift affair, barely raising the band above the grimy dance floor.

It was Saturday night and "Green River" by Creedence Clearwater Revival blared from the cheap amps. Tight-jeaned women swung sweet-faced on the arms of lean, stiff-legged men. When the Sioux Playboys performed, the dance floor would be crowded early in the first set. Matthew sat beside the stage with Mary, their eyes glued on his brother. On stage, Billy's awkwardness and self-consciousness disappeared. He smiled and sang, and the audience as usual was caught up, enchanted by this Lakota boy and his marvelous voice.

After the set was over, Billy sat with Matthew and Mary. This was the part Matthew liked best on Friday night. The conversation was light. Billy and Mary, reluctant to spoil Matthew's evening, spoke of the band's sound, and then asked what songs he would like to hear.

During the second set, Bill Hollow Horn signaled the band to wait a moment between songs. He took the mike from Billy Jealous, who, guessing what was up, shook his head, frowning at Bill. Bill could see the lead singer was angry, but proceeded anyway. "If I could have your attention for just one moment! I'd like to make an announcement!" Matthew stood looking up at his brother, a puzzled look spread across his broad dark face.

"I am sad to announce that this may be the last gig for the Sioux Playboys." The room of boisterous cowboys fell silent. "Billy Jealous, our lead singer and your MC, has gone and joined the army!"

Matthew's narrow eyes opened wide, then he turned and looked for the back door. Mary grabbed for his arm, but he pulled free. She chased him to the door, but he was too fast. "Matthew!" she called after him, but he only ran faster down the dark alley.

Inside, a slow-building applause filled the room. Upset by the surprise, Billy turned to look where Matthew and Mary had been sitting, but his brother was gone. He tried to leave the stage, but James Hollow Horn grabbed him and with a big smile pushed him back center stage.

Bill Hollow Horn went on. "The boys in the band would like to do something, if we could have your patience. We would like to tie this special eagle feather on Billy's guitar, 'cause when he's plucking that guitar in a swamp or some jungle, we want him to think of his people. He's a warrior now!"

The audience started buying shots for the new recruit before the band could even start the next song. By one o'clock he was too drunk to play. By two he was sound asleep in Mary's arms on the floor of a motel room crowded with sleeping band members, their girls, and a few hangers-on. Mary could not sleep. Her mind swam with the events of the past week.

It was past three when she saw Matthew come in. Hers were the only eyes open, so he walked over a jumble of sleeping bodies to sit near her. Mary gently released Billy's head and sat up.

Matthew spoke with his head down. "He should have told me; I wanted to go too . . . Billy lied. He said he wouldn't go to the army till I could go with him. He said he wouldn't go without me. He said we'd wait till we could go together. He didn't even tell me!" The younger boy's voice cracked.

Mary tried to think of something to say to comfort him. She put her arm softly around his shoulder. "Maybe he just couldn't bring himself to do it, Matt. Sometimes we think Billy is brave because of the way he acts, but most of the time he's real scared of hurting people by saying the wrong thing, doing something stupid."

Matthew sat there against the wall listening, trying to clear his head of anger and grief. Mary sat with him, sharing his heartache.

Beside her Billy's eyes fluttered. Then he rolled onto his chest, still so drunk he was barely able to push himself to his knees. When he saw Mary's arm around Matthew, "Wha' the hell are you two doin'? God Mar-ey, you and Congo? You sonuvabitch!" Billy staggered to his knees. He lunged at his brother, landing across Mary's legs. He tried to claw at Matthew, who, frightened by the look on his brother's face, swung at Billy's nose, knocking him back. Matthew jumped to his feet. "You're crazy, Billy! I just got here!"

Billy wobbled to his feet, blood flowing down his face. "I'm not even gone yet and my brother is tryin' to pick up my woman!" he screamed in drunken rage.

Mary stood and yelled at him. "Don't be stupid, Billy! We were just talking; it was nothing, Billy!"

Two men awakened, Lloyd One Bull and a guy Matthew didn't recognize. Lloyd hit the light and rubbing his face asked, "What's the matter?"

"Thatsonofabitch brother of mine was messin' with my old lady." His speech was as slurred as his thinking. "I'm not even in the army and, he, he's tryin' t'move in!" The blood on Billy's face seemed all the proof needed.

All three men lunged for the younger brother, knocking him against the box springs on which Billy had been sleeping. When Matthew, fists swinging and snarling mad, had been subdued with a flurry of hard-hitting if clumsy punches, they threw him out onto the concrete sidewalk.

Billy Jealous Of Him woke the next morning, confused by the blood all over his shirt; he dismissed it as a nosebleed. Mary sat dozing against the far wall. Walking and hitchhiking, Matthew found his way back to Wounded Knee, but was absent when Clayton took Billy to Martin on Monday. It was something he would come to regret.

18

ON FEBRUARY 6, 1968, WHEN THE LONG HAND CLICKED TO TWELVE, DALE wound up and threw his wet towel into a soapy bucket with a finality that brought laughter from the guys in the garage. "After six weeks of this crap, I'm never washing another fucking car again! Even if it's my own!" A loud applause arose from the mechanics at the busy Ford dealership.

Shorty Bob, the shop foreman, came around the side of a new yellow Mustang. "Quittin' time, boys. Time to give the Car Wash Man a beer!" Again a cheer went up from underneath the numerous grease racks. The shout was heard clear into the showroom, beckoning the salesmen and their customers to join the party.

Shorty Bob reached into an ice-filled, galvanized horse tank, then slammed the cold bottle of Budweiser into Dale's right hand. Someone else filled his left. The beers, the "good lucks," and the "go get them gooks" came fast and heavy till Gail walked in two hours later and found Dale leaning precariously over the wheel alignment pit.

A stupid grin covered his boyish face. "Is that you, Gail?" he asked, tottering back. The guys roared with laughter.

. . .

Early on following snowy Monday morning, like in a scene lifted from a World War II documentary film, the entire Nielsen family, grandparents, aunts, and uncles, showed up in front of the old Fairmont Hotel to wait for the bus. Gail showed up a few minutes later with her mother. The talk was forcibly lighthearted. Dale's father greeted Charley Hickham. "Hi Charley, your son going off too?"

"Yep, he joined the air force. Where's Dale headed?"

"The army," he answered, still gripping Hickham's hand.

"Into the army? Hmm. Well, I wish you luck, son. At least there will be someone you know on the bus."

The way Mr. Hickham said "army," with a combination of sarcasm and sorrow, made Dale's stomach a little more queasy than a weekend of hard partying had already left it. The buzzing of voices seemed to close in around him, as fearful relatives, wearing forced smiles, participated in one of the oldest human rituals.

In the crush, he looked for his younger brother. Mark had said nothing to him. He stood off to the side, sadness in his thin face. Surrounded by relatives with forced smiles, it struck Dale that Mark, like the honest boy in "The Emperor's New Clothes," was the only one who was acknowledging what was really taking place this bitter cold February morning. Mark's haunting face conveyed clearly that his only brother was beginning a journey from which he might not return.

"Bus is leaving," the driver yelled out. Mark moved in front of Dale, then took his older brother's hand and said, "Keep your ass covered. I'll miss you real bad."

"That's a hell of a send-off." Dale smiled. "Between you and me, I'm pretty close to getting cold feet, but I guess it's too late for that." A thick cloud of exhaust had formed around the bus. Behind him Dale heard the rounded aluminum door of the Jack Rabbit Lines bus bark open.

"I'll write!" Mark said, finally managing a smile.

"I'll write, too. And I'll see you in a couple of months, after boot camp," he said, hugging his brother.

Then it was his mother's turn, tears glistening in the corners of her eyes. "I know you're coming home to me, son," she said in his ear as she hugged him. "You hear?"

Finally, Gail pushed herself into his arms. "You're not going to forget me, are you?" She kissed him hard on the mouth; she tasted like beer.

"No, honey, I won't and I'll call when I get to wherever I'm going." He slowly released her.

Then his father reached out a gloved hand. "Take care of yourself, son."

"I will," he responded decisively, stepping up onto the bus. "I will."

. . .

Out the frosted windows, endless fields of corn and wheat stubble stretched to the horizon. Occasional banks of old snow, their crests polished by the wind, added to the bleakness of the land and Dale's worsening morale. Four hours out of the Black Hills and there were still only five lonely boys on the bus. Partners in misery, they hadn't said a word to each other.

Dale had never liked Chuck Hickham. They'd gone to the same high school, even graduated together; but they weren't friends. Dale remembered how many times Chuck had come up from behind to rub his wool-thick, wavy hair and yell, "How ya doin', Brillo Joe?" like he was an important jock or putting on a show for his friends. Unconsciously, he reached up and ran his fingers through his woolly hair. He hated that nickname.

Now here we are on this freezing cold bus and Chuck is heading toward some cushy job in the air force, Dale muttered to himself. He's too dumb to go to college, but smart enough to stay out of the army. He leaned his head back trying to sleep away the rest of the trip. His cousin's advice about college and Vietnam replayed in his mind, taunting him till he dozed off.

. . .

It was 6 P.M. when the bus pulled slowly up to a faded wooden sign that read, "Sioux Falls, Jack Rabbit Terminal." Dale cleared the frost from the window and noticed that the city streetlights only pushed back the moonless night in tiny yellow circles.

After eight hours of silence Chuck Hickham finally found his voice. "Brillo! Uh, Dale, you heading to the Y? I'll, uh, walk with you."

Dale picked up his suitcase. "Sure," was all he said.

19

FROM THE OUTSIDE, THE BUILDING WAS NONDESCRIPT; TWO STORIES OF yellow-painted cinder block with very few windows. If it hadn't been for the little sign in front that said "U.S. Military Induction Center," Dale and Chuck would have walked by. They looked at each other, forced a weak grin, and walked in.

. . .

Arriving earlier than most of the recruits, the first thing Billy Jealous Of Him had noticed was that as the morning wore on, there were as many Indians as whites in the large cinder-block room. Now he leaned toward a big full-blood, and in Indian said, *"Wasicu hoksila,* White boys, must be in short supply."

"O han, Yes," the big man said.

Billy noticed Dale and Chuck walk in and said, "and the ones they got look pretty scared."

The larger man laughed, then said disdainfully, "Most white boys go to college and get a nice deferment; these ones are probably too dumb!" Then he introduced himself. "My name is Garfford High Pipe, from downtown Parmalee, on Rosebud Reservation."

Billy smiled. "Parmalee. I played at a dance there once, almost didn't find the place. Nice ladies though! I'm Billy . . ." he stopped and quickly made a decision. "Ah, Frank Jealous Of Him, from Grass Creek, a suburb of Wounded Knee."

Garfford grinned and extended his big hand. "Is it Billy or Frank?"

"Friends call me . . ." Billy paused momentarily, a pleased smile spreading quickly across his face. "Frank. You can call me Frank or just Jealous. You can call me anything but late for dinner."

Garfford laughed at the bad joke. "Friends just call me Pipe."

Dale stood there alone, his natural shyness exaggerated by misgivings. He looked at the Indian boys and noticed none of them had the slightest bit of hair on their faces. He thought it made them look even younger than the white kids. When he'd imagined the army he imagined the life he knew at home, and therefore had created in his mind a recruitment center and an army with white faces. He next acknowledged how naive that idea had been and wondered how he would get along with these Indians.

A loudspeaker crackled, interrupting the commotion. "All those enlisting today please report to the room listed with your service preference when you hear the number. Those being enlisted into the army, please report to room thirteen."

Dale groaned. "Wouldn't you know it! Room thirteen!" He looked at Chuck, shook his hand, and said, "This is it! See you in the war."

The stark room with the ominous number was soon occupied by Dale and fourteen other tense draftees.

"Gentlemen!" The recruits looked up to see a ruddy-faced man with perfectly butched strawberry-blond hair. Dale studied the man. As hard as the man's expression looked, it did not disguise the fact that the staff sergeant was less than thirty. Fifteen teenagers stood stock-still. Dale found himself beside a slightly built Indian kid. On his other side was a short, muscular white kid.

"Gentlemen," the sergeant handed each man a set of forms, "you are about to be honored with induction into the meanest fighting machine the world has ever known. I want you to conduct yourselves with that in mind for the rest of the day and the rest of your lives!

"Today, and in the future, you will hear various things said about the army by members of the air force, the navy, and of course the marines, but let me tell you, they don't know a thing about this man's army! Do you understand?"

"Yes, sir," a few of the men responded, nodding their heads.

"That's pretty weak, boys. By this afternoon you'll be men, and you'll respond like men." The acne-scarred sergeant looked at them one at a time. "Pretty sorry lot of humanity, but we'll change all that. Now, my good men, you are in for the treat of a lifetime, the pre-induction physical."

He handed each man a set of forms. "After filling these out, you will, on my command, report to room twenty-six on the second floor. Once there, you will strip to your Skivvies. If you do not own a pair of shorts, you may requisition a towel from the table in the corner of the room."

When it appeared that most of the men had completed the forms, the sergeant returned. Finally smiling, the man proudly exposed the biggest gold caps Frank had ever seen. Slowly he looked at each man, then shook his head. "Gentlemen, I will have the distinct pleasure of visiting with your sorry faces again later in the day. Report to room twenty-six for your induction physical."

As Frank moved by the sergeant, he leaned and said genuinely, "Nice caps, sir!"

Dale could not help but grin at the man's shocked expression.

The near-naked men moved from station to station, were weighed, asked to spit, drop their shorts and cough while the doctors listened, poked, and prodded. Finally, the line of timid enlistees got to the station where the proctological examiner sat waiting. The first man was called forward and the curtain drawn shut. "You're kidding me?!" came from the draftee behind the curtain. Twenty-eight eyes widened, then narrowed.

Frank looked at Garfford, who rolled his eyes indicating second thoughts about this whole thing, especially about this little, fat, white doctor that was about to shove his finger where no finger had ever been. He reacted to this awkward situation in the only way he could as a Lakota, with nervous humor. He grinned and whispered to Garfford, "*Wanyanka,* Watch this!"

When it was his turn, Frank handed over his stack of forms, deliberately removed his towel as the doctor pulled the screen. In as perfect English as he could affect, he said, "Well, sir, go for it and if by chance you find something good up there, I'd like to send it to my stepmother!" All the boys, white and Indian, laughed nervously.

Now the men at the other stations were watching. When the doctor had removed his index finger, Frank opened the curtain, turned toward the other men, and bowed. The room went crazy.

• • •

After mess, Dale turned to the short, blond-looking farm boy and said softly, "Now we all know why they don't call it lunch." An Indian draftee overheard and grinned broadly at Dale, who sheepishly returned it.

Again the public address system crackled to life. "Enlistees and draftees will now report to the following rooms specified for your intelligence and aptitude testing." The chatter died down. "Navy and marines, room eleven; air force, room twelve; Coast Guard need not report, as their choice of service is taken as proof of intelligence!" A brief chuckle rang out. "All draftees report to room fifteen; all army enlistees report to room thirteen."

In room thirteen the same pock-faced sergeant passed out tests and pencils. After he'd read the test instructions aloud, he paused long enough to look up at the clock, then said, "Please begin."

A series of low moans drifted through the small room. It was obvious to Dale that some of the men could barely read. And surprisingly to him, there were as many moans and rubbing of erasers from the whites as the Indians.

To him the questions seemed tragically simple, almost humorous, certainly nothing to anguish over. When he was about three quarters finished with the Stanford Binet Standardized Military IQ test, the smaller of the Indian boys, the same one who had joked during the physical, finished, set his pencil down, and smiled at the sergeant.

• • •

By four o'clock all the air force, navy, and marine enlistees had completed their tests. Their paperwork had been filled out, and they had taken their oaths. Branch by branch they filed out for waiting buses, first the air force, then the navy left with the marines. The recruiting center was left in relative silence.

Standing outside room thirteen with the other army enlistees, Frank Jealous Of Him joked with Garfford High Pipe about the invisible if intelligent Coast Guard recruits. By 4:30, the fifteen future GIs still hadn't taken their oath or been given transportation orders.

Frank furtively studied the lanky white kid across from him, the one that had smiled only once all day, then the shorter blond one that smiled all the time. Standing there in this fluorescent-lit hallway, Frank looked at them remembering how his father had always said, "Hatred is against the spirit of Christ's message." He would occasionally preach, "It doesn't matter if you are red, yellow, black, or white; God made all the four sacred colors into people. All races are equal; he does not favor one over the other."

But another memory made Frank reach up and trace the long scar that ran through his scalp. He remembered that dark night in Gordon two years earlier, when four cowboys had come up behind him and Matthew, and how the tallest one had said to his buddies, "Hey, boys, how'd you like to scalp us some prairie niggers?!" The laughter from the three other whites was all too short.

Frank stood in the sterile hall, breathing deeply. Looking across at the tall white kid, he remembered the dark Nebraska street, relived how scared he had been when he'd seen the white kid's knife flash in the lamp light. He winced visibly, feeling again the awful burning sensation from the blade tearing at his scalp.

Shaking the flashback from his mind, Frank's eyes came back to the freckle-faced blond kid who stood across from him. Of all the men in the hall, he noticed this kid was the only one still managing a smile. Never the loner, he moved toward the blond.

"Hey, man, my name is Frank, Frank Jealous Of Him," he said, and extended his hand.

The strawberry blond smiled, offering his hand, "Ron Gilbert from Hitchcock." Somehow that sounded silly to both of them.

"Hitchcock?" Frank looked quizzical. "That's got to be smaller than Wounded Knee!"

The other man's face broke ear to ear. "Ah, jeeze! I believe it just might be!"

20

ON THE WAY TO SALT LAKE CITY, THE AIRCRAFT'S TURBO-PROP ENGINES rumbled so loudly that Dale could not sleep. *Sports Illustrated* had bored him even more than the *Field and Stream*. A walk down the darkened aisle to the magazine rack had produced a new *Life* magazine. The cover of it read "U.S. under fire in Vietnam: SUICIDE RAID ON U.S. EMBASSY." The black-and-white image was of two American MPs escorting a Vietcong captive. Dale put the magazine back unread and returned to his seat. Around him the fourteen other recruits idly chatted.

Moments later behind closed eyelids, a barrage of images played and replayed. "Gentlemen, you are about to be honored with induction into the meanest fighting machine the world has ever known." Dale had noticed that the sergeant stood a little straighter when he said that.

He remembered, after they were sworn in, the cold intensity that had flooded the sergeant's pale blue eyes when he said, "Gentlemen, now that you have been sworn in as new members of the United States Army, I'll let you in on a little secret. Many of the men who were here today will end up in some cushy assignment far away from the fighting. Most of you, however, will end up in the embattled Republic of Vietnam. So, gentlemen, prepare yourselves well, because the majority of you will end up in the thick of it, just as many brave country boys from states like South Dakota have fought in every war this nation has fought." That speech sent a mild shiver through Dale's thin torso.

From that moment on, the word "Vietnam" sounded different to him. Yesterday, it was a TV news story, and a strange place in the letters of his cousin. Yet tonight, his first as a soldier, Vietnam had been transformed in his mind, becoming a surreal landscape formed of frightening TV images. Waves of excitement and dread alternated inside him until, almost asleep, his thoughts wandered further back, to home.

"Well, I suppose you'll get a job." His father's face had been painfully cold. Scrubbing cars for six weeks was a strange way to end civilian life. Then he remembered Shorty Bob handing him a beer. That beer had felt like a membership card to manhood. It seemed strange if not silly that the first time an older man treated him as a man had been with a beer.

In the soft glow of the overhead lights, above his closed eyes, a wrinkle formed; another recollection came to him, which soon turned into a nightmare. "People really die. Dead patriots no longer care about the inherent right or wrong of war." Dale's head bobbed, his chin dropping to his chest as Dr. Cummins's bearded face stood out against the stark tile walls of his biology lab. The professor stood behind tables covered with bags of embalmed animals. On a black Formica table was a six-foot-long, orange, plastic envelope. Dale walked up to it and slowly tugged on the zipper. As it opened he froze. Inside he saw a huge black face, oozing blood from a gaping hole in the neck. Dale's own head snapped up painfully. "Shit!" he said half-aloud, half-awake. In the dim light of the plane's cabin, the buzz of conversation went on, now perhaps a little quieter than before.

When they landed in Salt Lake City at midnight to change planes, Dale realized he hadn't really slept well in three days. Exhausted, he didn't want to think or make decisions; so he was glad that the kid named Tim had been put in charge of the group.

As the plane taxied to the gate, Tim, acne-scarred, voice cracking, stood up in front of the enlistees. "Boys, I guess the sergeant put me in charge because I admitted to a year in ROTC. Well, aside from a few classes it didn't mean a thing. I'm here now with you guys, an enlistee ... only I'm standing here with this silly armband. So let's hang together. I'm just as new to this as you are."

Tim led them off the plane and over to a different concourse. There he pointed to the plastic letters behind the counter that read, "Pan Am Flight 212. Departure 12:45, Arrives SEA-ttle/TAC-oma 2:45."

"You guys want ... ah, you might as well find a pop or cigarette machine. Just make sure you're back here by 12:30." Tim sounded even less sure of himself than he had on the plane. No one left. Finally Frank and Garfford walked down the concourse toward what looked to be an all-night smoke shop. One of the men who remained in the cluster of tired boys quietly asked Tim, "Where's Sea-Tac?"

• • •

A half hour later the men had boarded a plane for the last leg of their journey. In flight, the stewardess brought them beer nuts and Cokes. In time, with the help of caffeine and sugar, Dale's head began to clear a little. Across the narrow aisle Ron Gilbert and the smaller Indian, Frank, were engaged in a contest to see who could roll the best cigarette. The larger Indian, Garfford, knelt on the seat in front, grinning down at the contestants.

These guys don't look like the "monkeys" my uncle described, Dale mused, and they certainly don't all look alike. His mind fell back to the summers he had spent on his Uncle Doyce's ranch. He could smell the cows in the middle of a broad pasture of prairie grass and sagebrush. He could feel the horse beneath him, the sun warm on his back.

Once again, in the distance, he saw his uncle's tan Chevy pickup speed through shimmering heat waves down a gravel lane. Further up the dusty road was a small man with a satchel. The man, clearly an Indian, walked slowly toward the horizon. When the truck got close, it picked up speed and swerved toward him, sending the tiny satchel flying and the Indian jumping for his life, sprawling into the drainage ditch. Dale could still hear the hooting that came from the cab.

Never close to his uncle before, he hated him after that; angry at a man who was a high school teacher with a mind so small that scaring or killing another human being was a joke.

Back in the present, in the dim light of the overhead lamps, Dale studied the two Indian men. Both had clear piercing eyes and easy smiles; neither had the gray stubble of beard slowly forming on the white boys' faces. The bigger one had thick, curly hair, not unlike his own; the other had straight, gun-barrel blue-black hair, cropped short.

After Frank had produced for Ron Gilbert an almost factory-looking cigarette, Garfford High Pipe said, "That's pretty nice. Mind if I give it a try?"

Frank grinned at the man, handing him the sack of Bull Durham. With the utmost care the husky man pulled one thin paper from the tiny bundle, his massive fingers deftly forming then smoothing a crease. When he had it to his liking, he smiled, then laid the paper on his tongue; next he sprinkled loose tobacco on the paper and closed his mouth! Dale had never seen this one.

The Indian concentrated on his mouth: after a few grimaces, he reached in and pulled out a well-formed cigarette. Frank broke out laughing. Even Dale muttered, "Holy shit!"

"I learned that from an uncle who spent time in prison," was the only comment the big Indian made.

The cabin eventually darkened and, except for a quiet unrelenting cough coming from another Indian guy up ahead, all was silent.

Mr. Finch appeared under Dale's burning eyelids. He was talking to the basketball team in the familiar locker room. Behind Finch stood Dale's father. The coach admonished the team: "Regardless of what some people want to believe, Indians are just like us! With the exception of minor surface differences, they are identical in every way to every other people on this earth. They don't have better lungs and they don't run faster, so I want you to go out there and show this Eagle Butte team what you're made of." Dale could almost feel his throat constricting as it often had on the court in high school. The coach reached out his hands, as did the rest of the starting team.

Across the aisle, the pale white kid named Ron and the Indian, Frank Jealous Of Him, now dozed. Dale sat remembering halftime, when the score was 64 to 48 in favor of the team from the reservation. From the bench, Dale had watched as one after another of the Indian boys lit cigarettes, laughed, and drank Coke. He couldn't help but notice his exhausted teammates, sweat dripping, as they huddled with the coach. Across the court only the smallest of the Indian players seemed to show fatigue.

Dale smiled to himself thinking that Mr. Finch may not have been right. He had never seen the big Indian's cigarette trick!

21

FRANK WATCHED A LANKY KID FROM HIS OWN RESERVATION NAMED BLAIR Two Crow, who stood in line flipping long black locks from his eyes. He had done this out of habit since the induction center and, as Frank knew, long before. Moments later Blair sat surrounded by a pile of his own hair, still nervously flipping back the missing locks.

Soon, in one of the four barber chairs, Frank Jealous Of Him was undergoing the final stages of his own transformation. When the barber was finished, Frank rose and rubbed the bristled nubs of his black hair, shook his head, and growled, "Shit! Scalped by a white man!"

The whole line laughed. It seemed to him that most of these white boys laughed easily, and he liked that. After the haircuts they were shifted to a table where basic measurements for uniforms were taken, including a tape around their shaved heads for caps. As the men stood in line, they reached up every few seconds to feel the prickly reminders of what had been only moments before a symbol of manhood. Their heads now seemed to represent submission. When the corporal measured Frank's head and yelled out "Seven," he turned to Blair and with exaggerated indignity said, "That's the first and last time I give a man my head!" The line chuckled, while the corporal shook his head, smiling as if he knew where this kid's mouth would land him.

At noon the company was organized into a basic formation and marched at double time off toward a testing center for aptitude tests. Once there, the temporary drill instructor called them to attention. "Boys, and you are nothing but boys. You are about to take the United States Army Basic Aptitude Test. When you finish it, you will have a ten-minute break. You will then complete the Military Occupational Aptitude Test. How you perform on these tests will determine if you are to become a member of the United States Army, or will be sent to the Marines!" A nervous laugh rose up from the men.

"How you answer the questions on the aptitude test today, and in the next few days, will determine your Military Occupational Specialty, in other words, what you do in this man's army. So apply yourselves!"

The men groaned and twitched in their seats. Two of the Indian guys kept coughing in a manner that was distracting. Dale thought the whole thing was an exercise in silliness; answers to the questions seemed so obvious. How this could test intelligence was beyond him. He arrived at the conclusion that it was designed to test the low end and weed out those too stupid to load a rifle. Long before the time was up he set his pencil down and went outside for a smoke. The Indian called Jealous, the short blond, Ron Gilbert, and the taller Indian the guys called Pipe soon followed him. "So what did you guys think of that intelligence test?" Dale asked, moving toward them.

Frank smiled as he reached up to light his cigarette off Dale's. "That test was kind of fun." He chuckled. "If that test is supposed to see how smart we are, I must be a Geen-ee-ous! I mean those questions were almost ree-dick-you-lous."

Dale laughed, and saw this as an opportunity to get to know these men. "I think it was just supposed to weed out the group! How smart can any of us be? We're all here!" he said, poking Ron Gilbert on the shoulder.

Shortly before the test period was up, two men, who had been overheard bragging about being from California, stepped into the cold, mist-laden air of late February, lit a cigarette, and spoke in hushed tones. Apparently the recruits were mostly rural kids from South Dakota or white and Mexican kids from urban California. Dale noticed only one black. The only common denominator seemed to be that most of them came from poor families.

The four boys from South Dakota stood watching as the others slowly left the test hall. A dark-complexioned kid from California looked worried. He leaned toward his white buddy. "So what you think, man?"

"I think I passed it this time for sure!" He tried to sound positive. "I think 'cause I took it twice before, I figured out what answers they want!" Overhearing this, Frank poked Ron in the ribs and grinned. Dale shook his head.

• • •

The next day was filled with inoculations and medical tests, including chest X rays. The men still wore civilian clothes, and on a base filled with thousands of uniformed men they felt like bald visitors.

That evening, a half hour before lights out, the barracks were freezing. The temporary DI came in. "Ten Hut! I've heard that some of you women don't like the accommodations. Believe me, we feel just awful about that. Girls, these barracks were built during World War Two, and they have no heat. To make matters worse we have experienced an outbreak of meningitis in this section of old Fort Lewis. We have been ordered to leave all of the windows open for circulation. It is for your own good. The base surgeon has decided you won't die from the cold, but you could die from meningitis! By the way, until this meningitis thing is under control you are restricted to the company area. Lights out is at twenty-two hundred hours. Get a good night's sleep, ladies!"

Assigned to bunks the day before, Ron Gilbert lay under Garfford High Pipe; Dale Nielsen under Frank Jealous Of Him. The four were at the rear of the barracks, upstairs and against the wall.

All night Dale lay under the single wool blanket, shivering miserably. Like the first night, he squirmed, shifted, turned, gathered his lanky body into a fetal position, doing anything to keep the warmth in. Halfway down the row of bunks two men coughed incessantly.

Ron Gilbert noticed Dale's constant movement and whispered, "Bad enough we're freezing; those poor kids are going to die of pneumonia."

A moment of silence went by. Then Frank said, "No, they're not. I recognize that cough. If they die, it will be from TB."

• • •

At 0930, the platoons from Training Company E stood in long lines waiting for fatigues, winter dress uniforms, helmets, packs, rain gear, canteens, web belts—all the things that would make them feel and look like soldiers. At the station where nametags were made, Dale noticed that the two Indian guys with the chronic cough were gone.

Almost afraid to ask, he finally whispered to Frank, "What do you think happened to those two guys who were coughing?"

Frank answered matter-of-factly. "Man, it's too bad. Probably they got put under quarantine somewhere. Some people still think they're gonna be sent somewhere to die. That's why they don't tell anyone about their symptoms. A lot of folks in my family died of TB."

Dale looked away, then back at Frank. "My, ah, grandfather died of it when

I was a kid." Frank stood there surprised. He had never thought of white people dying like that.

As the recruits visited this last station, each stuffed all his gear into a green duffel bag and hauled it back toward the barracks. Under a dark gray Pacific sky that spit frozen rain on them, Dale half-carried, half-dragged his gear while Frank struggled beside him.

Thirty yards from the barracks, Dale tripped, hitting the ground hard enough to lose his breath. When he rolled onto his back and looked up, he saw, standing above him, the biggest black man he had ever seen. The sergeant glowered, "What's wrong with those feets of yours, boy?"

"No, nothing, sir."

"Look, soldier, I ain't no 'sir.' I am Sergeant Jones, your permanent drill instructor; 'sir' is for officers." He extended a large hand and pulled Nielsen to his feet. "Now put on those pretty new fatigues! Dismissed."

"Yes, sir," Dale blushed, as the tall black man frowned and walked away. Dale looked over at Frank. The Indian wore a smile that would have dazzled a blind man, but said nothing.

Soon forty men in crisp new fatigues stood outside the barracks admiring themselves. Some were quiet; others were making small talk. All were waiting for the next step in the enlistment process. A few of them looked down, lost in thought. Some were already homesick.

Like the Pied Piper of Hamlin, Frank walked out of the building with a basketball. No one asked where he got it and he didn't say, but many of the men rose and followed him toward the nearby court.

Dribbling slowly toward the middle of the concrete court, Frank said, "I know what you guys are thinking! We got all these guys standing around missing their girlfriends, when we could be playing basketball!" He tossed the ball over to Ron Gilbert, Ron tossed it to a guy named Les Amdahl. Les stood there trying to think of whom he should toss it to. He finally tossed it to his older brother, Lee.

"Nielsen, let's pick teams!" Frank called out.

Dale was surprised the Indian kid called his name, till he remembered the new nametags. He flashed on the games in high school with the reservation teams and chuckled to himself. He stroked his chin and looked for the tallest Indian kid in the group, then yelled, "Clayton, I'll take you!"

Frank acted shocked, then looked for the tallest, leanest, white kid and said, "I'll take him."

Dale looked around and saw Garfford High Pipe. "I'll take him!"

Frank looked for the tall black kid, pointed to him, and after looking at his nametag yelled, "Mardell, Sam, you're on our side." It went on like that until last pick. Frank stood beaming, while he took his time looking at who was left. He looked at Ron Gilbert, then past, then came back to Ron, then moved his eyes again. Finally, after exaggerating the decision, he said, "Ron from Hitchcock!" and the game was on.

Pretty soon it was the white kid with the Indian team against the Indian kid with the white team, and the entire company was screaming and laughing.

At 1145, a tall, handsome, brown-skinned sergeant stood unnoticed in the back of the group watching the game. After five minutes he cleared his throat loudly. The ball bounced vacantly across the pavement.

"Gentlemen! My name is Edwards, Sergeant Edwards to you, and I will have the distinct honor of being your baby-sitter the next eight weeks. From now on you will have a common identity; you will be Second Platoon of E Company, Fifth Battalion; I will be your platoon sergeant. You will address me as "Sergeant" or "Sergeant Edwards," show respect for my uniform and my rank at all times, and we'll get along just fine. I will be working with Sergeant Jones. You will also show him respect and courtesy or life will not be fun. Is that understood?" They all stood staring attentively.

"Is that clear?"

A weak "Yes, Sergeant," went up from a few men.

"What is the matter with you fellahs? When I ask a question of the platoon, I will get a platoon response. Is that clear?!"

"Yes, Sergeant!" the recruits joined in.

"Since you can't remember what to call me, I'll give you a little reminder. Drop and give me fifty push-ups! One, two, three . . ."

Dale's arms burned until they turned into quivering hot jelly. The sergeant was only on thirty-six.

• • •

At mess hall the men were lined up by Sergeant Edwards, who stood in the lead. "Some of you men are fat, soft; others are thin as stray cats. But it doesn't make a difference. You will all get three minutes to eat. When three minutes are up you will police your trays into these bins, and report to me."

Frank stood there grinning. "What the hell are you grinning at, boy?" Edwards stalked over to him. "What's your name, boy?"

"Frank Jealous Of Him, sir."

The black man almost broke his composure. "It's not 'sir'! You got wax in your ears, soldier? Maybe some push-ups would improve your hearing! Drop and give me fifty!"

After Frank had struggled through the last ten he stood at attention beside the sergeant.

"Jealous Of Him, is that some sort of Indian name?"

"Yes, Sergeant, Sioux!"

"Well, what is there to grin about?"

"I just do that Sergeant Edwards. I don't know why; I guess it's 'cause the food smells good, Sergeant."

"Well, now, that's an interesting idea, son," he laughed, then glared at the other green trooper who had dared smile at Frank. The sergeant shook his head in disgust, then barked, "Chow time!" The men scrambled for the line.

22

IN A HUGE BARN THAT LOOKED LIKE AN OLD HANGAR, THE BOYS OF Second Platoon, E Company stood in line or sat with officers reviewing their aptitude tests. Dale had never seen anything like it. Frank sat beside him speaking with another officer. While the captain in front of him shuffled papers, Dale glanced over and noticed the high scores on Frank's tests.

The officer across from Dale addressed him. "Nielsen, in our rating system for intelligence and leadership potential you ranked near the top. At the completion of basic training we would like to encourage you to consider Officers Candidate School and become an officer. As you may know this would require that you sign up for four years, but it would ensure that some men in the field have a good leader and that you would be out there giving orders."

Dale sat for a moment, surprised by the offer, but with a gnawing sense that he just wanted to do his time and get out. After three days of being tested, screamed at, poked at, and herded around, two years seemed like an eternity. "No, sir. I just want to serve as a soldier and return to college."

"Well, son, I want you to consider what I've said. You have superior skills in all areas and could do us both a favor. If you should change your mind any time during your basic training, let me know. Next."

Outside, while the rest of the company completed their interviews, he stood thinking about what the captain had said. Ron Gilbert walked up to him, and Dale offered him a cigarette. "Jeeze, ya know. I don't smoke. My dad would kill me!"

"What did they tell you in there?" Dale motioned toward the building.

"Jeeze, they want me to become a helicopter pilot, said I'd be making real use of my talent and all that." He laughed. "'Course I'd have to sign up for four years."

"What did you tell them?"

"Well, I come from a family of fourteen brothers and sisters. Heck, never thought I'd admit it, but I'm so homesick right now all I can think about is going home to Hitchcock. I told them no. What did they tell you?"

Dale shook his head. "Said that I should consider becoming an officer. I told them I just want to do my thing and go back to college, but it was nice to know they asked."

Dale noticed Frank exiting the large building. "Hey, Frank, what did they say?"

Frank smiled broadly. "Said I scored real high, said I should think about being a helicopter mechanic or going to jump school."

Dale wondered why the test officers had not mentioned Officers Candidate School to Frank. It was already apparent that he was the natural leader of the group.

At ten the next morning, under a breaking sky that threatened to produce some sunshine, the men stood in formation shouldering World War II vintage M-1 rifles. "Right Shoulder Arms! Left Shoulder Arms! Present Arms! Order Arms! Right Shoulder Arms! Left Shoulder Arms! Right Shoulder Arms! Present Arms! Order Arms! At ease!" Sergeant Jones's dark face was intense. "Man, you bad! Some of you peoples don't know your damned right from your left. You downright clumsy. But that's going to change. You know I got some pride and right now I don't want to be seen with you! Do you understand?"

"Yes, Sergeant." A weak response hung in the cool air.

"What the hell was that?" He shook his head. "Didn't you hear me?"

"Yes, Sergeant!" It was louder but still not what the man was looking for.

"What did you say?" The big man glowered at them.

"Yes, Sergeant!" the platoon called out as if one voice.

"Very good. Now, Sergeant Edwards will explain something to you about unit pride. Sergeant Edwards."

The tall, thin, paler-skinned DI stepped forward. "Men, right now you are a sorry collection of losers. Sergeant Jones and myself are professional soldiers. We are not in this for a hobby. Our job is to see that as many of you get home to your mama's arms as possible. I will be honest with you! All of you will not return. How many of you return depends on how you do in the next eight weeks, and what I have seen in the last half hour tells me you better be paying some powerful attention." He stayed silent for a moment to emphasize his words.

"Company E will be the best-trained unit on this base or die trying. You will develop a pride and esprit de corps that will sustain you in battle; a pride in yourselves that will last a lifetime. Now let's get this drill right!"

. . .

After mess hall, Sergeant Edwards stood in front of the tired men and said, "This is what we call cadence. You might as well learn to like marching, 'cause we will be doing a lot of it. For today, Sergeant Jones will return my calls. In a few days you will return them. Let's try to look sharp, Platoon Attention! . . . Forward! March!" He swung the men across the base calling cadence.

"Jody this and Jody that."

"Jody is a real cool cat," returned Jones.

"Ain't no use in callin' home!"

"Jody's on your telephone."

"Ain't no use in going home!"

"Jody's got your girl and gone."

"Ain't no use in feelin' blue!"

"Jody's got your sister too."

"Ain't no use in lookin' back!"

"Jody's got your Cadillac."

"Going home on three-day pass!"

"Gonna kick old Jody's ass!"

Back and forth it went while the sweating men smiled at the lyrics. They were beginning the long process of leaving civilian life behind and becoming a military unit.

After twenty minutes Sergeant Edwards called "Platoon . . . Halt!" He walked to the middle of the line and stood before a pudgy kid from California. "What's your name, son?"

"Massey!" the boy panted.

Sergeant Edwards's brow wrinkled. "I believe this boy called me Massa! That's not necessary." Jones laughed.

"Massey, you got two left feet. We're going to try something easier for you: I want you to call your right foot 'right' and your left foot 'left.' Got that?" The platoon snickered.

"Platoon . . . Forward. . . . March! Left, right, left, right, left . . . left . . . left, right, left! Platoon . . . Halt! Sergeant Jones, do you see what I'm seeing?"

Jones responded. "Sure do! This whole damn outfit trying to make Massey look bad."

Edwards spit on the ground. "Well, Sergeant Jones, what should we do about it?"

Sergeant Jones furrowed his dark brow like he was actually making a decision. "I think the whole platoon should do one hundred push-ups in honor of Mr. Massey's fine footwork. Drop and give me one hundred!"

A groan went up. "On your faces, and count off!"

At the end of three minutes Sergeant Jones blew a whistle. Men moaned and slowly stood. Only Frank Jealous Of Him and Garfford High Pipe wore smiles. That night eighty arms ached so bad they could barely lift food off their plates.

• • •

By 1800 hours the men were back in their company area resting on their cots. Some were playing cards or sat bullshitting, when Sergeant Jones walked in. "Attention!" The men jumped to their feet.

"Ladies! Most of you will be sent to Vietnam. A few of you gonna ride in tanks, others might be assigned to motor pool, but the majority of your sorry asses will walk from point A to point B. Since we don't know which ones you are, you will all be considered infantry and trained to survive as infantry soldiers.

"As an infantry soldier you will have to rely on your feets. You will learn to pay attention to your feets. They will carry you on patrol. They will carry you into a firefight, and if you pay attention during the next seven weeks, they will carry you on out! And speaking of feets, what the hell is that smell?" A few of the men looked over at Bill Cord, the sole recruit from Montana. "Well, whoever or whatever it is better do something about it or you'll all be doing a few push-ups." The sergeant looked at Cord and narrowed his eyes, then continued. "What you peoples will learn today is how to take care of your boots so your feets will stay dry! That's rule number one for the infantry soldier." He paced up and down the line looking at the men, sizing them up.

"At ease . . . I will go through the process one time, and you will have shiny boots from this day forward. You will learn to take pride in your appearance from bottom to top, because you are in the United States Army! Is that clear?"

"Yes, Sergeant!"

By eight the lesson was over and the boys from Second Platoon entertained themselves in the frigid air of a late February night. Ron Gilbert lay below Garfford High Pipe on his bunk reading. Dale lay below Frank looking at the addresses on two letters. "Hey, Ron, you got a girl at home?"

"Yeah, sure do. Her name is Mary."

Dale leaned to look up at Frank. "Hey, Frank, you got a girl at home?"

Frank responded straight-faced, "Hell no, man. I'm kind of shy with women." He slid a letter from Darlene Ghost out of his pocket and under the mattress. "Why?"

"Oh, I don't know . . . I got two girls writing to me and I only need one. If you need someone to write to, you can have one of these addresses."

Frank stayed serious. "First you offer this girl to Gilbert, then you offer her to me. She must be a real dog."

"No, that's not it. It's just that I'm thinking of marrying this other one, and I don't want to string this one along."

"Hey, that's damn white of you. What's her name?"

"Elaine," Dale replied. He handed Frank the empty envelope.

23

SUNDAY WAS THE FIRST DAY THE NEW SOLDIERS WERE ALLOWED TO SLEEP past 0530, and most of the company was sleeping in. Dale was awakened at 0700 by Frank singing "Mule Skinner Blues" in the shower.

"God, Frank, what the hell are you doing up so early?" he yawned as Frank walked back into the main barracks.

"I'm going to church and you're going with me. You and Ron, and . . .," he banged on Pipe's bunk, "Garfford. We'll get cleaned up and get out of here for a little while. Besides you guys could use it."

Ron's eyes fluttered awake. "What's up?"

"You are! Dale was just telling me how he was going to church and that he wanted us to go with him." Frank's eyes danced.

"He's crazy!" Dale moaned.

"Seriously, I'm going to church at the main area and I want you guys to come with me."

Dale was annoyed. "I'm not going to church today, next week, or ever. It's not my thing!" He rolled over.

Frank persisted. "Well, my dad is a preacher, and I promised him I would go to church, and take the guys in my outfit with me." He nudged Garfford.

"I don't go to church, Frank." Garfford sounded grouchy.

"What? You got no religion?"

Garfford did not turn over. "I got religion; I just don't go to a white man's church."

"Would you guys shut up about church!" Sam Mardell, the company's only black, yelled out. "Hey man, some of us want to sleep!"

Finally, Ron said quietly, "I guess I wouldn't mind if you really want to. Give me a few minutes and I'll go with you."

• • •

Later, the four men lay on their bunks, taking advantage of two hours of free time the Sunday schedule allowed. The conversation began when Ron Gilbert mentioned being homesick. It shifted to the topic of how much basic training "sucked," then on to Vietnam, and drifted finally to the topic of dying.

It was Ron who pressed the others for their thoughts. "Something bothers me and I can't make it go away. You know how Sergeant Jones is always saying how some of us aren't going to come home. Do you guys ever think about that? I mean about dying and all? Dale, what do you think? Do you think that when you die there is something else?"

Dale turned on his bunk toward the freckle-faced inquisitor. "I try not to think about it. I was raised Catholic and I know what the church says about it. How you meet St. Peter who sends you to God for a final judgment and how you could end up in heaven, hell, or a place called purgatory, sort of stuck in between. That's probably where I'd go," he chuckled.

"No, really, what do you think?" Ron insisted.

"I guess it's like a permanent blackness, like when you turn off one of those old black-and-white TV sets and the light gets smaller and smaller until finally it's a pinpoint and then it disappears. There's a part of me that thinks people invented religion because they don't want to believe they're going to end up worm pudding! What do you think, Frank?"

Frank put down a worn magazine. "I guess it's like in the Bible. It's a really nice place, where you'll be at peace and it will be bright and warm. I guess you'll see Jesus and that will make you happy. It will last forever but it will seem like a second. And I guess I believe there is a hell, where some people end up paying for how they hurt people on this earth. They stay there forever, suffering." He smiled. "What do you think, Ronnie?"

Looking pensive, Ron said, "Jeeze, ya know in my family, every Sunday in summer we play softball in the farmyard. Everybody knows the rules: which part of the barn is a home run, which part of what tree is a foul ball, so there's no disagreements. Everybody comes: cousins, aunts, and uncles. Between them and my own brothers and sisters there's enough for different teams and people to serve the refreshments and cheer on the players. Mom is in the kitchen with my sweetheart, Mary, organizing a family feed. My dad is standing out there behind first base, worn out from three hours of work that morning. He's pretending to umpire, he's got a lemonade in his hand, and he's laughing and smiling at everyone. It's the happiest memories I've got. I hope heaven is like that and it goes on forever."

"Jeeze, ya know, Ron." Imitating Ron Gilbert's wide-eyed innocence, Garfford broke his usual silence. "Your idea of life after death is like what Indians believe. I'm not a Christian, that's the religion of the white man's missionaries. They tell you if you take the Bible that's all you need. I don't believe it 'cause the white man has the Bible and all the land and money, and he's still trying to get more. In the Indian way, you got what you need if you got how we say, *Wicozani, na wiconi cage* . . . your health and children. Everything else is up to man."

Garfford rolled on his side to face the others. "We Sioux believe that when you die, if you've been a generous man, someone who has a heart for people, then you go to a land beyond the clouds and Milky Way. It's the Milky Way you follow to get there. There is an old woman who greets you on that path; if you been good to people, generous and all, she lets you travel on. If not, well, you're sent back to start all over again.

"When you get to that Spirit Land, there are no white men. The Great Mystery will ask, 'How was your journey?' If you answer well, you will stay in that land. Everything is green and fresh. The air is sweet and no one is hungry. No one hates, nobody is drinking." His voice dropped. "Nobody is fighting themselves or anyone else. People are free and happy over there. Besides, I'm not going to get killed in Vietnam. I already know how it's going to turn out."

"So how come you know?" said Frank. "Did you go to a medicine man or something?" His voice teased.

Garfford nodded his head. "I'm an Indian just like you, Frank. Ain't nothin' gonna change that. Fighting in a white man's war doesn't change that. So I got some Indian help.

"When it comes to power, the white man's religion is weak. A long time ago our warriors could ride into a hail of bullets and come out without a scratch. They had a medicine. They wore it on their shields or tied in their hair. Mine is here." He tapped his fatigue pocket.

Dale lifted onto his elbow. Intrigued by the quiet Indian's eloquence, he asked, "So if you're not fighting for the white man, why are you here?"

"I'm fighting for me, and my people, I guess. So I can go home a veteran. In the Indian way you ain't nothin' unless you're a veteran. And being a veteran don't mean much unless you been to war. It's just part of being a man."

"Is that why you're here, Frank?" Ron asked.

Frank thought for a moment. "Well, I guess that's part of it. My dad was in World War Two and he got a bunch of medals. I told him I'm going to top him. And there's another thing that Indians believe, that Pipe forgot. If you die on the battlefield, you go straight on from there." As he pointed, their eyes drifted toward the ceiling. "Besides, we're all here for the same reason," his voice serious, "'cause a-l-l women love a man in a uniform!" With that he had them chuckling again.

Dale looked at Frank. His new friend always seemed to hide behind humor.

"So you think you might die over there, Frank?" Ron asked innocently.

"Not until I get some foreign pussy!" Frank answered.

24

COLD, DAMP AIR BLEW IN OFF PUGET SOUND, CREATING A GROUND FOG that shrouded the physical training track at Fort Lewis. Sergeants Jones and Edwards had just demonstrated the proper technique for lifting a wounded comrade. Now Edwards nodded and grinned at Jones, knowing the fun was about to start.

Jones stood before the platoon. "Men, what we are doing today may save your life or that of a buddy. With proper technique and a little adrenaline the smallest man can rescue the biggest man. If your friend dies because you could not or would not help him, you gonna live with that the rest of your life."

Edwards added. "Despite the technology of the United States Army, when it comes to a firefight, in life-and-death situations, all you really have to fall back on is the guys you are serving with. The saving of a fallen comrade is a sacred duty."

The men hung on every word the big man said. Sergeant Edwards was a Vietnam combat veteran and that gave him a mythical quality. He seldom made direct reference to it, but when he did the men listened intently. "I want you to divide up into pairs and practice the lift. Your comrade has a serious leg wound and cannot walk. It is your job to lift and rescue him."

The recruits sized each other up, generally trying to pick someone their own size. At 130 pounds, Frank walked over to 160-pound Dale, flashing that irresistible smile.

Dale returned the grin and lay down on the ground feigning unconsciousness. "Do it to me, baby!" Dale whispered. With an ease that shocked all within eyesight, Frank boosted Dale to his shoulders.

Dale laughed at how silly and helpless he felt being held by a man six inches shorter. Frank reached up and tickled his victim.

Within minutes everyone had been the rescued and the rescuer. Sergeant Jones stepped forward. "Boys, now we gonna have some fun. You and your partners will be timed at a distance of one hundred yards. Each man will have a turn carrying and being carried. Sergeant Edwards will keep track of the times. The fastest team in combined time will get unlimited chow tonight." As if the prize were a trip home, a raucous cheer went up.

"Do I have some volunteers to show the rest of the men how it's done?" Ron Gilbert and Garfford High Pipe lifted their arms, followed by Frank and Dale. "You'll start with your partner lying flat on the ground. Pick him up, carry him to the end of the field, switch positions, and run back here. Is that clear?"

"Yes, Sergeant!" the platoon resounded.

"First two teams on the line!" Frank pointed at Dale and then the ground; Dale shook off the call and Frank took first man down.

"Place your bets!" Sergeant Edwards yelled. "Take your mark! Go!"

Dale strained, boosting Frank to his shoulders, then drove with sinewy legs.

At the same time, "Ahhggg!" Garfford High Pipe screamed mournfully as he picked up the smaller Ron Gilbert and sprang ahead of Dale. Jostling, bouncing, groaning, the two teams pounded toward the far end of the field. Midway Dale passed the big Indian. At seventy-five yards Garfford pulled abreast of Dale while Frank swatted at Ron with his cap. The platoon roared with laughter.

Despite two weeks of marching and physical training, with fifteen yards to go Dale's legs burned red hot beneath him. His calves wobbled, thighs twitched until he could drop Frank to the ground at the goalpost.

Meanwhile, the newly grounded Ron Gilbert grunted loudly as he hefted his larger Indian partner to his shoulders and took off for the starting line.

Frank sprang to his feet while Dale lay down. To everyone's surprise the Indian stopped for a moment, spit on his hands, then tugged his fatigue pants up. Dale looked up. "What the fuck are you doing?" Frank only winked at him.

By now the other team was fifteen yards ahead and gaining more ground. Frank snapped his partner off the ground like he was weightless, then sprang ahead so fast Dale had to hang on.

At midfield Frank was smiling so broadly, Sergeant Jones slapped the laughing Sergeant Edwards on the back, pointing at the Indian.

Frank called to Ron, "Move over, train coming through!" His combat boots grinding loudly into the cinders, Ron Gilbert fought desperately to keep the lead. Garfford took to whipping Ron on the butt like a frantic jockey on a winded racehorse. With fifteen yards remaining, Frank came abreast of the other pair.

The crowd exploded with the craziness of the spectacle.

At five yards, Frank leaned into the finish fairly catapulting his helpless partner ahead of him. Dale bounced and rolled across the finish line.

Just a yard behind, Ron Gilbert's legs tangled and both men slid painfully across the finish.

Sergeant Edwards stood smiling like a proud father. Then he said, "You were a little sloppy. I want you to do it again!"

25

ON SUNDAY, RON AND FRANK WENT TO CHURCH AT 0900. AT 1000 SAM MARDELL walked back from his shower. Dale signaled him to come over to his bunk. "Sam, what do you think of Bill Cord?"

"I think that smelly bastard give guys from Montana a bad rap! Everybody know that man. He don't bathe, he don't brush his teeth! He's disgustin'! Why? How come you askin'?"

Dale leaned over toward the smaller soldier and whispered. "I got an idea how we could have a little fun and maybe teach him a lesson." The two sat on the bunk whispering and snickering until the black soldier stood up, gave Dale a high five, and walked back toward his own bunk.

At 1300 the platoon had two hours to kill before a company parade was to be held. Bill Cord lay on his bed snoring while the other men polished boots, wrote letters, or talked quietly.

Dale signaled Mardell to move over to Cord's bunk. Mardell waved for the rest of the men to keep silent. Dale reached into his footlocker and took out a thick, round wad of toilet paper, then wet it down with water from his canteen. Frank watched curiously. Quietly Dale walked over to the sleeping man and sat down on the bunk closest to him. A low buzz filled the room as everyone realized something was about to take place.

Mardell stood adjacent to Cord's open mouth and unzipped his fatigue pants and withdrew his Boy's Club membership card. It's flaccid length hung precariously close to Cord's face. Now, all the men on second floor stood stock-still in anticipation.

Dale took the wad of wet toilet paper and held it up for the room to inspect, then reached over and rubbed it across Cord's lips. Waking with a start, his eyes opened to see Mardell slipping his cock back into his pants.

"Oh shit! You fuckin son of a bitch!" Cord yelled. The room rocked with laughter. "You black son of a bitch! You stuck your cock in my mouth!" By this time Mardell had gotten a safe distance away. "God damned nigger! Come over here where I can beat the shit out of you!" He stood, the veins in his neck and forehead distended.

By then some of the men were on the floor laughing helplessly.

Sergeant Jones burst from his office. "Who's got a problem with a nigger?"

Cord stood there stammering, knowing he'd been had. "No one, Sarge, it's just that Mardell, well, he . . ." Now Cord's face was a brilliant scarlet. Jones towered above him glowering. "Well, it's just that Mardell stuck his fuckin pecker in my mouth while I was sleeping."

Jones turned toward the black soldier. "Mardell, this is a pretty serious accusation; you know how the army feels about homos. Did you stick your clean, black dick in Cord's filthy mouth?"

Mardell stood straight-faced. "No, Sergeant, I did not! He must have imagined it or dreamed it." The whole barracks roared with laughter.

Jones began to realize something was up. "Did anyone in this barracks see Mr. Mardell stick his dick in Mr. Cord's cavity-filled mouth?"

"No, Sergeant Jones!" A chorus rose up.

"Well, Mr. Cord, it seems you been hallucinating, maybe dreaming about a chocolate bar or a chocolate dick or something." The men howled. "I suggest you return to your bunk and best not be callin' folks nigger. Better yet, take a shower. You stink bad, boy. Now!" A loud cheer ended the matter.

26

"KILL! KILL! KILL!" DALE YELLED AS HE LUNGED FORWARD THRUSTING HIS bayonet into a human-shaped dummy. "Kill! Kill!" came from a line of six men as they fiercely attacked other dummies. The remaining recruits stood back waiting their turns.

"Massey!" Sergeant Jones screamed at the flabby recruit. "Massey, you've been here five God-damned weeks and you're about as aggressive as marshmallow in hot cocoa. If you gonna make it over there, you gonna have to get mad!" He grabbed the weapon from the wide-eyed boy and thrust it through the dummy, practically snapping the chains that held it. "Like that, boy!"

When it was Dale's turn, Jones stood over him screaming "Kill! Kill!" so loud it went right through him. To his surprise, Dale could feel his adrenaline rise as he attacked the enemy. He could see the man, his imagined Asian eyes and black hair taunting him. "Kill! Kill!" he pushed, muscles straining, until Sergeant Jones tapped him on the shoulder.

"Better give someone else a chance while we still got a dummy!" Dale got hold of himself and relaxed. It was the first time he had felt this worked up, and he liked the sensation. After all, he thought, this is why I joined up. Despite his natural cynicism, he had to admit he was getting sucked in, excited by the idea of killing.

After mess hall that afternoon the sky overhead threatened with a cover of low-flying dark clouds and the air had turned bitter cold. The training company moved toward the classrooms marching in cadence. Sergeant Edwards started the call: "I don't know but I been told."

Frank picked it up: "Sergeant Edwards' getting old!" He poked Dale in the ribs. "I don't know but I would say . . ."

Dale picked it up: "U.S. Marines are mostly gay!"

Frank took it back: "I don't know but I been told . . ."

Dale responded: "Air Force guys got nothing to hold." Sergeant Edwards was all teeth, fighting back laughter.

"I don't know but I would say . . ." Frank's voice floated over the men.

"U.S. Army rules the day," Dale snapped back.

"I don't know but I been told . . ."

"Massey is about to fold!" Dale grinned.

"I don't know but I would say! . . ." Frank sang out.

"Army's got the worst damn pay!" Dale fumbled a little.

"I don't know but I been told . . ." Frank pushed his luck.

"Cord's old jock is filled with mold." Dale shook his head and shrugged his shoulders as the troop moved forward laughing.

The sky opened with a vengeance as Sergeant Edwards signaled the column to a halt. "Rain gear." Each man reached for the small pack he carried and quickly slipped into a waterproof jacket. Within thirty seconds Edwards motioned with his hand for the company forward. Behind them Massey stumbled in his half-raised rain pants and tripped, falling onto his hands.

Sergeant Edwards wore a scowl as he waved the column to a halt once again. He walked back to where the frightened Massey struggled to simultaneously stand and pull up his pants.

Edwards stood in front of him, lips quivering. It looked for a moment as if Edwards might actually strike the nervous man. "Massey, you're a dud!" was all he said.

"Yes, sir!"

. . .

Then it was Sunday, and the few hours of free time seemed a blessing. Frank and Ron Gilbert were back from church before Dale and High Pipe were even up. After noon chow, Ron sat on his bunk looking glum.

"What's the matter with you? Did you get a 'Dear Ron' letter or did your favorite sow die?" Dale taunted him quietly.

"Nahh, I, ah, I'm just feeling down, I guess."

"You want to talk about it?" Dale asked.

"Nahh, I'll be okay, I guess."

"In a pig's ass—you look like your best friend died. What is it?"

"It's all your damn farmboy pig jokes. You know I've never had a favorite pig. I like them all."

"Seriously, what's up?" Dale said.

"Not here. Let's go outside."

Dale could now see Ron had moisture in his eyes.

Walking through the gray coldness toward the base store the recruits had soon learned to call the PX, Dale broke the silence. "What is it, Ron?"

"Ah, I don't really know. I mean it's like you and Frank thrive in this place. No matter what they do, you guys make a joke of it. It's like you actually like it here." His voice dropped.

"I thought you were doing fine," Dale offered.

"Jeeze, I'm hurting, Dale. You know having a big family is something some people complain about. I mean you never have enough clothes, we have to eat in shifts, but, damn, I miss them. It's like I got sixteen people pulling on my heart. With Mary, it's seventeen. Damn, I miss her so bad I can't stand it. Every day I get lonelier . . . I've been getting these crazy thoughts about getting killed over there and never seeing my family again. To tell you the truth I been getting crazy thoughts about going AWOL." His voice cracked.

Dale stopped and turned to his new friend. "You know, I never would have known that, Ron."

"Really? I mean I thought it was written all over my face."

"No. You've been hiding it pretty well and so, I suspect, have a lot of other guys. There are lots of times when I could kick myself for dropping out of school and signing up for this abuse. If I thought I'd be putting up with this for two years, I'd be going AWOL myself, but it will end in two weeks and we'll be home on leave. I know you'll make it."

Ron smiled. "Come on, you're just saying that. I mean you and Frank are the greatest. I can't believe you're homesick."

"Well, maybe it's not always homesickness that bothers me so much. It's more like the army bullshit, like being in a prison you volunteered for. I don't like being treated like I'm stupid from morning till lights out . . . I guess I didn't know how much I'd hate the bullshit and regimentation.

"As for Jealous Of Him, I think he's the best one here, not just at the tests, but at hiding his feelings. Maybe he's running away, or to something you're not. Maybe if you were, it would be easier. You'll make it, man. You're no slouch; I mean, I doubt Sergeant Edwards or Sergeant Jones have anything but respect for you. You just got to believe the other guys are as scared and homesick as you are, and that you're tough enough to get through it. Hell, just fighting over food at the dinner table, with all those brothers and sisters, has got to make you tougher than some of these California guys." Dale slapped Ron on the back, indicating they should keep walking.

• • •

Monday morning they were at the track by 0830. Each recruit had on combat boots, full fatigues, and a web belt and carried an M-14. Sergeants Jones and Edwards stood by with a clipboard and stopwatch the men had come to dread. "You children are in for a treat! You've had six weeks to toughen up those sorry excuses for legs. Now we're going to find out who's the fastest and who's the slackest." Sergeant Jones glanced over at Massey, who was distractedly lighting a cigarette.

The tall black man was at Massey's side before the fuzzy-faced blond could react. "Massey, do this look like a smoke break?" he asked, whispering loudly.

Massey's hand began to shake as he pulled the cigarette from his lips, but he did not answer.

"Massey! You deaf, boy? I'm asking you a God-damn question. You think this a smoke break?"

Finally, the quivering recruit answered. "I guess not, Sergeant Jones."

"You guess not? What the hell kind of answer is that? Sergeant Edwards! Massey here don't know yet when he on smoke break!" Sergeant Jones took the cigarette from the boy's trembling hand. "Stand at attention, boy!" Massey stiffened.

The sergeant took a long drag on the offending cigarette and studied the man. The whole company was watching. "Since this boy's already got hearing problems, thinks he hears 'Smoke break!' when no one said nothing, I think I should put this fucking cigarette out. What do you all say?" He exhaled on Massey.

The training company responded in trained unison, "Yes, Sergeant Jones."

The sergeant went on. "I think I should put this cigarette out in Massey's God-damn deaf ear. What do you think, men?"

This time the response was more muffled. "Yes, Sergeant."

Sergeant Jones slowly moved the cigarette toward the shaking man, but Massey did not pull back. Dale watched with horror as the glowing cigarette inched toward the plump recruit's pink ear. Jones's palm was now on the boy's fuzzy red cheek, the cigarette's orange heat only millimeters from Massey's ear canal. Still Massey stood his ground.

With calm precision the hot point entered the canal. Massey's eyes were wide with fear, but he did not move an inch. Before it burned the skin, Sergeant Jones tossed the butt to the ground. "Well, will you look at that, Sergeant Edwards! Maybe there is something more to this useless sack of shit than we thought!" He turned and moved back toward the starting line.

"All right!" Sergeant Edwards bellowed. "This is a mile run! For those that need an explanation, that is four times around the track. Fastest man gets unlimited chow for two days! We need four volunteers for first flight." In a moment Frank was standing on the line. That was a clear signal for Dale to step forward. Then, as usual, it was Ron Gilbert and Garfford High Pipe who filled out the foursome.

Dale bent toward Ron and whispered, "I'm going to kick your homesick ass." Ron only smiled.

Frank stood smiling self-confidently as if he had already won.

"Runners, take your mark . . . go!" Sergeant Edwards roared. The four boys sprang from the start, pumping their heavy combat boots forward, straining to capture the lead. Four men hit the first turn dead even. By the second turn, Frank had moved into a delicate lead only a step ahead of the other three.

By the end of the first lap, Dale had made his plan. He knew that Frank would not run any faster than he had to in order to win. He would lay back a few feet and let Frank think he was out to a comfortable lead, then maybe, just maybe, he would make his move. Pipe and Ron were still only a few feet back, yet Dale knew it was a race between himself and Frank.

At the second lap his legs were beginning to burn; the hard boots ground at his feet; his shoulders ached with the weight of the rifle. Ahead, Frank loped along, seemingly at ease with the awkward equipment. Dale wanted this one. He wanted just once to beat Frank at something. He forced his mind to remain calm.

Three laps into the test, and Frank had a comfortable lead. Dale glanced back to see the big Indian and the flush-cheeked farm boy running shoulder to shoulder. It was as if a sacred pact had been struck between them, as if they were becoming brothers, and if they were to be beaten it would be together.

As a side cramp gnawed into his ribs, Dale's game plan began to collapse. Fuckin Jealous isn't even trying, he thought. The Indian's short, muscular legs kicked high; his strides were long and even.

Dale's lungs burned, his throat was thick with dreaded asthmatic phlegm. Despite the screaming of the men, all he could hear was the noise of his wheezing breath, the pounding of his heart, and the loud crunch of his tortured footfalls.

With one hundred yards to go, and confident with his lead, Frank actually let up a little. Dale, five yards behind, wobbled on spindly legs, his brain starving for oxygen. Straining for every breath, even his vision had begun to narrow, shrinking with each thrust of his wasted, red-hot thigh muscles. He could see the men screaming, waving their arms. He could see Frank so confident that he had slowed slightly. "Push!" his pounding brain screamed at itself. "Now!" it taunted his failing body forward into a shrinking tunnel of light.

At ten yards he passed Frank, who was too surprised to respond. Dale sprawled across the finish line, totally panicked by his inability to breath, sure his asthma could cause him to suffocate. Ron and Pipe, who finished only seconds behind them, pounded each other on the back and grinned breathlessly.

Frank stood off by himself, hands on his knees. This skinny white kid had beaten him, and it did not feel good.

When he had regained his composure, he walked over to the gasping, wobbling victor and reached out with his hand. "You beat me, man," he said, quickly pumping Dale's clammy hand. Then with what Dale heard as resentment, he said, "But it will never happen again."

27

THAT SAME NIGHT BEFORE LIGHTS OUT, RON LOOKED OVER AT DALE. "MAN, that was quite a run!" Turning loudly onto his side, Frank said nothing.

"Yeah, that was really something," Pipe said, trying to get a charge out of Frank. Still, Frank did not respond.

"Lights out!" the sergeant yelled. Dale lay wide awake for a few moments, replaying the event, wondering why Frank should be so angry. Above, still smarting from his defeat, Frank, too, lay awake.

Frank never slept that night. Angry with himself, he tossed and turned until 0430. He was the first one up.

Stepping into the shower, Frank could see Sergeant Jones walking down the quiet barracks between the bunks with a cup of coffee in his hand. Grinning, he turned on the shower and began singing the "Mule Skinner Blues" at the top of his lungs.

"Well, good morning, Sergeant! Good morning to you, sir! Hey! Hey! Yeah! Do you need another mule skinner? Well, let this old shower run. He he he eh eh! He he he he!"

Frank's perfect pitch reverberated from the shower room. Sergeant Jones stood stunned at the beauty of the voice. "Jealous. It must be Jealous," he muttered to himself. Laughing, he chimed in singing the refrain, "Oh da ley hee, hey hey hey hey hey!"

Frank's voice echoed through the barracks. "Well, I'm a mean mule skinner, from down South Dakota way, and I'm in this army. I can make any mule listen, but I won't accept your pay! Hey! Hey!" Back and forth the song went until the entire two floors were awake and either moaning in disgust or laughing till tears ran from their eyes.

"Yoh da ley hee! Hey, hey, hey, hey, hey!" Jones crooned back.

Then Frank: "Well hey, little water boy, won't you bring your water round. Hey, hey! Well yes you can. . . . If you don't like your job, then throw that bucket down. Throw it down, boy. Well, throw it down!"

"Well, I been working out in Washington State in the U.S. Army's pay. In this army making fifty cents a day! Well, I'm sick of it! 'Cause I just want to be a mule skinner! Skin them mules all day."

Sergeant Jones jumped in once more. "Oh da ley hee! Hey hey hey!"

At chow that morning, Sergeant Jones caught up with Frank at the slop bucket. "Man, you sing all right!" he said admiringly. "You sing at home?"

"Yeah, a little," Frank said. "We had a band called the Sioux Playboys. Used to play for dances in the towns around the reservation."

"Jealous, you got one hell of an ear," said the sergeant. "Did you ever think of making a living with it?"

"Not really," Frank said, remembering the TV show. "Guys who make a living don't just have good ears; they got real talent."

"I think you got talent, son. Do you play the guitar?"

"Not well," Frank said, showing his irresistible, toothy smile.

"Well, I do a little pickin', I got a guitar at home. If I bring it would you sing a couple songs for the guys?"

Frank hesitated. "Sure, I guess that would be okay," was all he said.

• • •

The day broke bright and warm. Beyond the athletic field, giant spruce swayed gently in the coastal breeze. At the obstacle course that morning, as men grunted and strained over the walls, Sergeant Edwards turned to Jones. "I think that's the first time since this batch started that Nielsen and Jealous have not volunteered to go first." Jones only wrinkled his brow and nodded.

At evening chow Dale needed to settle his problem with Frank. Hating to be the one to pursue what he saw as Frank's problem, he sat down next to Ron. "Man, Frank is acting like a kid about that run the other day. Have you noticed how he's been acting?"

"Yeah, it's been pretty obvious all day. Maybe he's just used to winning." Ron stabbed at the rock-hard steak on his mess tray.

"No, it's more than that. He hasn't even looked my way all day," Dale said, staring with disgust at the dried beef on his own tray.

"Jeeze, if it bothers you so much why don't you talk to him about it?"

As Frank walked from the mess hall, Dale rose quickly, scraped his tray, then hurried toward the door, bumping Jones's arm and knocking some pale peas off the sergeant's spoon. Irritated, the black man stood and followed Dale to the door ready to collar him with some push-ups. He stopped short.

"Hey, Frank, I want to talk to you!" Dale called out.

Frank ignored him. Dale grabbed him by the elbow. "Talk to me, man! I thought we were friends."

"There's nothing to talk about!" Frank said, snapping Dale's hand from his arm.

"Why don't you admit it," Dale pressed, "you're pissed off about yesterday!"

"Yeah. So what of it?" The Indian's face was expressionless. To Sergeant Jones, who stood in the doorway, the two looked like boys on a schoolyard.

"Is it that you can't stand being beaten? Are you that good?" Dale was getting angry.

"Man, you don't know shit. Just leave me fuckin alone, man." Frank turned abruptly away. Dale stood there, heat running up his back, not sure if he should press it. Then he walked slowly back toward the mess hall and Ron.

Dale could see Sergeant Jones just outside the door, leaning against the door jamb. As Dale approached, the sergeant stood directly in front of him. In the darkness the sergeant's yellow eyes and white teeth seemed illuminated against his black skin.

"What is it, Sergeant?" Dale asked.

"You and Frank having a lovers' quarrel?" the man chuckled.

Dale stood for a moment trying to calm down. He looked at Sergeant Jones. He had never known what to make of this Negro man who said "feets" instead of "feet." "I don't exactly know. I think it has to do with that run I won yesterday."

"Yeah, it might have something to do with that, white boy," the man taunted him.

Dale's eyes narrowed.

"It's something you're going to have to figure out, my man, if you're ever going to be a colored man's friend," the black man said, quietly.

"What do you mean, Sarge?" Dale asked.

"Well, my man, all your life you've had it all. Nice house, nice life, respect." He paused. "It's 'cause you were born white. You never had to really wonder about yourself. Colored folks got to think about themselves all the time. White folks see to that, planting that little seed, when you're a boy, about how maybe your skin color makes you less human than othah folks. But your brain tells you 'Come on man, you is just as good as that white man. You just got to show him!' So you got this argument in your head. Some of us finally stop arguing and settle for being colored. Some of us convince ourselves that actually we is better than the white boys. A few realize skin color don't mean nothing. Others still have that argument in them forever. You a bright boy. You understand, don't you?"

• • •

That evening Sergeant Jones announced, "Listen up! At twenty hundred hours we got a special treat. I want all you men in the recreation hall on the hour."

When the platoon arrived, Sergeant Jones stood in front holding a worn guitar. He motioned the room to sit, then handed the guitar to Frank. "Mr. Frank Jealous Of Him has agreed to sing us a couple songs." He nodded at Frank, who sat there, afraid to show he was pleased.

Frank took the guitar. "Thanks, Sarge, but I told you I'm pretty bad on the guitar." He looked up at the smiling faces of the platoon. "Well boys, here goes nothin'." He started with an energetic rendition of "Long Tall Texan," then he teased the sergeant into a repeat of "Mule Skinner Blues." But it was on "In the Shadow of the Night" that the beauty of the man's voice finally hit Dale.

"Frank is right about his guitar playing," he nudged Garfford High Pipe, "but by God he's got perfect pitch!" Pipe nodded in agreement. Dale thought for a moment of the choir director at Ames, Iowa, his cherubic face basking in the glow of blessed sound.

"Match Box" by the Beatles gave way to Frank's version of "Bony Maroni." Then it was Sam the Sham's "Woolly Bully" followed by a soulful version of "Lodi" by Creedence Clearwater Revival.

In the middle of the song his eyes briefly met Dale's. From across the rec hall, Sergeant Jones stood looking at these American boys, propped quietly against pool tables or sitting on the floor, and thought about Vietnam. There wasn't a noise in the room as the Indian moved effortlessly from one song, one style, to the next, finishing with Merle Haggard's "Branded Man."

An hour had passed when Frank handed the guitar back to Sergeant Jones, grinning broadly, and said "Next!"

Later that night at the latrine, Dale stood at the mirror next to Frank. "That was great, Frank. I'm talking great. I've done a little singing . . ." he put toothpaste on his brush, "and I've got about an eight-note range. For those eight notes, I'm pretty hot, but you're a natural."

Frank did not look over. He simply smiled quietly into the mirror and said, "Thanks."

• • •

Before the boys from South Dakota knew it, eight weeks had passed, a cold wet winter had turned into a greening and blooming April, and a sunny graduation day was upon them. Advanced infantry training assignments had been handed out that morning. The graduates looked like veterans in their helmets and crisp fatigues. They stood talking, waiting for the base photographer to arrive for the traditional graduation photo.

Frank, smiling as usual, walked over to where Ron and Pipe were standing. "What's the word?" Garfford asked as Frank drew closer.

"It seems that all the best guys are being shipped off to Fort Polk for advanced infantry training. Massey's even goin'!" He touched the paper protruding from his pocket. "All the lesser types are staying here, I guess." He poked Ron in the ribs. "Where you headed, Ronnie?"

Ron grinned. "Jeeze, I guess we're losers!" He slapped Garfford on the back. "The two of us are staying here."

"No shit?" Frank dropped his bravado. "What about Nielsen, where's he headin'?"

"He's staying here." Ron could see Frank's face sober.

Later when the photographer snapped the shutter, Frank stood there beaming, thinking about his Dad, Clynda, Matthew, even Bernice. He wanted them to see what kind of a soldier he was going to be.

Three rows up on the extreme left, Dale smiled too, not so much to send a message, but because it was over. In three days he would go home and see Gail.

That afternoon Dale stood outside the old barracks shaking hands and making small talk as the men left. He saw Frank come out and almost sheepishly look his way. Dale left his duffel bag on the ground and walked toward his friend. "I hear they're sending you to Fort Polk," he said.

Frank forced a smile. "Yeah, that's where they send the best, I guess." His voice fell.

"I'm going to miss you, man!" Dale stuck his hand out and pulled Frank into a hug.

Frank's voice cracked. "Yeah, me too, man, me too."

28

ONLY BACK IN WOUNDED KNEE TWO DAYS, FRANK HAD ALREADY BECOME restless. He was sitting in the little trailer, strumming simple chords on his old guitar, when he said, "Hey, Congo, I got most of my pay left; let's go partying over in Alliance. I'll bet some of the other guys who joined when I did are back. Maybe we could hook up with them."

Matthew smiled at his brother's idea. "Yeah, you're forgetting one thing; none of us are old enough to drink in Alliance or anywhere else. Besides, if you're not up in front of them white guys playing, and if we go in there, they'll probably want to fight us."

"That's you, Congo! Always thinking too far ahead!" Frank jabbed playfully at his brother's chin.

"Well, somebody's got to look after your foolish *onzé*. You know how many times I got in fights for you?" Matthew shook his head.

Slightly insulted, Frank thought for a moment. "Well, how's this? There's a war going on, and brown skin soldier boys are going over there fighting and dying just like I'm gonna be. If we're fighting the white man's war, they'll let us drink with them. Might even buy us a few drinks.

"Probably treat us like heroes, and we can keep our money!" Now he stood reaching for his uniform pants.

Matthew had not moved. "Just one problem. You may be a soldier boy going off to be a hero, but I'm not. I'm just a skin and I don't have no ID that says different."

Frank sat back down, thinking again. He looked at Matthew, then quietly said, "You know I miss you brother . . . even with your fuckin down-at-the-mouth way of thinking." Frank broke out laughing.

Matthew was annoyed. It was typical of Frank to almost say something, then make it into a joke.

"I got an idea. In that duffel bag I got most of another uniform. If you can get the wrinkles out of it, you can wear it. Then we'll all get the war hero's treatment."

Matthew sorted through the big bag for the uniform. They stopped in at a log house in the village of Manderson, and, sure enough, John Steele, a childhood friend, was also home on leave. He joined in their plan. "Matt, you need a cap. I got my brother's old green beret; you'd look snaz in it!" He reached up, took it off a deer antler on the stuccoed log wall, knocked the dust off, and plopped it on the younger brother's head. Matthew stood in front of a chipped mirror admiring himself, adjusting the hat to the angle he had seen in a John Wayne movie.

An hour and a half later they were standing in uniformed glory in the Buck Horn Bar in Alliance, Nebraska. No one bothered to ask any of these warriors for their age or their IDs. As Frank had prophesied, the uniforms were like a passport to equality, maybe better than that, because his other prediction was also coming true.

No sooner had they walked inside the darkened bar than a big weathered cowboy yelled, "Hey barkeep! Get these soldier boys a drink! Whatever they want!" Soon it became a personal challenge for the civilian men in the bar to show their patriotism and "Buy them Indian boys a drink!"

"I'm home on leave," Frank said, "heading to Vietnam in a few weeks." His mind, now affected by Canadian Club whiskey, skipped over his impending advanced infantry training, and the small fact that he didn't really know where he would be assigned. "Don't know when or if I'll be coming home." His white teeth shone as cowboys slapped him on the back. Soon drinks stood waiting for him on the worn bar.

Even Matthew had gotten into the spirit. A small crowd had formed around him. "Yeah, it was rough," he said quietly, then reached up and touched his hat.

"They put you through a lot gettin' that beret?" one of the white guys asked.

"Yeah, it's pretty bad; most of the guys don't make it."

Twenty minutes later a couple of Indian boys in navy uniforms came in, adding to the mood of the warrior's welcome. By now each boy stood with a small knot of attentive white men. The same people who might have thrown these Indians out, or worse, were now buying them drinks. Matthew was warming to the attention. "We go pretty heavy into the martial arts, stuff like that . . . We're taught to be killers," he added.

"Well, killer, what'll it be?" one of the men yelled loud enough for Frank to overhear. He glanced over at Matthew and noticed that he had attracted the biggest group of fans. His heart began to beat more rapidly.

"Whiskey," Matthew beamed.

"The best whiskey for the best man here!" a pock-faced man yelled toward the bar.

The comment made Frank's neck warm, but he turned back toward his inquisitors and tried to ignore it. "I'm heading for the north, you know, to be a scout up in the mountains." He had picked up enough folklore from Sergeant Jones and the gossip on the reservation to string them along quite easily. Playing on his listeners' sympathy, he dropped his voice. "Most of us Indian guys end up as scouts, walkin' point, we call it." His chest puffed slightly.

Within an hour Frank was beginning to have to think about how his mouth worked, but still the drinks kept coming and the little wad of army money remained in his pocket. "Mosepointmendon'tlastaday," he said, his eyes already staring out with the first dullness of intoxication.

"It's not that I'm into killing." Matthew stood, falsely protesting the attention. "It's just, well, that's what I'm good at."

Frank overheard that comment and his ears burned. I'm the soldier! he thought. I'm the one going off to war and might get killed. His mind swam in the booze. He's not even in the army and he's the one getting all the attention. A drunken hatred rapidly replaced the cordial numbness of the whiskey. He stood on unsteady legs, glowering at his younger brother.

He walked over to Matthew and grabbed him by the elbow. "Fucker's gotta piss!" he said with force.

"No, I don't," his brother said, snapping his elbow from Frank's grip.

"Yes, you do!" Frank yelled, pulling Matthew violently off the stool.

As soon as they were in the tiny men's room, Frank swung. Matthew ducked to the right. The punch grazed the younger brother, leaving scratches from the buttons on Frank's uniform sleeve on Matthew's left cheek.

"Jeeze, Billy, what the hell is your problem?" he asked, grasping his brother's arm.

"You li'l fucker; you're a big shot with all your stories and that fuckin green beret."

Matthew's eyes widened. "Well, big brother, it was your idea!" He pointed angrily toward the hat, then brushed the uniform jacket with his hand. Frank stood there a moment thinking, then relaxed enough for Matthew to release his grip.

"Oh yeah . . ." Frank smirked foolishly, "guess it was."

Someone had recognized Frank and come back with a guitar. The attention shifted back toward Frank. Hurt and confused, the younger boy stood alone now, off to the side, dabbing at the scratches and slight bruise on his cheek. He thought about the motel room brawl the night before Frank had left for the army. That memory could be seen burning on Matthew's boyish face, if anyone in the noisy bar had been looking.

Frank soon forgot his jealousy and rage. He stood in the front of the room and played a medley of favorite songs. Men, white and Indian alike, whistled and stomped their feet. Musical enthusiasm grew with each round of drinks. His singing reduced his own drinking, and he performed late into the night.

For two days more the party continued. The small group of Indian soldier boys, plus an impostor, moved from one bar to the next. From one dusty reservation border town to another, they drove until their uniforms were a dingy mess. The collection of Sioux sailors and soldiers finally annoyed a bar full of white men in Chadron, Nebraska so much that the cowboys, with angry grunts and comments, made it clear the disheveled Indians were to leave. With that, the party was over.

29

THE YELLOW- AND WHITE-STRIPED CANVAS OF A REVIVAL TENT SNAPPED IN the light prairie breeze not far from the Body of Christ Church in Grass Creek. Here and there a tethered horse coughed gently into the cool spring air. It was past midnight, and a few of the faithful had retired to their wall tents. Some strolled around visiting; others stood quietly at the meeting tent openings, listening. The remaining faithful sat on folding chairs under the yellow cast of ten bare bulbs that now swayed with the motion of the Big Top.

Inside, on a small platform in the front, a middle-aged Lakota man stood speaking rapidly in English of God, Hell, and redemption: "That is why God lifted up the armies of this American nation in the face of Hitler, in the face of communists. In a few days our brother will be in a war, fighting for his country and all of the Oglala People. Praise God, he will return to us safe."

"Praise the Lord!" rang out from the congregation.

"We know that when we went to war in the old days we took a *wotawe* with us . . . something holy to protect us in battle. We don't need that today. No, we don't use that now! We have Jesus' love to protect us!"

In devout unison, "Praise the Lord!" punched the air.

"We want to send our brother Billy wrapped in the protection of Jesus' perfect love!" His head dropped as he dragged out the last word.

"Praise God!" rang out again.

"We want to pray with all our faith that the love of our congregation goes with him into battle. We have a growing number of young people Sun Dancing, leaving Christianity, going to Yuwipi men, going back to the devil for help, when all they would have to do is find Christ, to put their faith in Jesus as Billy has done. Praise God!"

"Praise God!" the faithful shot back.

"Now I would like us to join together in the glorious song 'Jesus Stands over Me,' and then Billy himself is going to give testimony!"

Two men on either side of the tiny stage stooped to plug in their instruments. Bass and lead guitars crackled to life, then struck the first powerful chords as men, women, and children joined in singing an emotional rendition of the hymn.

Eyes closed, heads swaying, the singers were caught up in the power of the moment. Some of the women dabbed at their eyes, sobbing in quiet admiration for this soldier boy.

After the hymn, Frank, still called Billy by his people, walked slowly to the front, then mounted the worn plywood platform. "Praise Jesus!" Frank smiled at his fellow church members.

"Praise Jesus!" came back.

"I won't be around to give testimony for a while, so I thought I would speak this evening. I want to thank all of you for coming, all of you for your prayers and words of encouragement, but most of all I want to thank Jesus for bringing us together this evening!"

"Praise Jesus!" the people shouted their agreement.

"All of you in here know my mom, Bernice, and you know her heart. She took Matthew and me as small children, she has watched over us, sometimes treating us like her own kids." He looked at Clynda. "Well, I want to testify that Mom prayed for me not to pass the army entrance test. And I want to say a word of greeting to my father. He knows how much I care for you and this little church. He gave me this cross!" Frank reached into his shirt and withdrew a mother-of-pearl and silver crucifix. "When I wear it each day, I will think of him, and this congregation. Praise God!

"Dad knows that there are never simple reasons for what people do. He knows his wife's heart." He looked across the tent at Clayton's watery eyes.

"It's tough to raise kids these days. Sometimes there is barely enough food. Sometimes there are barely enough clothes, barely enough love or money to go around." He looked at Bernice, but she was not looking.

"Matthew is not here this evening, and that is why I want to say that sometimes there's barely enough brothers to go around!" The congregation burst into laughter.

"Back in the fall I decided it was time for me to leave, to go out into the world. I didn't know where I wanted to go or what I wanted to do, but I prayed to God, prayed to Jesus, to direct me."

A soft affirmation rose from the assembly.

"That's when I decided to join the army. I was scared to go out into that world. Afraid to leave this place." He looked around. "But I decided I needed a change. So I went to the recruiter and I signed up, and here they told me I have to take a test because I don't have high school. I was scared to take that test, afraid that this dumb Indian would flunk it." Again the congregation chuckled.

"I told Bernice I was scared to take that test. She said she would pray for me to flunk the test because her and Dad need me here! But Praise the Lord I passed my test!"

"Praise the Lord!" rang out.

"I prayed for God's help and he listened to me!" He enunciated the last word, looking toward Bernice. Still her eyes were down.

"With the Lord's help I passed my test, I got my GED, and I got into the army. And I want you to know that I've done good so far representing my family, my church, and my Oglala Lakota people." Now his eyes were watery. "I am not a perfect man. I am a sinner! I know that the seeds of sin flower in hell, but I try and that is all we can do!"

"Praise God!" rose up.

"I don't know what will be over there; only the Lord can know that. I don't know if I'll come back. I can only pray for God's will to be done." His voice cracked.

"But I pray, as I have these last few days of Christian revival, that I will see your faces once again; if not here, in heaven." His eyes were filled with tears. "Again, I want to thank each and every one of you, and whatever it is in your hearts, I pray the Lord could make it that way. Praise the Lord!"

"Praise the Lord!" came back one last time.

30

THE GRASSY VALLEY FLOOR WAS CRISSCROSSED WITH CREEKS AND FILLED with ash, cedar, and box elders. Pine trees, a few at first and then in thickets, spread up the sandstone-covered hillsides. On a hill above this holy valley, stark white and steepled against a cloudless azure sky, sat the Sacred Heart Catholic Church. On the crest of the same hill, only feet away, in a hallowed earthen trench lay the remains of Big Foot and his Howoju followers. This northern Lakota band of Ghost Dancers had left Cheyenne River Reservation the day after Sitting Bull had been killed and, in fear for their lives, journeyed south to find food and safety among the Oglala Ghost Dancers. They had been intercepted and disarmed by the reconstituted Seventh Cavalry. The next day, December 29, 1890, with Big Foot dying of pneumonia, these freezing men, women, and children were slaughtered in the cross fire of Hotchkiss guns.

Below, on the site of the 1890 massacre, a circle of cars and pickups surrounded a busy dance arbor. Its fresh pine shading stood out like an emerald ring against a prairie not yet fully green. In the arbor sat rows of Lakota people of all ages. With a signal from a tall elderly man standing near the singers, everyone except those too elderly or those in wheelchairs stood, the men and boys removing their caps.

For the sake of the few white visitors, the *eyapaha,* announcer, said in perfect English, "Would all of those present please rise and remove your hats for the singing of the National Anthem!"

"Tunkasila yapé tawa pa ha ki na we cin-jin! Grandfather (the President) under your flag staff we stand." The first words of the Sioux National Anthem floated clearly from a pair of dented metal speaker horns tied in the support beams of the round arbor. The women gathered their flowered shawls around themselves; the men removed their hats. Below the bullhorns, a microphone was handheld inside a large ring of Lakota singers. With their short hair, bristling shiny black and thick as that on a bear robe, three of those lending their voices were young boys just learning the trade. The other six were mostly gap-toothed, grizzled veterans of the duties the traditional way of life demanded of the *hoca wica,* singer man. Some of these men wore braids; others sported thinning crew cuts. All held in their left hand felt cowboy hats whose sweatbands were deeply stained. Armed with simple cloth-wrapped willow rods, the men struck the worn bass drum in perfect unison. Behind them stood four solid-framed older women, their silver braids tied behind their heads, which were covered with flowered scarves. Their broad shoulders draped in colorful shawls, these women sang the *wicaglata.*

As the "Flag Honoring Song" was reverently sung, two uniformed World War II veterans from the Wounded Knee Legion Post slowly hoisted an American flag up a slender pine pole. After three verses the flag had reached the worn brass pulley at the top of the staff, and the singers ended the song with a simultaneous and resounding drumbeat.

In seconds another song was struck up. As was custom, this one, with its faster rhythm, honored the veterans. Beneath the blue sky and green pine boughs, a small line of Indian dancers moved into the grass-covered arena. Their roached deer and porcupine hair *wa pésha,* headdresses, bounced gently around the arbor in rhythm with the drum. The two black-and-white eagle tail feathers that swung in bone sockets on each dancer's headpiece spun with the breeze and the action of the dancer's head and shoulders. These older men filed slowly into the dance arena in a long single line until all had circled the arena and the drummers struck the stretched steer hide and hollow pine a final blow.

The dancers returned to the rough benches that circled the powwow ground, and all sat. With gray hair highlighting his dark, creased face, the announcer stood, microphone in his right hand. In Lakota he announced, "Mrs. Jealous Of Him welcomes you and extends a cordial thank you for coming here today and honoring her grandson." With that the nine men sitting near the worn bass drum banged it four times, loudly signaling affirmation that honoring was in order. Some of the women made the same high-pitched, staccato trill Lakota warriors had heard for hundreds of years when they rode off to battle: "Lee-lee-lee-lee-lee!"

Frank sat taking it all in. His head hurt from two weeks of welcome-home parties and the friendly white men in Nebraska. He felt embarrassed, though not because he hated attention—he was honest at least in the confines of his head.

It was his grandmother's generation, with their old-fashioned "Indian ways," that embarrassed him. It was all of it, he reasoned: the feathers, the bells, and the traditional dances that to him had become irrelevant.

He sat in his freshly pressed uniform and was about to be marched around, dancing like an Indian. His head ached, his stomach was queasy, but he sat there and politely smiled at the two or three hundred people that had gathered for this warrior's send-off.

His uncle, Sam Jealous Of Him, stood away from the dance arbor, tending a large cook fire under a big cauldron of deer meat and wild turnips. He and his boys had rounded up these precious ingredients gathered and dried that summer by their female relatives. Close by was another cauldron filled with freshly slaughtered beef Frank's relatives had purchased for the occasion.

With both pots boiling briskly, the midday air hung heavy with the rich promise of delicious soup.

After conferring a moment with Grandma Alice, the announcer held up the mike. "Mrs. Jealous Of Him, her relatives, and friends will feed all of you soon, so you need to be getting an appetite." The crowd laughed as the *eyapaha* went on. "Mrs. Jealous Of Him, Grandma Alice, is proud that her grandson Billy is going to war for this country to be a soldier for his people, and therefore wishes to share her pride with all of you. This is why we are here today! On behalf of the Jealous Of Him family I would like to say thank you to all those who have come to honor Billy. We would like to call Billy and his grandma forward for the honoring dance."

All those gathered stood in place, the women hoisting embroidered shawls to their shoulders, the men removing ten-gallon hats or caps. "After Billy and his grandma have circled the arbor, I would ask that all the rest of you file in and circle with him. Mrs. Alice Jealous Of Him wishes to mark this day by giving her grandson a new name. From this day forth, to us he will be known after her uncle who was a brave warrior in the Rosebud fight! He received the name for his actions and was known by that the rest of his life. This brave man saved some lives because the warriors turned to him for advice, and they won the fight that day. Billy's name will now be Aná Kita, They Run to Him."

"Lee-lee-lee-lee-lee-lee-lee!" Tongues rattling, the women's victory trill rang out.

The announcer held the microphone aloft in agreement, then cleared his throat. "Grandma Alice tells me that her reason for giving him this name is that she knows him, his nature, and that where he is headed, overseas, people will run to her grandson for help, they will turn to him for security."

Leaning together, the singers whispered among themselves, then nodded. *Wham!* They banged the drum in slow unison as the song built. The lead singer, in a brassy voice, sang the first verse, then the second singer joined in matching the lead singer, and finally the rest, young and old, added their voices till the sound was powerful, flowing through the ground itself.

To this old "honoring" song, used to send off Lakota warriors for the past two hundred years, the singers added Billy's new name. Their feet pumping gently up and down with the drum, he and his grandmother slowly made their way around the circle. Feeling it was she that Billy would come home to, Mary moved around the circle to stand behind Clynda. When the couple, grandmother and grandson, passed by, their relatives filed in behind, Mary with them.

Heel, toe, heel, toe, in dignified, subtle steps, the slow-moving dancers circled around the dance ground for the second time. Then the crowd filed in. Each person moved forward with the drum, showing his or her unspoken spiritual support. There were few smiles, because sending a man off to war has always been serious business.

When the long line of people had returned to their seats, the announcer turned toward the family and announced over the PA system: "Clayton Jealous Of Him will now lead us in a prayer of thanks for this food and this wonderful day." Clayton walked toward the microphone and, like the others, spoke in the language of the people, "*Tunkasila* . . . Grandfather above, may the power and grace of our Blessed Savior Jesus Christ bless this food our relatives have prepared. May this food strengthen our bodies and these prayers strengthen us spiritually, now and in the days to come. I pray you watch over this soldier boy wherever he ends up. I pray you bring him home to us in our Lord Jesus' name, Amen."

When the prayer ended, Frank's extended family moved like a catering service, the male and female cousins, aunts and uncles, passing out a lifetime collection of mismatched bowls, cups, spoons, and knives, enough to feed all who had come. Many of those who had come produced additional bowls and small, lidded porcelain kettles. Some sat on wooden benches, others on folding chairs. Just as many sat on the ground, men with legs folded before them, the women with them folded modestly to one side. The men of the family moved quickly, ladling out beef and deer *wahanpi,* soup, mixed with hominy and *wastunkala,* dried sweet corn, and *tinpsila,* wild turnips, and *psin watogla,* wild onions, harvested and dried the previous summer. And then there was the *taniga wahanpi,* beef intestine soup, with its rich, familiar smell. Mary handed out *wiglí ungagapi,* fry bread; others served *gabooboo,* skillet bread, cake, and pie until each man, woman, and child sat behind a virtual mound of food.

As the guests ate, the women in the family carried forward laundry baskets full of Pendleton blankets, hand-sewn star quilts, homemade shawls, beadwork, towels, and inexpensive blankets still in their department store plastic wrappers. The menfolk now carried forward boxes of oranges, apples, and cigarettes. The older women spread out the finished quilts, blankets, quilt tops, and squares of fabric inside the arena on the dance ground.

Later, when all that could possibly be eaten had been consumed and the rest carefully packed away in the *watecha,* leftover containers, the announcer blew on the mike, testing the system. In his most formal Lakota he said, "At this time I would request Frank's immediate family to please come up and stand with me. The family has worked for many months gathering and making gifts for all of you, so when you are called please come forward and receive a gift in honor of Aná Kita."

First the *eyapaha* called the singers forward. They were each given twenty-five dollars, a carton of smokes, and a quilt. They moved in unison down the receiving line, gently shaking the hands of Grandma Alice, Billy, Bernice, Clayton, Clynda, Julie, Carol, and little Verla.

Soon the band members and other special friends were called up, one at a time, to receive a gift and shake the hands of Billy, his grandma, and family. The older women moved down the receiving line shaking hands until they reached Billy and hugged him. Some, especially the aunts, cried as they passed.

As the *o tu kĥan,* giveaway, progressed and those to be honored were called up, the quilts, blankets, and beadwork pieces were dispersed. The men and younger cousins passed out cigarettes, cloth handkerchiefs, and oranges to the men. Even if just a potholder, all who came that day received a gift.

Wham! Wham! Wham! the drummers struck up as the men joined the lead singer Matt Two Bull in a fast-paced, high-pitched song from another time. With that beat, the decorated Lakota veterans of United States wars, the Grass Dancers, in their finest regalia, strode back out, their horse hair-streamered, eagle-feather bustles rustling in the breeze, their chrome bells jangling loudly with each footfall.

In the manner of the old warrior societies, many wore the bone breast-plates, and in their deep bronze fingers some men held eagle-wing fans, others a war club or beaded and feathered staff, some both. As they moved, their heads bobbed and swayed on their shoulders. Behind painted faces their eyes snapped up and down, back and forth, always looking for the enemy, imitating the way a bird inspects the ground before it.

The men moved slowly forward, scanning the ground, then crouched down, dancing low for a better look. Like birds circling the battlefield, dancing low in small circles, they stepped out the four honoring beats. Long woolen breechcloths swaying, their sinewy legs pumping briskly up and down, these birdmen rose and then dropped low, circling the arbor in unity with the drum.

Just inside the arena the women stood dancing in place, bouncing gently with the drum. Some were decked out in tribal finery, hair braided and wrapped in red wool or otter skin, and their navy blue dress capes, decorated with narrow dentalium, coins, or elks' teeth, glistened in the spring sunlight. Three of the women wore fully beaded buckskin dresses, leggings, and moccasins. On all their necks were *wáoslata wanapin,* the heavy, broad, hair pipe necklaces, that descended almost to their knees. These horizontal rows of thin white bones swayed in wavelike rhythm with the dancers' bodies. Around their waists each had a *maza wapiyaka,* a concho belt made of German silver, whose conchoed trailer touched the ground. Still others wore civilian clothes and a simple shawl. The women held themselves with a quiet dignity as they watched the men dance clockwise around the inside of the small circle.

When the dancing had ended, the announcer again stood with the micro-phone in his hand. "We're now going to ask the Sons of the Oglalas for a Mastincala Wacipi, a Rabbit Dance. Ladies choice. *I na ĥni ĥíyupo!* Let's go! Now everybody dance!"

Mary Hollow Horn had for the most part stood quietly in the background, apparently unseen by Frank. Although she had done her best to hide it, her chest ached because he had ignored her. With the announcement of the Rabbit Dance, she moved bravely across the arbor and headed straight for Frank. When he noticed her moving toward him, he blushed.

She pulled him reluctantly to his feet and moved him out to where a line of dancers was forming. Standing on the right side of their partners, the men encircled the women with their left arms and held their partner's right hand in their own. In time with the drum, they took three steps forward, and one back, slowly moving around the arbor until the drum signaled a change, and the couples circled in place like square dancers.

"Wey hey yah hey, yah hey, yah hey hey yah," the singers sent their voices out.

"So why haven't you come to see me?" Mary said quietly but directly.

"I, ah, haven't had a chance. I was meaning to," Frank said weakly, trying to stay in step with the music.

"But you've had time to see Darlene Ghost, and a few other women." The hurt was clear in her accusing tone.

"I guess I didn't want to encourage you, little cousin. I'm going away for a long time, and well, it's different with those others. You're too good to wait around for me."

"I'm not your little cousin!" she said with a reluctant laugh. Mary knew Frank always did that, made people laugh just when things were getting serious. Now she hated him for it. "I'm old enough to know if I want to wait for you. That's a decision I have to make, if you care for me."

Frank squeezed her. "You know I do, but I'm going away. I don't want to leave someone waiting at home like in the movies, especially not you, Mary."

The delicate woman did not know what else to say. She shook away tears and lifted her head. At this moment Mary was with her man, whether he knew it or not.

31

BY LATE APRIL 1968 FRANK'S LEAVE WAS COMING TO AN END. ON THIS NIGHT a million stars, floating in a cobalt sky, glowed down on the Wounded Knee Community Hall. Indian couples, young and old, stood waiting on the edges of the little meeting hall for this "White Dance" that would be Frank's final send-off. When Frank William Jealous Of Him, now known to his Oglala people as They Run To Him, climbed up on the little stage to join his band, the crowd broke into applause.

Smiling broadly, already a little loose from an all-day party with the band, Frank stepped up to the mike. Although he was drunk, the stage transformed him. His smooth voice instantly quieted the low buzz of Lakota words and loud bursts of female laughter that filled the hall. "Since this will be the last time that I'll be singing with the Sioux Playboys, I'd like to play some of my favorites. I'd like to thank those of you that organized this, and tell you that I'll take this memory with me to Vietnam. Now grab your sweethearts and everybody dance to this Merle Haggard tune; it's my favorite." Guitar strains stirred the air.

I'd like to hold my head up and be proud of who I am . . .
Now I'm a branded man out in the cold.

Guitar strains picked up the melody while Frank closed his eyes.

After "Branded Man," the band played through a medley of their best tunes, first "Woolly Bully," then "Matchbox" from the Beatles, and on to country-swing classics.

An hour had passed when the band finally broke into an instrumental. Frank stepped off the stage and walked over to a mixed-blood girl named Joyce. She wrapped her arms around him, and they moved in unison across the dance floor. Around and around they went, people nodding and smiling as the man they still called Billy made the circuit.

It was after ten when Mary Hollow Horn arrived, peering through the crowd. Looking over the heads and between the dancing couples, she noticed that Billy was not up in front of the band. The small woman pushed her way through the crowd until she saw them. Stomach queasy, eyes watered up, Mary almost knocked down her uncle, Adolph Hollow Horn, as she ran out into the night.

By eleven bootleg whiskey had taken its toll on the soldier boy. Still he sang, barely missing a lyric, until moving forward he stumbled and slipped from the low stage, banging his head loudly on the edge of the wooden platform as he fell.

Matthew let go of his girl and ran up as Billy Hollow Horn jumped off the stage. Clayton placed his hand under his son's head and felt a lump rising. Despite coaxing and gentle slaps, for five long minutes Frank did not move. Then his eyes fluttered open, and as if he had been teasing, he jumped to his feet. Only the wobbling betrayed him. "Who the hell hit me? Let me at him!"

He feigned a boxer's stance. "Must have been a big guy! Where are you now, you coward?" The room broke into laughter as Frank dropped his hands and stepped back up onto the stage, laughing at his own joke.

At midnight Adolph signaled the band to take a break. He stepped up on the little stage and took the microphone. "As you all know, Billy is leaving soon for Vietnam. That's why we wanted to have this here farewell dance for him. I know every one of us wishes him the best and prays for his safe return. No one could fill his place in the band, so we want him to know that when he gets back, we'll be waiting. Now if someone could hand us up a chair, I'd like to ask Billy to sit for a moment." He motioned to the floor.

A folding chair was placed on the stage, and Frank sat down.

"When a warrior went off to war, our people paid him honor, and that's what we're doing tonight. My wife has made something for Billy and I'd like her to bring it up now." Adolph's wife stepped out from the crowd holding a laundry bag.

"She's going to give me her laundry?" Frank smirked, swaying a little on the chair. The room roared with laughter.

"No, it's not her laundry," the manager laughed, as his wife pulled a hand-stitched star quilt from the bag. With her husband she held it up for everyone to see. It had a white background against which blazed a red, white, and blue eight-sided star. Small American flags had been stitched into the corners.

"Billy is a warrior now, and while this is not a buffalo robe like our ancestors had, it is a warrior's blanket. We would like to place it on Billy's shoulders on behalf of all the people of Wounded Knee." The women joined their voices together and a loud victory trill filled the room: "Lee-lee-lee-lee-lee-lee!"

As they placed the blanket on his shoulders, a tear formed in the young soldier's eye. He leaned over to Adolph. "I want to say something."

The manager motioned with his hand for the room to be quiet. "Billy has something he would like to say."

With the quilt over his shoulders Frank stood and approached the mike. "Before I say what I'd like to say, I want to honor my dad with a song from World War Two."

His voice started in slowly, then built in intensity, singing an a cappella version of "The White Cross on Okinawa." When he finished, the room broke into a long applause, and Clayton came forward to shake his hand.

Frank signaled that he wanted to speak. "I want to thank all of you, again, friends and relatives alike, for all that you've done for me over the years, and especially for this farewell dance. It is a farewell dance for me because I am leaving and I'm never coming back to this place." His voice trembled on those words, then he sat down hard. Shocked silence filled the hall.

As if in response, the band climbed back on the stage and one last time struck up "Branded Man."

32

DAYS WERE GETTING LONGER AND WARMER, YET LATE APRIL 1968 WAS STILL wet. It seemed to Dale Nielsen that the Washington sky resented blue, much preferring a kind of monotonous gray. Advanced infantry training was moving quickly for him, although he had not found someone to share it with as he had shared basic training with Frank. Now he stood in the growing pall of evening by the side of a dirt road. One hundred yards north the spruce and hardwoods were thick, the forest floor already black.

A young, white drill sergeant surveyed the company. "All right! Listen up! The manner in which you conduct yourselves in the next few hours will determine whether this evening will end in total fatigue or total pain. That's the choice you've got. Get through this without being captured and you'll be happy campers!" A nasty grin spread across his face. "Get caught and you will be in a world of hurt!" He enunciated each word: "Is that clear?"

"Yes, Sergeant!" the men called out.

"Now buddy up. You got five minutes till the search team arrives." He glanced at his watch.

Dale looked for a familiar face. Ron Gilbert and High Pipe were already teamed up. A twinge of jealousy passed through him. He spotted a kid from South Dakota named Bryson and waved him over. "You by yourself?"

"So far!" was all the thin blond said, grinning nervously. "I heard they really mess with you if they catch you."

"Yeah, it's definitely something I want to avoid," Dale said, returning the nervous look.

A troop truck rumbled up the road. Aboard were a group of men, who, by the evening's rules, would have the complete upper hand. They were hurling jeers and laughing when the truck pulled to a stop.

In the dying light, their drill sergeant's teeth were pearly against his black face, his smile a leering intimidation. "Ten-Hut! I want you men to dismount." When they had jumped off and were standing around him, he continued.

"Try to remember how you felt just one week ago when you were the bait."

As if rehearsed, a loud grumble rang out.

"Some of you were caught. Try to remember what you felt like in that prison compound. How you swore if you got the chance you would get paybacks on whoever you could. Well, take a look at these young men and try to remember how they feelin' tonight!" Now he couldn't contain himself and started to snicker.

His inky face went expressionless as he addressed Dale's drill sergeant. "OK, line up your men, Sergeant. They will have five minutes to get into the woods and decide their course of action. Then I'm going to send in the hounds!"

Moments later, heart pounding, Dale was sprinting toward the safety of the trees. He couldn't have run faster if a bogeyman from his childhood dreams had materialized behind him.

When he reached the edge of the woods, he heard a whistle and then a heart-stopping scream as the pursuers leaped forward.

The forest floor was a tangle of roots, short shrubs, and saplings. Like ghoulish arms, they seemed to reach up and slam into a shin, bang against a thigh, or grab a foot, throwing Dale and Bryson repeatedly to the soggy ground.

Frantically, Dale's mind raced for a plan. It seemed foolish to think they would make it through this darkening forest. Still they pressed forward, vaguely aware of the curses and screams of their equally hapless companions on either flank.

Within moments the pursuers were on the edge of the woods yelling. "Over here!" resounded from the rear right, while "I see 'em!" came closing in from the left.

In the dim light, Dale's eyes strained to pick out a clearing, anything that would give him reason to think he might increase his lead. "Oomph!" he sprawled onto his hands.

He spotted a large tree, its lower branches within grasp. "I'm taking to the trees!" he panted. "Let 'em get ahead of us!"

Before Bryson could disagree, Dale had swung like a gymnast and was scrambling up the thick trunk. His partner ran forward into the gloom.

Moments later a group of panting men stood directly beneath the giant alder tree. Dale squatted high in the branches, his breath roiling between pursed lips, his ears straining to pick up the conversation.

"It'd be a hell of a place to hide," he thought he heard one of them say as he tried to reduce his silhouette. "Sergeant Williams says all the ones that think they're smart climb trees." Dale heard that clearly. A cold sweat broke out between his shoulder blades.

The men on the ground peered up into the leafless branches. One of them murmured something and then pointed right at Dale. His stomach churned. "You can come down or we'll come up and get you!" the man yelled.

Well, I'm sure as hell not going to come down! he thought, but no plan came to mind. Two of the men started up the tree. Fear snapped something inside, and he tried to kick their hands, knock them out of the tree. Then two hands were squarely around his right ankle, and he was pulled from his perch.

His hands were soon tied tightly behind him. He resolved, Damn! If I'm stupid enough to get caught, that's the only thing they're going to get. Shoved forward in the darkness he tried to imagine what torture awaited him. He had heard horror stories but tried to beat back his growing dread with the thought that they couldn't actually kill or maim him.

Thirty-five minutes later, in the glow of mercury arc lamps, he could see the twists of concertina wire above the twelve-foot-high hog fence enclosure. A panicky sensation grew inside him like a fast-spreading cancer.

A tall gate swung open and he was shoved through so hard he fell on his face. His cheek slammed into the ground. Now a knot of anger began to form deep inside. Newly born anger battled with panic for room in his consciousness. He thought briefly of escape, but another quick look at the tall fencing and the awful lights ended that. Like wood smoke, all sense that this was just a game dissipated into the damp night air.

Moments later a husky, black staff sergeant came to greet the captors. "Well, will you look at this sorry sack of shit! Someone always has to be the first. Good job, men," he said to the pursuit team. "We'll take over from here." He smiled menacingly.

Dale thought, Maybe everything I've heard about this was blown up like some college fraternity hazing. Maybe they'll just play with me, scare me a little, then put me in that frame building at the end of the compound and let me sleep. Yeah, that's it ... I'll simply be allowed to sleep till morning and that will be all there is to it. This conclusion momentarily calmed the growing waves of panic.

The sergeant grabbed Dale by the elbow and pushed upward, shoving him in the direction of the little building. The pain was excruciating. All delusions of sleep slid from his mind.

In the little building sat a dour-faced officer behind a desk. The guard slammed the door behind him and maneuvered Dale in front of the man.

"Sir. We have captured an enemy soldier, sir, and await further instructions."

The young white officer stared at Dale for a moment. His eyes were the unmistakable, chilling blue of a soldier who's been over there in the jungles and rice paddies. His mouth was expressionless. "Man, you are one stupid fuck." The man's voice was calm. He shook his head slowly. "What is your mission in these woods, soldier?" The yellow glow of the bare incandescent bulbs gave the light a surreal quality.

Wrists burning, hands numb, Dale tried to think of the classes they had conducted on the Geneva Convention. He would give them name, rank, and serial number and no more. "Private E-3 Dale Edward Nielsen, United States Army, Serial Number 551-64-3912. Sir!"

"Now, son, we know that you are here for a reason." Again the voice had that same flat quality. Dale's eyes darted from side to side studying the room. Along the walls were a number of cots. Again he tried to calm himself, thinking, This is just a game; what can they do to me?

"Soldier, answer me, or you will not forget this night as long as you live and that is if you live through the night." The voice was southern, no evidence of threat or humor in its tone, yet it brought back Dale's instinctive panic.

"What is your mission here, son?" The man looked bored.

"Private E-3 Dale Edward Nielsen, United States Army, Serial Number 551-64-3912. Sir!"

Now the captain grinned at the sergeant. "This stupid dickhead thinks that this is a girl's summer camp, Sergeant. He thinks well, hell, what can they do to me? I'll write my folks or tell someone if they hurt me." His voice now had a razor edge of sarcasm. "Haven't you ever heard of men who die accidentally in the army? Do you think anything ever comes of the investigations? We do the investigations!" Now he openly laughed at Dale. "Show the enemy we're not kidding, Sergeant."

The black man moved forward, spun Dale around, and drove his fist into his stomach. When he bent over in pain, the man caught him in the jaw, sending him to the floor. Before he could catch his breath the sergeant grabbed his bound hands, jerking the helpless captive painfully to his feet. Then the sergeant smiled, placing Dale back in front of the bored-looking inquisitor. "Son, what is your mission in these woods?"

Bowels aching, shoulders burning, Dale stood looking at the man through watery eyes, trying to focus his thoughts.

"You might as well tell me and save yourself a lot of grief. In a few minutes we'll have another hapless dickhead and he'll just tell us anyway."

Dale's mind reeled. Who the hell are these crazy fuckers? God, how could I have been so stupid? A part of him now accepted the blame for his predicament. It tore at him, weakened him with shame. He was a country kid, not some barrio kid from downtown LA, and he had been the first captured. Maybe I'm buying into all this bullshit about war and the fight in Vietnam, pumping myself up. After all this training, he scolded himself, I've failed my first chance to be a soldier. The boy in him wanted to cry out, but he said nothing.

The captain's eyes dropped to an open magazine on the green desk. "Sergeant, I think this dumb fuck wants a tour through our little amusement park. Don't you, son? Then we'll see how talkative he is."

Before Dale could react, the big man yanked him around, opened the door, and shoved him through. Two more men armed with M-16s grabbed him by the elbows, almost lifting him off his feet. White pain lit the interior of his skull.

Dale thought his shoulders would snap out of their joints. He thought for a moment about his folks, then Gail, and then the captain's comment about investigations. He felt let down, hated himself. Shoving aside the shame, a sense of futility now shared space with the panic in the back of his mind.

Half-shoving, half-lifting him across the white-lit compound, they brought him to what looked like a black trench. The cords were removed from his wrists, and without comment he was pushed into the narrow ditch. As he tumbled forward, he could see it was filled with water.

He fell forward, splashing into large blocks of ice. Sparks blazed in his skull as his face slammed into a small iceberg. For an agonizing moment his face went under. Never a strong swimmer, he now fought to get his head above the surface. An excruciating, burning cold completed the job of sending him into a brief but total panic. He pumped his legs trying to right himself. Shoulders aching, he flailed his arms to the jeers and hoots of his tormentors, only to find that the water was but two feet deep. He burst from it standing on the muddy bottom.

"Crawl, asshole!"

Dale turned to see the distorted face of a white kid pointing his M-16 in his face. As if a bullet might rip through his frozen cranium, caught up totally in the prison's illusion, he dropped back into the frigid moat. "Now crawl, fucker!" the man with the gun yelled.

When he had half-swum, half-crawled, through the ten yards of ice water, two more men grabbed him and, before he could find his feet, dragged him back to the leering sergeant. "What is your mission, boy!? Where is your company? How many men were with you?"

Dale stood stunned by the brutality. It was as if for a brief moment he had become separated from himself. He could clearly see a shivering, downcast boy, mud dripping from his scalp. He could see a bright blue-green bruise growing on the kid's cheek.

Falling back into himself, his mind raced: I've got nothing to tell them anyway! I could just tell them we're on a training exercise. Maybe that will be good enough. But his mouth did not open. Without warning a hand reached out and threw him backward into the frigid black drink. This time he gathered his thoughts: Just get to the other end, just get through this bullshit one step at a time, bad enough you're stupid enough to get caught. Don't give these assholes anything else! His brain commanded his body through the ice water.

The men pulled the shivering boy from the trench. The wet fatigues clinging tightly to his frozen skin made the burning worse and sent a steamy vapor into the chilly, damp air. Ahead of him was a set of four posts sticking a foot out of the hard clay. Without speaking his torturers threw him down, then slammed his boots on top of two of the posts, his hands on the others. "Now give us twenty!"

Mud and water dripping from his face, Dale lowered himself. His body shook so badly he could barely control his arms. *Wham!* His right arm was kicked out from under him, sending him sprawling into the dirt. Again he was forced back up onto the posts. Now it was his legs that were kicked out. It seemed to go on forever.

After a time the laughing men pulled him to his feet and repeated their questions. It now seemed as if the men were questioning him from the end of some sort of tunnel. Pain and fatigue and relentless fear had dug this grim shaft, and he retreated into it as far as he could. He could see his questioners' faces, twisting in speech, but he could barely hear their voices.

It had become a nightmare, and like all nightmares, all one had to do was get through it, find a way out or wake up! Soon it was back to the ice water. He thought he heard someone say something about "this bad-ass fucker." Between sessions in the water and interrogation sessions on the posts, he heard someone say something about how "There's always assholes like him who have to get to the pit before they'll talk."

It sounded like someone said "Put him back on the blocks" when dragging his head up. Dale recognized the young officer from the guardhouse

Photograph taken during basic training, April 1968. Men from South Dakota: *Front row*, first from left, Wilbur Smith. *Second row*, seventh from left, Gabriel Two Star; ninth from left, Garfford High Pipe. *Third row*, fourth from left, Frank Jealous Of Him; seventh from left, Ron Gilbert; ninth from left, Private Harford. *Fourth row*,

tenth from left, Private Star. *Fifth row*, fourth from left, Bill Yardley (from Montana). *Top row*, second from left, Les Amdahl; third from left, Dale Nielsen; fourth from left, Clayton One Star; seventh from left, Lee Amdahl; eighth from left, Bill Ford. Photo courtesy Ron Gilbert.

Ron Gilbert and Frank Jealous Of Him at Fort Lewis during basic training, January 1968. Photo courtesy Ron Gilbert.

Frank William Jealous Of Him in dress uniform. Photo courtesy Ron Gilbert.

Frank *(third from left)* and three unidentified comrades, somewhere near LZ Baldy. Photo courtesy Beth Farinelli.

Frank *(standing)* wearing the infamous Olive Drab "poncho" towel; eventually some of the men copied this. Carl Schofer is furthest from the camera. Photo courtesy Beth Farinelli.

Lieutenant Albert Farinelli with M-60, on a patrol off LZ Professional. Photo courtesy Beth Farinelli.

Ron Gilbert with Garfford High Pipe at Tay Ninh. Photo courtesy Ron Gilbert.

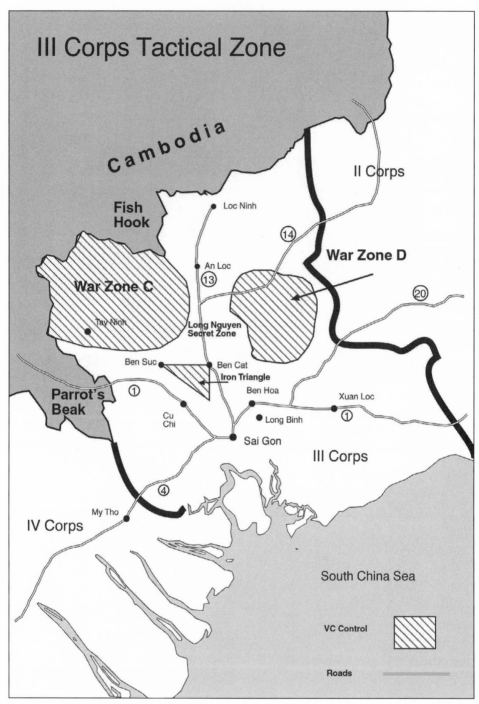

The III Corps Tactical Zone during the Vietnam War. Courtesy Donald S. Frazier, Abilene, Texas.

approaching. The man looked as serene as before. Dale studied the face, now pale blue-green in the mercury lights. It conveyed nothing. "Son, you've been one tough fucker, done real well so far. But we just caught three more of you losers and one of them will tell us what we want." Then with the same glass-sharp sarcasm he added, "It might as well be you, tough guy."

Flat-toned again, he said, "Believe me, boy, what you've been through so far is nothing. But personally, I think you've been through enough; I don't want to see you suffer anymore. If you tell us what you were doing in our neighborhood, there's dry clothes, coffee, and a bed waiting for you." With his chin he indicated the guardhouse.

The black sergeant stuck his face into Dale's. "Been educating this boy. He's a slow learner, sir! Don't want to give up on him just yet!" Dale's arm was kicked out from under him. He teetered but kept his balance.

"Talk, son," the captain said sincerely. *Wham!* His feet were kicked out simultaneously. In defiance Dale placed himself back on the posts.

"Well, look at that will you, sir. He wants more!" the sergeant said angrily.

His wrists and ankles now bled openly where they had collided with the wooden posts. The cold-blooded officer bent to see Dale's face. "Come on, boy, this man's going to hurt you. You might as well speak and then you can sleep."

It was the word sleep that connected first. Yes, sleep, he thought. Instead of waking up to escape this nightmare I only have to go to sleep. That's the way out of this nightmare and I found it. Yeah, I'll talk and then I'll sleep . . .

His body slid off the posts in slow motion; his chest hit the ground. I'll tell these bastards whatever they want to hear and then it'll go away. I won't be here, and I sure as hell won't stop in that damned tree again and this time I won't even go to the recruiters. It would all simply be gone, he thought, and he would be back singing in the college choir. Melodic Latin filled his ears.

"Looks like he's given up, sir." Laughter invaded the darkness as Dale was pulled to his feet. "Looks like you've had enough. Coffee will be good right now, and then a bed." The man seemed so sincere.

Sure, that would be fine, he thought, but "Private E-3 Nielsen, Dale Edward, United States, 551-64-3912" was all that came out of his mouth. Heart sliding downward in his bony chest, he realized with some horror that his brave mouth had betrayed his exhausted brain.

Moments later, in a dark corner of the compound, he stood before a black metal disk. He could see it was fastened to a buried fifty-five gallon oil drum. The angry sergeant signaled for two armed guards to remove the lid. Inside was just blackness. Dale's legs wobbled, his head spun, but he tried to focus.

Every time he did the panic returned; so he mentally retreated. *If only my mouth would have obeyed!* he almost cried.

Legs ripped violently from under him, the exhausted boy now hung upside down above the inky metal tube. When they had forced his struggling arms and legs into the barrel, his head collided with the bottom, hitting something soft. His face came to rest in something that seemed to move in ten directions at once. His brain lit up in a burning blue phosphorus of fright.

Left arm pinned behind his twisted legs, he kicked violently, for a moment frustrating all attempts to lower and secure the lid. Then all was black. Gasping for air, Dale groped wildly with his free hand. Ears pounding, blood began to rush into his skull. Whatever was in the barrel was much more active now.

Blind, suffocating, heart bursting, panic surged through his nervous system. "Snakes!" he screamed unheard. He wanted now only to die, or faint, or wake up.

The snakes crawled over his face, sliding across his bulging eyes and over his swollen screaming lips. With his free hand he tore madly at one, only to have it replaced by another. The harder he struggled the more he forced himself down into this writhing bed of reptiles. Lungs bursting, he screamed and screamed, but the lid did not come off.

· · ·

With gray breaking on the horizon, Dale stood dazed, shaking violently, in the little room where the nightmare had begun. "Looks to me like he enjoyed the pit," the man said quietly as he walked from behind his desk to stare at the bruised and bleeding face of his wild-eyed victim.

The snakes had left his brain numb. Dale only looked at the man in confusion.

"What were you doing in our perimeter, private? You must realize by now that it is our duty to make you tell us?" The man sneered. "I'm sure you want to sleep. You're shivering, and I've got hot coffee." Dale only returned the man's stupid grin.

· · ·

That morning Dale Nielsen awoke in the guardhouse. Somehow his wet fatigues were dry and he was lying on a cot. The tortures of the night before might have been just a nightmare, but he hurt everywhere and, as sleep left him, he could feel the bruises and cuts on his body. He could barely see out of his right eye.

Like one last torture, the cynical, steely-eyed officer appeared above, startling him. "Well, well, I can see you're awake." The officer smiled. "I'm Captain Tibbets. You should be proud of yourself, son. I have seen some tough sons-a-bitches in here, and despite being stupid enough to get caught, you proved yourself very worthy of your uniform. There will be a truck to take you captives back to the barracks at oh-eight-thirty. You may stay there in the barracks and rest as long as you want. Congratulations, son, you have my respect." The young captain reached down and shook the bewildered private's swollen hand.

33

EXCEPT FOR GOING TO MESS HALL, DALE HUNG AROUND THE BARRACKS THAT day. His eye was swollen almost shut, and he ached everywhere. He had tried to sleep but awoke with a jolt when his dream shifted to the snakes in the barrel. It was noon when his drill sergeant came by. "Heard what happened last night. Looks like the guys got a little carried away," he said, shaking his head. "How you doing?"

Dale looked a little sheepish. "Not bad, I guess."

"Not bad for a guy that's had the living hell beaten out of him?" the man chuckled nervously. "Captain Tibbets wanted me to, ah, compliment you on your courage last night, Nielsen. He hopes there are no hard feelings. He also wanted to let you know that if you'd like to be a prison guard during next weekend's evade-and-capture exercise, he'd be honored to have you."

Dale thought briefly about the offer but dismissed it. "Tell the captain thanks, but I'd just as soon not see that place again. I'd rather have a weekend pass like the other guys."

The young sergeant stared uncomfortably at the wooden floor. After a long pause he cleared his throat and asked, "Mind if I sit?" Without waiting for a response he sat on the bunk across. "There is one other thing the captain wanted me to ask you, Nielsen." Dale waited.

"He wanted me to remind you of the army's offer to put you through Officers Candidate School and send you to Vietnam as an officer."

Dale smiled at the man. "You've been to Vietnam?"

"Yeah, Tibbets too."

Dale sat up, taking full notice of the man for the first time. "Tell me, if you had the choice, would you go as an officer or an enlisted man?"

The man laughed. "Neither! I'd go as a supply clerk or maybe a tourist!"

"No, honestly," Dale insisted. "Knowing what you know now, what would you do?"

The man lowered his voice. "Well, we had a term for OCS guys in Nam. Some of them were great but a lot of them weren't. We called them shake-and-bakes." A nervous look crossed the man's face. "I heard stories of a few of them getting fragged. I never saw it myself, but I heard of it."

"Fragged?" Dale looked over at the man. "Isn't that when your own men toss a grenade in your direction?"

"That's the idea, more or less," the sergeant answered.

Dale looked in the man's eyes. "Thanks, but no thanks. Having one enemy over there would seem like enough. Besides, I've been thinking about last night and how I felt. I think it's helped me to make a decision. I'm going to do my thing as an enlisted man and take my chances and come home. I've been thinking about my girl. I promised her something once, long before I promised the army anything, and I've decided to keep my word."

· · ·

It was Saturday when Ron Gilbert and Dale Nielsen stepped off the bus in civilian clothes in downtown Tacoma. "You're really going to go through with this?" Ron grinned at his friend. "Yeah, I'm really going to go through with this." Dale's voice was strangely ambivalent. "Aren't you going to say you're happy for me?"

"Yeah, I'm happy for you, but I still think you should wait till you get home. From what the veterans say, you may see the world a little differently after being over there."

"I doubt it." Then he fell silent as they walked up the sunny street looking for a jewelry store. "There is something I've never told anyone except a girl I knew named Elaine. It's hard to talk about but maybe you'd understand. You see, last summer Gail missed a few periods, and I don't mean the kind on the end of a sentence." He blushed slightly.

"I mean four or five weeks went by when she passed something like a large blood clot and . . . I was off the hook. But when I was on the hook I had to think about things, I guess about what I believe is right and wrong. Last month I got a letter from Elaine. She said she hated me for giving her address to Frank; asked me what the hell I was doing to myself and to her. She said she still cared about me and thought that my ideas about marrying Gail and some of my reasons were immature. She said that even if Gail had been pregnant and had a kid, that it would be just as much her responsibility and that marrying her would be a stupid mistake.

"Well, maybe she was right and maybe she was wrong, but I have to live up to my beliefs. I could have cried uncle the other day, told them some bullshit, and gotten out of a night of hell on earth. I didn't, maybe because I couldn't afford what it might have done to how I see myself. Does that make sense?" Ron just shrugged his shoulders.

They spotted a jewelry store and stopped on the sidewalk in front of it. "So I'm going to go through with it. It's not like I haven't thought about it. There's a part of me that knows exactly what Elaine was saying about Gail and all, but there's a part of me that has to live with me." He ended the conversation by walking into the shop.

34

AFTER THE WEDDING SERVICE AT ST. PAUL'S CATHOLIC CHURCH IN LEAD, the reception was brief and informal. Late August sun shone over the pine-forested Black Hills, giving a warm glow to the house. Because the Nielsen home was larger, the quickly planned reception was held there. More out of duty than joy, Jean and Alan were gracious hosts.

As the mother of the groom moved from guest to guest, serving food and drinks, she smiled and chatted, but a nervous tension was growing in her. Jean Nielsen felt strange and frightening parallels here. She clearly remembered, from her childhood, brothers and male cousins marrying before shipping out for the Pacific. This wedding had served notice on her that their son was grown up and forever gone. Worse yet, he was soon going to the awful war that was bleeding and dying on TV every night.

In a corner of the dining room cousin Jim Smith, recently returned from Vietnam, stood shaking his head. Smiling a tight-lipped mocking grin, he said, "It won't be like anything you might expect. I mean, I could tell you lots of things, but I was on the Mekong Delta, and that's the only place you know you won't be going."

Dale sipped quietly on a bottle of beer. It had been some time since he had seen his cousin. Jim looked older, more like an adult. True to form, he was not trying to glorify Vietnam or his tour.

"I'm tellin' you, Dale, you'll probably feel like you're in a dream; I mean, I guess it felt like that for me, at least for a while." His voice dropped as he saw Grandma Rose push open the kitchen door.

Grandma Rose continued to quietly set food on the table. She looked at

Dale and Jim, gently shaking her head. Though one grandson was back, her face seemed to tell Dale that her tired heart was already aching for another who was going.

In her simple wedding gown, Gail was radiant. Even Alan, who had told Dale he was against the marriage, saw it. Dale stood there half-listening to Gail. An empty wineglass swinging in her thin hand, she chatted with her mom and an uncle.

". . . And then he'll be gone for a year," Gail's mother, Marie, added.

Gail smiled and shrugged her shoulders. "At least we'll have a few months before he goes. We're going to get an apartment off base. When he does go, I'll probably go back to school at Black Hills State."

The balding man standing next to Gail raised his glass and his eyebrows. "Well, yes, at least it's better than World War Two," the uncle proudly recalled. "We went in as boys like Dale and came back grown men years later. After all, how much can change in a year? In those days we were in for the duration!"

Grandpa Russell, Rose's husband, stood in a quiet corner talking with his grandson Mark. He glanced over at the much-younger World War II vet and frowned, yet continued his conversation without missing a beat. "It's only about fifteen feet across, looks like beavers formed it, but I'll tell you what, the cutthroat trout like it. I mean, it's almost not fair! You throw a fly in there and let them fight over it. When the biggest one's chased off the rest, you got him. Best fish I ever tasted." The grandfather's eyes twinkled, yet the teenager hardly seemed to have heard him.

The old man leaned closer. "But I suppose this story is not what you're thinking about, is it, son? You're standing here pretending to listen to your old grandpa, but you're thinking about Dale. About how he's moved out of your life."

The teenager only nodded, so the old man went on. "Folks act like weddings are happy occasions, but they're only partly honest. For the ones left behind, it's like a death. I know that better than most—we had all girls. Each time a daughter left, a piece of Rose and I died." He waved his glass in the direction of his wife, and said even more softly, "She'd never say it, and maybe if I hadn't had some champagne I wouldn't have said it either, but what you're feeling is natural, Mark."

Soon it was time for Dale and Gail Nielsen to open their wedding presents. One part of Dale stood there enthusiastically handing his bride gifts; the other watched her, noticing her genuine happiness. He wondered quietly, from far back in his thoughts, why he didn't feel that intense happiness. He rationalized that it was because he was a man and, after all, marriage was different for men.

Between the opening of silver-plated flatware and the dishes from Aunt Betty, the image of an angry Elaine boldly entered Dale's mind. He distractedly tore at and then dropped a box that held some thin crystal goblets. No one noticed him slide it back on the table.

By four o'clock Dale was looking anxiously for Gail's eyes, but she was sitting with some high school friends in animated conversation. From behind, Grandma Rose slipped her hand into his and squeezed it. "You were handsome up there." She looked into his eyes. "Let's talk," she added, pulling him into the now quiet kitchen.

"So tell me, Mr. Nielsen," her face softened into a gentle smile, "what happens from here? When do they send you to Vietnam."

"Oh, don't worry, Grandma. Thanks to some very convincing officers I've decided to take a detour through Non-Commissioned Officers School. I won't be going to Vietnam for months. When I graduate I'll be an E-6, that's a staff sergeant. When I get back to Fort Lewis, I'll be taking a company through advanced infantry training. Then I'll be back here for a few weeks. I'll come by for a visit."

"Your telling me not to worry is nice, but I will, and so will your mom." His grandmother paused for a moment, then said, "Jean is young, she does real well, but she's keeping a lot in. And that dad of yours, I suppose he'll do just fine . . . Will you be here for Christmas?"

"No, I don't think so; I should be just getting into Vietnam by then, unless they court martial me." Dale chuckled. "I was supposed to be back two days ago, but I figured what can they do to me, send me to Vietnam?" I'd like to take Gail on a honeymoon, but we'll be driving straight through to Tacoma. I don't want to push my luck too far."

"Do you think you'll be in trouble with your commanding officers?" Rose asked.

Dale put his arm around the old lady. "No, Grandma. I think when I explain that I was getting married, I'll be OK. Hell, I've been kind of lucky." He thought of Frank, Ron, and Pipe. "Most of the guys I went in with are already over there; some have been over there for months."

His grandmother hugged him. "Yes, you've always been the lucky one. I just hope it stays that way."

35

IN THE MOUNTAINOUS RAIN FORESTS OF NORTHERN SOUTH VIETNAM, NOT far from Da Nang, Frank Jealous Of Him stood alone looking across the helicopter landing zone called LZ Baldy. The LZ, about a hundred meters in diameter and built mostly of sandbagged bunkers and empty shell boxes, sat on a hilltop cleared from the jungle and overlooked a long range of coastal mountains. The terrain below the firebase ranged from flooded rice paddies interspersed with thick hedgerows on the valley floor to thick brush that covered the lower hillsides. Higher up the mountainsides the cover changed to thick triple-canopied jungle. LZ Baldy sat high above it all, and to Frank seemed perched like a lonely eagle's nest on a craggy mountaintop.

A misty ceiling at five hundred feet shrouded the distant forest floor where two lakes were fed by the numerous streams that cascaded down the steep mountains. Trails, which aided movement for both sides of the conflict, converged amid the thick brush on the valley floor.

Winter monsoons had brought rain every few days, keeping the sky a gloomy overcast, and sent him into dark thoughts of home and whether he would or, better, should go home again. Showers would commence late at night and leave the jungle floor a cool, slippery red mush in the morning that would turn steaming hot by noon.

Fog clung to the lower reaches of the area most days, creating an eerie isolation for the men of the landing zone. At 1100, in the command bunker at the center of the LZ, Captain Larry Stanford addressed the assembled platoon leaders. As usual, Frank was invited to the meeting by his lieutenant but felt out of place and squatted just outside the circle listening. "Intelligence from *chieu hois* and our own reconnaissance patrols indicate that NVA and Vietcong are again utilizing Base Area 116 as a hospital and training site." He indicated a set of circles in the northeast quadrant of the map.

"We have good information that a trail north of Alligator Lake is being used to purchase rice and resupply enemy units." Again the young officer's hand went toward the map. "We know they are getting rice from Dien Ban, Duy Xuyen, and Khe Sanh districts.

"This route gives the enemy access to Goi Noi Island in the northern part of the lake. Sniffer missions and aerial observations have us convinced that the Thirty-sixth NVA Infantry has reestablished their headquarters here at location 9656, while the Thirty-eighth Quang Da Provincial Headquarters are here at vic Bravo-Tango 0254. Our mission for the next two months is to discourage these people from thinking they've got control of this area." He studied the faces of the men in the half-light of the bunker's interior.

"Company C is to attack and secure position one, here. Company A is to seize and hold objective two over here, while Company D will seize objective three. B Company will secure LZ Baldy, including the immediate vicinity."

With that Frank slumped against the sandbagged wall, part of him relieved that for now at least life would be easy, but also a little annoyed that his company would see little action from this mountaintop stronghold.

Under cover of a makeshift roof constructed of empty wooden mortar cases, he looked out through the rain, down at the misty world below him. He drew some writing paper from his pack and began a letter home.

Dear Dad,

We've been moved again, this time further north to a place called LZ Baldy. Lieutenant Chellis who I've been working under is a short timer and will be leaving soon. He says that I am one of the main reasons he will be going home. These guys tell me I'm a pretty important part of the platoon because I'm so good on point. Point means that I'm like a scout out in front of the squad and the rest of the platoon looking for sniper trip wires and booby traps.

When our platoon goes on a company sized operation, I'm what they call point of point. That means I'm point man of our squad, point man of point platoon, out in front of the rest of the company. These guys tell me that the lives of point men usually only last a few days, sometimes only a few minutes or hours before they get blown away.

They think that because I'm an Indian, I'm good at this. How do you tell these guys how crazy that is? "Hey, I'm from the prairie where we can see for miles." It's kind of weird but I have gotten good at it. It's kind of up to me to see that we don't get lost, that we end up at night where we're supposed to be. Lots of times I don't even look at the maps. I try to feel where I'm going. Sometimes I look for animal trails through the jungle and just like hunting at home, here they kinda go towards water but I don't know really how I do it. The Lieutenant says it's something he calls instinct.

These Vietnamese people over here are all the same. By that I mean, the enemy and the civilians are the same people, so we don't know who is who. Remember I told you about the Chu Hois, they're former Viet Cong who now live with and work for us. They know I look more like them than the guys in the outfit. I feel like these people stare at me. They wonder why I'm even here with these Americans because I don't look like the other soldiers. Sometimes I think they are just curious. They never did hear of Indians. Sometimes I feel like they hate me for fighting here at all.

But maybe that's how I survive. I try to think like them. Like Crazy Horse fighting the cavalry soldiers with his mind instead of having the best weapons. That's how these Viet Cong are always having to outsmart the U.S. Army.

The guys in my outfit still call me "Chief" even though I tell them that I'm not a chief. I guess it's because I'm an Indian.

It's pretty rainy up here so when we're out on patrol our fatigues usually don't last long. I took to just wearing an olive drab towel, split down the middle, like a poncho over my head, instead of a shirt. Now all the other guys are doing that too. It's kind of become our uniform in the bush.

I think a lot of these guys are really scared, and they think that I'm going to get them home alive. I guess that's why I take point so much. Nobody orders me to, in fact we're supposed to rotate on point, but some of these guys are so bad at it that I figure they'll get killed or get the rest of us killed. Lt.'s calling me.

So much for now.

Tell Congo that it's a good thing he's not old enough to be here. Say hi to Bernice and give the girls a big hug. I miss you all a lot and think of you all the time. I sure look forward to the letters I get from the Hollow Horns too.

See you in the funny papers!

                                                    Spec 4 Frank W. Jealous Of Him

The next seven days were light duty except for occasional patrols in the vicinity of the landing zone. B Company enjoyed the meager comfort of the firebase, including sun-warmed showers and a steady supply of C-rations.

On December 22 Lieutenant Chellis called together the platoons of B Company. "We're ordered on a reconnaissance in force patrol at the base of LZ

Baldy tomorrow at sunup. Sniffer patrols say activity has been stepped up, so get some rest, we might be out for a while."

• • •

Because the platoon lieutenant was a short-timer, the pace of the patrol the next day was cautious. The first night the lieutenant sat reading a map. He called for Frank to join him in the command post at the center of the laager. What he did not need right now was to run into the enemy. "Frank, tomorrow I want you back on point. If you see or hear anything unusual, I want to hear about it first. Right now I'm one superstitious and nervous bastard and I'm putting my faith in you to get my tired ass on the Freedom Bird."

"You got it, sir," was all Frank had to say, and the lieutenant relaxed a bit.

The next morning, after coffee and beef chips, under a gray sky, Frank moved slowly ahead, down through the triple canopy, studying the ground. He didn't have a map, but as usual sensed where the location of that night's laager should be. With total concentration he took it all in: the matted jungle floor, the low-lying branches, and the trees had become his textbook, and he was an A student. The deer in these woods were tiny; the noise of the war in their mountains had made them rare and elusive, but they left tiny trails and in his heart Frank thanked them as he crept forward.

At noon he sat near a buddy named Carl Schofer. Both were reading letters from home. Frank's letter from Clynda carried news about school and volleyball. It spoke of Christmas and his dad's church and Bernice being pregnant again. All of it made him smile. He read parts of it to Carl, who had come in country not long after Frank. The two shared almost everything.

By 1300 he was out on point again. A sixth sense made him edgy, told him to stay on his toes. At 1400 he stopped, crouched, then raised his hand for the squad to halt. Chellis and his men froze. Lying on the dim jungle floor only a few feet ahead was an intact American C-ration can, looking for all the world like a discard. Only somehow Frank knew it wasn't. He had found the source of his intuitive nervousness.

His eyes studied the jungle ahead and to the sides and then went back to the mysterious tin. After a pause that unraveled the nerves of the men behind him, he turned slowly around and grinned at the lieutenant and pointed at the can. Sure enough, a fine wire was stretched tightly between the can and the trunk of a sapling. He signaled Chellis to come forward. The lieutenant moved up quietly and crouched nervously behind his point man. Frank said in a whisper, "Sir, I think I got something here you might want to see." He pointed to the can.

The officer stepped up beside him and returned a nervous whisper. "What is it, Frank?"

"It's a can of chipped beef and gravy, sir! The Vietcong must have good intelligence," he said chuckling.

"Why's that?" the officer asked, a little confused.

"Because they wanted one of us to pick it up! If it was ham and mother-fuckers, the booby trap wouldn't work." Frank laughed. Then he signaled the lieutenant and his men back. Stepping back quickly himself, closer to the squad, he pulled a pin from a grenade and tossed it toward the deceptive tin. A muffled blast and a spray of earth were followed by a loud explosion from the right side of the trail, toppling a small tree. Chellis signaled the squad to move quickly away from the noise, knowing every Vietcong in the area now knew exactly where they were.

Later, two klicks away, the RTO radioed in a situation report to base camp. Frank walked over to the lieutenant. "Wouldn't want you to miss that plane ride, sir!" he said, slapping the officer on the back. The other man shook his head and forced a nervous smile.

36

THE FLIGHT FROM ALASKA TO JAPAN HAD BEEN LONG AND UNEVENTFUL. Except for a short nap while refueling in Tokyo, Staff Sergeant Dale Nielsen had not slept since San Francisco. On the final leg of his flight from Tokyo to Vietnam, he had noticed that the left side of the refitted cargo plane was loaded with gaunt, tired-looking men from all service branches who were returning from R&R. On his side of the plane were fresh-faced enlisted boys in winter dress uniforms and starched-looking officers. There had been little conversation.

From inside the aircraft, Dale could see the size of the Tan Son Nhut Air Base at Bien Hoa. In the lifting darkness, he could make out numerous runways and control towers. In the dim gray distance were ghostly rows of jet fighters and helicopters.

It wasn't long before the "cherries," as rookies were called, looking out the windows on the right, broke the silence with excited comments. "Must be a welcoming committee," one soldier said, his voice tight.

"No, I think those are flares, and those red things, those are friendly tracers," another cherry threw in.

"Maybe they're under attack!" still another nameless kid said.

A veteran officer grinned across the aisle and said, "That's H&I fire, harassment and interdictory . . . don't mean nothing!"

From the small window Dale could see the flares and red tracers arcing outward into the black void. In the dim, flickering light of burning phosphorus he could also make out a core of large permanent buildings surrounded by what seemed like miles of large bunkers and supply sheds.

Around the base was a system of guard positions, thatched hootches, and the large village of Vietnamese civilians that had been Tay Ninh before the Americans. A growing sense of anticipation and tension filled his exhausted mind as the plane circled and then descended. Non-Commissioned Officers School had delayed this moment, but This is it! he thought as the plane rolled to a stop.

But so like the army he'd come to know, he found this wasn't it. Twenty-four hours later he sat on the floor of a windowless C-47 transport plane headed for the 25th Infantry and Cu Chi.

· · ·

When the huge aircraft was shut down and the green troopers were assembled on the tarmac, a tall staff sergeant stood smiling. "On behalf of the United States Armed Forces, I would like to welcome your cherry asses to the Republic of Vietnam. If you are reporting in country for replacement duty, please follow me."

He led the men across the air base toward a processing depot. On the way the boys with their fresh fatigues, sparkling combat boots, and well-fed, pale faces saw planes being loaded with flag-draped, military coffins and lines of thin, slow-moving men.

These haggard veterans, whose fatigues were worn, boots cracked and dull, seemed old beyond their years. Their eyes had a sunken, distant look. Some smiled from deeply tanned faces at the new men, and then shook their heads knowingly; others ignored them.

In the hot air drifted a strange mix of expended jet fuel, flowers, and burning dung. It was the stench of burning buffalo dung from the cook fires of the Vietnamese civilians, more than anything else, that flared the nostrils and created in the new men an unsettling sense of disjointed isolation.

They walked toward a huge three-sided hangar where a long row of tables and processing clerks awaited them. Standing in line filling out forms was the slice of army pie Dale resented most, yet its familiarity momentarily ended the worst case of homesickness he had ever felt.

Later that morning the men were assigned to a replacement company. At noon they were loaded on buses and quartered in temporary barracks on the base in Cu Chi. The only topic of conversation among these strangers was the assignments they might be handed.

Three days passed. Each day a list of names would be read aloud and posted for the company to review. Some of the men would return to the barracks to gravely gather their gear. Others would turn and walk toward the row of PX shops. Each day the men would spend twelve hours in the barracks waiting for assignment. As long hours passed, Dale's sense of anticipation, dread, and loneliness grew.

Lying on his cot those lonely hours, he thought often of Gail and how he had asked his folks to sign the marriage license for him. He was still a boy in civilian life, but here in Vietnam he was to be a man for the first time. He'd looked at the anxious, eager, sometimes scared faces of these men in the barracks, knowing he was two years older than most of them.

Eight weeks married and he was thousands of miles from home. What had started as a vague awareness, in the airport in San Francisco, had grown into a relentless sense of complete isolation.

After three days with total strangers he had barely uttered a word. There seemed little reason to speak to anyone. He had seen his share of buddies come and go, and idle chatter was more than he could bear.

To relieve his anxiety he went for long walks. There was a part of him that marveled at the civility of the base at Cu Chi, with its pavement and permanent buildings. He studied the little Vietnamese civilians that worked there. They seemed a tiny, rather delicate people. The high voices of the men and the incessant singing nature of their language gave him the impression that they would be barely capable of hefting a rifle, never mind waging a relentless war or the televised gore of the Tet Offensive.

It was on the third day, late in the afternoon, when the staff sergeant read the names that included Dale's: "To the Second of the Twenty-second, A Company, Mechanized Cavalry, Nielsen, Dale, E-6." For a brief moment he was relieved, grateful he was on a chain of events that would soon deliver him to the fight.

"What'd you pull?" a tall, black soldier asked from his bunk.

Dale smiled sheepishly at the man, not at all sure what kind of card fate had dealt him. "I'm going to the Second of the Twenty-second Mechanized Infantry." He grinned. "Sounds like an APC company."

"What ya know 'bout them APC?" the man asked.

"I know what they look like!" Dale grinned. They both laughed.

"You a lucky one," the black soldier commented. "I got assigned to an artillery group near Pleiku; probably won't see no gooks where I'm going!"

The next morning the men were joined at mess by another batch of unseasoned soldiers and then escorted to an indoctrination center. Here veterans told them what the insiders knew of the enemy. They were told about the combat methods of the North Vietnamese regulars and Vietcong. Some sessions presented experts who told them about the geography; others explained the history and politics of the country. Despite the distracting feelings that flooded his soul, Dale noticed that all the lectures were carefully tailored to support U.S. involvement.

At 1000 hours the entire group was marched to an open area for a firearms demonstration. His young face tanned and already lined, a tall, muscular staff sergeant stood before them. "Men, what you are about to experience, and the degree to which you pay attention and absorb what you see and hear in the next few days, will increase your ability to survive and be an effective weapon in this conflict. At my command you will belly-crawl into this simulated battlefield."

"We will be using live ammo. Do not! I repeat, do not raise any part of your body above the wires or you will lose it. This demonstration of Russian, Chinese, and American rifles will familiarize you with sounds you must remember. Whether you are a rear-area clerk, cook, mechanic, or a soldier on point, you will likely be placed in situations where knowledge of enemy weapons and how to react to them may save your life."

A flat matter-of-factness, a lack of embellishment, made the sergeant's words ring with clarity.

For two sweltering hours a day during the next three days they heard the staccato crack of the AK-47, the pop of Chinese carbines, and soft banging of the nylon-stocked M-16. Along with the men assigned to fighting units, those headed for combat-support MOSs, who had not handled a weapon since basic, were given additional training with M-16s and grenades.

At 1400 and then each day that followed, a black-pajamaed Vietnamese man was brought before them. The stiff-faced sergeant introduced the frail thirty-year-old. "This is Trin Hoc. He is what we call a *chieu hoi*. That is a man who, although trained by the North Vietnamese, has decided his fate and that of his country would better be served by teaching you how to survive and win this war."

Trin showed the men how the Vietcong could move under the wires, carrying satchel charges. In broken English he told them how he was "train to build bomb, look for command area, and blow dem up," creating confusion, chaos, and death. He told them of the fervor of the enemy and their willingness to sacrifice themselves for the common goal of a "Vietnam, united under Hanoi." There was something in his voice that Dale could not trust.

The new men had daily classes that taught Vietnamese history and stressed the heroic role and mission of the United States in the ancient conflict between North and South. Along with classes on communist political and military tactics, they were instructed in local religious beliefs and culture. On the afternoon of the third day Dale sat wondering why the Buddhist majority tolerated a Catholic government, but did not ask.

On December 23, 1968, Bob Hope came to Cu Chi. As he had for two previous wars, Hope brought with him an entourage of leggy dancers, musicians, and comedians. Dale sat far enough away so that the whole thing seemed surreal, but he took it for what it was worth. For two hours he felt Christmas and the power of his culture and its technology pulled like a security blanket tightly around him and the other men.

They howled at Hope, whistled at the pretty girls, and grinned at the silly sketches.

37

ON CHRISTMAS EVE THE MEN ON LZ BALDY FEASTED ON SHIPPED-IN CHRISTMAS dinners. In I Corps a meal of anything but C-rations was a treat. Warm turkey with all the fixings succeeded in boosting spirits, had the men talking in animated tones, and feeling relaxed.

They listened to Armed Forces Radio and the familiar Christmas music of everyone from Bing Crosby to Glen Campbell. Most men got cards and small packages. Everything received in the mail was shared.

Frank Jealous Of Him sat in the red dust behind a shallow berm position that overlooked thick jungle. He cradled his M-16 and ate some cookies Bernice and Clynda had sent him. In his hand was a letter written on military notepaper.

Dear Frank,

How the hell ya doing. It was great to run into you at Jump School and been wondering what became of you? I hope this letter finds you OK, seeing I don't exactly know where you're keeping yourself these days. We got a stand-down for a few days including Christmas Day in Cu Chi. I know that's probably a long way from where you are but if you are on stand-down and could make it we'll be cruising the PX bars looking for a party.

Things here have been pretty quiet for the last few weeks. No serious casualties.

Ever since they made Pipe an M-60 gunner he's been teasing the shit out of me saying he's got to take care of me and insinuating I'm just a little guy who needs protecting.

Well four weeks ago I got my own M-60, so he's been having to eat crow. He's quite a guy and we both feel lucky to be out here together. Well so much for now, hope this finds you in time and look forward to seeing you in Cu Chi.

Merry Christmas,

Ron Gilbert

By 1800 most of the men in Company B were doubled up in pain. Salmonella in the turkey quickly brought on fevers and violent stomach cramps.

Over the shrouded mountains came a steady stream of evac helicopters that landed, filled up with sick men, and then headed to Pleiku and the field hospital.

Frank had wisely puked at the first queasiness and so was able to help with the evac. He was one of the last to board a Huey and participate in the medical stand-down. In the *whop-whop-whop* of the rising bird, Frank sat grinning about how strange life was and looked forward to the shock on Ron Gilbert's face.

38

ON CHRISTMAS DAY, DALE TOOK ADVANTAGE OF THE HOLIDAY AND SLEPT IN.

Later, wandering the base for hours, he wondered about where he was to be sent and what life might be like in the months ahead. Behind every location where there were MARS phones, lines of anxious men who could no longer bear the separation from mothers, wives, and children stood waiting their turn.

As he walked alone among the long metal buildings and sandbagged machine-gun emplacements, he knew only that he was to be sent some place named Dau Tieng. He thought constantly of the war and how he would handle it. The time for imagining was passing quickly; two days and he would finally be a soldier. Despite his anxiety, the boy in him longed to be reborn of fire.

It was 1300 hours when he turned up a paved lane he had been down an hour before. It felt better to walk off the growing anticipation than to sit idly in the barracks, trying to evade small talk.

At 1400 he came up the street again. On the other side, some fifty yards away, walked three men. There was something familiar about them. The way they moved, their relative sizes, the dark faces on two of them. Something that made Dale quicken his step.

For a brief instant, he thought he was dreaming. There were perhaps half a million U.S. servicemen in Vietnam by this time, but these three sure looked like Jealous, Gilbert, and Pipe!

"Nielsen?! Is that you?" Ron Gilbert shouted. "By golly, Dale!" Check out those stripes, boys, he's a staff sergeant!" The three broke into a run while Dale stood too shocked to speak or move.

There was Pipe, his muscular frame even bigger now, and Ron with his reddish-blond hair, freckles, farmer's tan, and Frank, thinner, his Sioux cheekbones now clearly visible beneath the dark skin of his grinning face.

After excited hugs, handshakes, and backslaps, they stood silently for a moment marveling at fate and each other.

"I think we need a beer!" Frank proclaimed, pointing to a bar across the street. "Beers!" the others shouted and followed him across.

In the dim light and thick cigarette smoke of the enlisted men's club, they found a free table and sat down. Dale spoke briefly of his non-commissioned officers training, his marriage, and his assignment to an armored personnel carrier company. "You're going to miss out on all the humping we do, man." Frank grinned and tossed down half a beer. "Hell, you won't even have to carry a ruck! And Third Corps, that's a pussy assignment! That's a place where they send guys like Ronnie and Pipe!" He slapped Ron on the back, then drank again, and slammed down the empty.

"The real war is up north!" He laughed his infectious laugh. "God, it's good to see you guys," he said, signaling the bartender.

Dale had little to say. He sat studying these soldiers and couldn't help but sense that Frank's sense of competition had taken on an ironic twist. The pink, cracked skin on Ron's face and the dark tans on the others made him feel pale and childlike. They spoke casually of ambushes, firefights, and patrols as if they were playground activities.

"I've seen a lot of guys get it." Frank was suddenly serious. In fact, Dale could not recall ever seeing Frank so serious. "It's like they're alive one minute, and dead the next, or they got both legs one minute, the next minute they're lying in the wet jungle screaming about the pain in legs that are gone!" Again in a single tilt half a beer slid down his throat.

Frank went briefly silent. Then finally just sipping his beer, he said, "It could be worse—some units in the American have been completely wiped out and whole platoons never found." Then he fell silent, staring off, at what Dale could only guess. While the others took up the slack, Dale noticed Frank slumped a little and noticed that the Indian's dark eyes grew glassy, distant.

Ron Gilbert took the floor, and with his eastern South Dakota twang told of earlier in their tour when they had come upon a "friendly" village, of how they had taken heavy casualties and been driven back to the tree line.

Pipe sat there working on his second beer. "Tell them how scared you were, Ron. Tell 'em about how you burned out the barrel of your sixty! I got to keep a constant eye on this little guy," he said, hugging his buddy. They all laughed.

"Yeah, it was late afternoon," Ron went on. "It was a battalion-sized operation about a month ago. Once we started receiving incoming fire, the battalion commander told us to move up to the berm that surrounded this little village and use it as a defensive position. Well, we snapped in a couple extra belts, moved up, and surrounded the place. Pipe was too far away to hold my hand! Man, the damned world exploded. That village was full of VC and they weren't scared of us. I don't know why he told us to go up to that berm. It left us completely exposed . . . When it was dark we moved up to the top of the berm, and they opened up on us. There we were, they had us in their sights, and there was nothing to protect us. In a minute we had several guys wounded and that many more killed. I mean instantly!" He shook his head, reliving his sense of shock. "There were green tracers flying towards us, and guys screaming for help.

"We had to fall back and leave the dead. All night the firing went back and forth. We'd fire tracers into the roof of a hootch, and when it caught fire, we'd use the light to see what the hell we were shooting at. Anytime something would move we would shoot like crazy. That's why I lost my barrel!

"The next day all these farmers came out with their hands up, and by golly, they all had South Vietnam citizen IDs, and these people never carry IDs! Our Kit Carson Scouts questioned them and they said the VC were gone. We searched the village and of course we didn't find a thing!"

Setting down his third beer, Frank was grinning. "It's lucky for them gooks we weren't there. We do it different in First Corps, we'd a wasted all of them." He took a long draw on his beer.

Ron finished. "Well anyway, Pipe and I have been guarding this Marine Rock Crusher for the last month, and it's been pretty slack."

Dale looked at Frank, remembering how happy and gentle he'd been.

The conversation drifted from one firefight to another. Hearing these things from guys he knew well gave them a strange quality, unlike a training movie or a drill sergeant but just as unreal. He could do little but listen and absorb. It was as if the fates had brought these combat-hardened men together, and he, the cherry with staff sergeant stripes, was to be the beneficiary of their experience.

At 1700 the group broke up. "I've got to get going and find a ride back to Pleiku," Frank said as he stood. "It's been great seeing you guys, even you, Ron!" he said, slapping the grinning redhead on the back. "And Sergeant Nielsen, whatever you do on that APC of yours, watch your skinny ass." His voice slightly cracked. "You're too good to get fucked up over here." They hugged farewell and then they were gone, leaving Dale to walk back alone, wondering, as new soldiers do, what his own war would be like.

39

BELOW THE NOISY HELICOPTER WAS A SIGHT AT ONCE EERIE AND HUMOROUS. Dau Tieng was a large firebase within the rubber plantations of central Vietnam. As the helicopter descended, beneath them grew a classical French villa. When they had dropped to a few hundred feet Dale could see walls, still intact, but pockmarked by the war. In a courtyard at the center of the villa was an empty pool, a white Playboy bunny emblazoning its blue tile work. Surrounding the villa were artillery batteries, thatched hootches, bunkers, and numerous tents.

Once on the ground, E-6 Sergeant Nielsen was directed up to the villa where he reported in. The red tile and white stucco buildings surrounded by arrow-straight rows of rubber trees did not match any of the televised images of the war he had seen.

He was sent to company supply, issued an M-16, web gear, mess kit, poncho and liner, a helmet, and a flimsy duffel bag to haul it in. At 1600 he was temporarily assigned to a bunker. The veterans explained he was to pull his share of perimeter guard that evening. On berm duty that night, the only fireworks he saw were H&I fire and occasional flares used to light the perimeter. Still, he was exuberant: he had a gun, he was in Vietnam, and he was on guard duty.

At 1000 the following day an armored personnel carrier approached driven by a copper-haired kid with ragged fatigues. The man stopped and jumped off the machine. There was no false military formality, no salute. "You must be Sergeant Nielsen. My name's McGregor, guys call me Big Red. Stick with me and I'll show you how to get through this! Captain says you're headed toward my outfit. In fact, we were sent in for supplies and to fetch you." The burly, sunburned soldier's grin was infectious.

Dale dropped his pack and shook the man's calloused hand. "Dale Nielsen . . . So this is what they call an APC," he said, pointing to the big machine.

"You guessed it," the smiling man said, lighting a cigarette. "This is what the army calls an M113 Armored Personnel Carrier, but that's kind of a bad name for it, because nobody in their right mind would ever ride inside it!"

"Why not?"

The soldier looked pleased at having the upper hand. "Well, you see, Sarge, APCs are made out of thick aluminum so that they can float. This thing is supposed to be amphibious, which it's not, on account of it's too heavy with men on deck and gear and all, and even if it wasn't too heavy, it's mostly mud we go through anyway. Well, because it's only aluminum, Chinese rocket-propelled grenades go through it real nice. We just call 'em RPGs." He pointed at a quarter-sized hole in the metal siding. "When the RPG gets inside," he stepped around to the metal door in the back and pointed in, circling his hand, "they throw shrapnel all around and tear things up, including GI Joes. So mostly we walk beside them or ride on top." Dale stood there looking confused.

"Don't look so hurt, Sarge; they do make excellent cover for small-arms fire, and it beats the hell out of walking everywhere. And the best part is they carry lots of extra beer and C-rats. Another nice thing about them is with a fifty and a sixty, they carry lots of firepower. So when you're making an assault on a tree line with the other tracks in the company, you can scare the living shit out of the gooks. Hopefully they'll *di di* and that makes our lives a whole lot easier and longer." He laughed at the expression on Dale's face. "Oh, *di di* is short for *di di mau.* That's Vietnamese for 'get the hell out of there' or something!

"Climb aboard; I'll give you a tour of your new home." The shaggy redhead slapped Dale on the shoulder. "After all, we're both goin' in the same direction."

They were soon joined by another soldier who jumped behind the fifty-caliber Browning and slid into the turret. "This is Donovan, best gunner in the outfit. I'm two months short, but Donovan here is so short he can smell the jet fuel on the Freedom Bird!" The unshaven man tipped his fatigue cap and grinned tobacco-stained teeth. It was hard for Dale to believe these men were his age.

On the way to Alpha, McGregor jabbered incessantly. "This baby has got a two hundred fifteen-horsepower Chrysler engine, will go about three hundred kilometers on a tank of diesel, cruise at sixty kilometers an hour, and can turn on a dime." He pulled so hard on the steering levers the spin all but threw Dale off the vehicle. The cherry sat on top laughing as he hung onto a metal support bracket.

40

THE MORNING SUN HUNG SUSPENDED SWOLLEN AND QUAKING IN A cloudless sky. Heat waves ascended from the red clay of the countryside, baking the foliage. Inside the firebase reveille floated in the hot air, and one by one the boys of war woke to play with fate. Sergeant Dale Nielsen was the second up. The last two days of light duty and anticipation had robbed him of any real sleep.

It was later that morning when the first of many such calls came in via a thin crackle over the radio. Corporal Smitz handed the phones to Captain Crocker. All the men could hear clearly was a nervous "Shit!" when the captain slammed the headset in its cradle.

"Hau! Sergeant Hau! Assemble the platoon and squad leaders ASAP! There's trouble." The captain's face was tense.

Hau's husky Hawaiian form made the circuit. "Captain wants a quick conference. That means you, Nielsen!" he said flatly as he passed. A slight nervousness started slowly in the young sergeant's stomach and spread upward, tightening his neck and shoulders. By the time he reached the assembled men, Dale was fully awake and more alert than he had ever felt before. Every fiber of his body was fully charged, electric, waiting.

The captain wasted few words. "Men, we've got a situation we have to attend to. It seems a large fortified NVA bunker system twenty klicks west of here has ambushed a convoy. It's created quite a ruckus. We've got U.S. and civilian casualties. Charlie is dug in. Intelligence says they are in a large fortified bunker system on both sides of the road. The enemy has decided to stay and fight. Prepare to mount up."

Fifteen tracks on line cruised at sixty kilometers per hour. In perfect spiral plumes, red dust boiled into the morning brightness. Spec Four Donovan, the unshaven fifty-caliber gunner, turned to look at the face of the grinning Sergeant Nielsen, knowing what this cherry could not. With only a month left in country he had seen these eager faces before. He stared for a moment, as if he knew that he would never see exactly the same face again.

The splendor of the steel cavalry at full gallop sent a dose of self-confidence into Dale. After only three days with his new unit he was filled with a feeling of thanksgiving and well-being. Of all the assignments he might have gotten, this was the best. Remembering McGregor's words, "I don't have to walk much and these things are great to hide behind," he thought about touching the thick aluminum armor as a final reassurance.

Jets screamed in the general direction the company was headed, spewing rockets before them in a display that paled the Fourth of July fireworks back in Deadwood. It was almost grand, Dale thought.

After twenty minutes, Crocker signaled the company to halt, then instructed the platoon sergeants to relay the essentials to the men. "NVA regulars in fortified positions about two klicks ahead. We're going to assault their position to determine their strength. We'll pull back if need be, then call in another air strike." Sergeant Hau relayed the message as precisely as possible.

The fifty-caliber gunner's face went ashen. He turned toward Dale and, with a look in his gray Irish eyes that scared the replacement, tipped his metal pot forward and fastened his flak jacket.

In seconds the vague clatter of Russian AK-47 automatic rifles could be heard above the roar of the huge Chryslers. Dale could see muzzle flashes coming from the thick foliage of a hedgerow on the far side of this dormant field. Sergeant Hau ordered a dismount, and all but the drivers and gunners slid to the scorching earth.

Fear turned to adrenaline as the men got the signal to advance. Now the heavy machines crawled forward warily like cats stalking unseen prey. The dismounted men moved behind the tracks. With claws of tremendous firepower, these cats looked invincible. Dale settled into a crouched steady walk just enough behind the APC to shield himself and still see the trees now only a hundred meters ahead.

Gunfire from the trees popped sporadically, sending sprays of red dirt into the air.

From the command unit Crocker gave the order for the big guns to open up. With a roar Dale could not have imagined, thousands of heavy rounds with bright red tracers flew toward the strip of jungle. Fifty meters to go, and things began to go wrong. Dale noticed a man behind the track to his left drop his rifle, stagger, then pitch forward, his gurgled murmur of death covered by the noise of the machines.

Dale looked over his shoulder at the man, half-expecting him to rise or maybe to see his soul wing upward. The man only lay there facedown in the weeds and dust.

Bullets ricocheted off the plating on the far side of the track, making an odd metallic sound. Dale tried to swallow, to push the man's slow descent from his mind, when the whole world lit up. In a blinding flash accompanied by a deafening explosion, the heavy track stopped moving.

Dazed, confused, with smoke and a strange wet spray that filled his eyes, Dale instinctively fell on his chest. Wiping a greasy smear from his face, his only thought was to get out of there. Why were the rest of the tracks pulling up? He lay there trying to make out his platoon leader through the smoke and dust. Before he could see anything the tracks on either side began to pull back, slowly at first, then faster as the men repositioned themselves.

Seconds turned to eternity as he lay in the powdered red dirt wondering why his APC was not reversing, wondering why the huge machine would not obey, would not back up like the rest. Then he saw Hau signaling him to get his ass out of there and behind the track to his left.

Pushing himself to his feet he flung himself to the left, almost forgetting his M-16.

Fifty meters into the retreat it was obvious that his track was not going to pull back with the rest. Instead it sat largely undamaged and strangely quiet, a steady stream of gunfire whining off its surface.

Crawling behind the retreating track, Dale's thoughts briefly returned to the excitement of the ride in and of the ashen look he had seen earlier on Donovan's face. It was then he saw Big Red. His fatigues were torn, smeared with blood; but he appeared unhurt, alert. One hundred meters back, and the gunfire from the distant line of trees diminished to an occasional pop and ping.

Crocker ordered in an air strike that rocked the earth in the trees, sending debris, black smoke, and orange fire into the blue sky.

Hau signaled Dale over to his position. "Doesn't look good for a few of the guys." He seemed to be speculating out loud. "No, Sarge, it sure doesn't," was all the replacement could think to say.

"Well, son," the huge Hawaiian spoke calmly. "In a few minutes we're going back up there. Hopefully the air strike killed them little bastards or sent them scurrying back toward Hanoi, but empty or not, we're going to reassault that position and recover that track and our men. When we advance I want you and Big Red to recover that vehicle if possible, and, Nielsen, if Big Red can't get it started in the first sixty seconds, get your asses out of there."

Half-thinking that Hau must be addressing someone else, Dale looked unconsciously over his shoulder before it sank in he was now the one expected to move on command.

When the second air strike stopped shaking the ground, Dale was sitting smoking a civilian Lucky Strike and draining a warm Coke. "Mount up, men! We're moving back up," Hau said with the same indifferent tone.

They advanced slowly, carefully, while the fifty-caliber and M-60 gunners sent a deadly spray before them. Like grieving elephants the tracks moved slowly toward their stranded brother.

With twenty-five meters to go Big Red signaled Dale to follow him. The two crawled in the powdery dirt slowly assessing the damage. Only there didn't seem to be any. "I think we can get it started; she looks okay. The concussion just blew me out the hatch, knocked me stupid!" was all the short-timer said. He looked neither scared nor excited, only intent on getting the APC out of there before the NVA recovered their positions and opened fire. "Okay, let's do it!"

The two men pushed open the rear door, met only by the sound of huge buzzing flies. Dale crawled out of the brilliant sun into the acrid smelling semidarkness of the track's metal belly. The buzzing of flies filled the hot silence. Over the ammo cans and gear strewn inside, Dale crawled forward toward the hatch of the fifty-caliber gunner, sliding over something soft and cool. Above him was the hatch, the gun, and the sky. He wondered what had become of the worried gunner.

In the harsh sunlight, Big Red cranked the engines to life behind him. Dale pulled himself up behind the small half-inch thick shield, punctured by a small jagged RPG hole. No sooner had the engine fired up when the staccato cracks of AK-47 fire began to tear the boiling air. Dale checked the belt, then grabbed the handles of the big gun. A strange greasy film covered the splintered wood. In fact, it covered everything around him, smearing his green fatigues, a strong, sweet, coppery odor sticking to his fingers. He removed his hands, staring at the pinkish smear, before the chilling reality of the slick handles hit him. It was Donovan!

Until the track pulled back behind the rest, he poured round after round into the shredded tree line, cursing the enemy, the heat, and the greasy paddles of the fifty caliber.

41

SERGEANT DALE NIELSEN SLEPT RESTLESSLY BESIDE THE APC. EVEN ON watch the night before, his thoughts had been dominated by the sight of Donovan, or what was left of him, being slid into a body bag for the dustoff.

It seemed unreal, almost unimaginable, that what they would return to his parents was a pair of legs. In his hazy dream the legs struggled with a life of their own, resisting the rubbery enclosure, kicking and squirming on the ground. "Sarge! Sarge! Time to go." Hau was nudging him. He came out of sleep with a jolt. The sky was already ablaze with its fat Vietnamese sun.

• • •

A small chunk of C-4 plastic explosives flared under the pork and beans until they bubbled. Dale sat poking at them until Hau came by a second time. "You okay, Sarge?" His face an open book, Dale returned the question with a wrinkled brow. "Yeah, sure, Henry, I'm okay; it's just, well . . ."

Hau sat down. "Since you're not eating those lovely pork and beans, mind if I have at them?"

"Sure, I'd be glad for the company." He looked at the huge man sprawling to the earth beside him. He thought how old Hau looked, silver hairs hidden among the coarse-bristled blackness of the man's scalp. Hau's skin color had from day one reminded him of Frank. Maybe there was a small comfort in that.

"Yesterday was kind of rough, Donovan bein' so short and all," Sergeant Hau said.

"Yeah," was all Dale could muster.

"Well, son, shit happens. I mean I've been here nine months and shit happens all the time, but the worst I've had were mosquitoes and foot rot! What you got to focus on . . . is staying alive yourself." The Hawaiian spoke between bites. "I mean, like I was home in Hawaii one day . . . raising my family . . . going to work like any other guy, when they activated my reserve unit, and here I am, thirty-eight years old and in the middle of hell. I don't think for one minute about not making it. I can't afford to. I mean, like, you're married, aren't you?"

"Yeah," Dale said, fingering the thin gold band on his finger.

"Well, then, that's what I mean. You got to get home and make some babies. Someday, this place," he turned his broad Polynesian face to survey the dusty red savanna, "this place will be just a damn memory. You fix on that, boy." Standing, Hau tossed the empty tin, slapped Dale on the shoulder, and moved away toward the command track where Crocker stood shaving.

Dale sat there thinking about how lucky he'd been, how if he had been a few feet further forward he'd have been hit by more than the gunner's greasy spray.

• • •

By 0900, Crocker had assembled the platoon and squad leaders. His jaws were tight. "Men, today we go back up there and recon yesterday's firefight. We're looking for bodies, or parts. We need to confirm enemy dead for the higher-ups. You know the routine. We mount up at oh-nine-thirty."

He turned toward the young sergeant. "Nielsen, you did pretty well on that fifty yesterday during that recovery. I want you to take Donovan's place until we get a proper replacement." A wave of nausea flowed into Dale's empty stomach.

• • •

Bomb blasts and mini-gun fire had pretty well shredded the strip of jungle. Dale noticed that even individual leaves had holes in them. Heat poured in through the ruptured canopy, raising a glistening sweat on his neck and shoulders.

He walked slowly, carefully, from crater to crater looking for, but half-hoping not to find, "signs" as Crocker had said. But what if I find a foot or an ear? The thought of picking up a leg sent revulsion through him, and then he saw it.

Instead of calling out, he just stood there staring. On the ground, lying at the edge of a deep, jagged crater, was a body. Except for fléchette punctures, the young face was relatively intact. Huge, black blowflies buzzed around the dull, moon-blue eyes. They crawled hungrily in and out of the gaping mouth and tiny nostrils. Where the khaki shorts ended so did the legs, except for the jagged stumps of bone and the drying pulp of muscle and skin.

Dale tried desperately to move his eyes, to call out, but he couldn't. Instead he slowly inched closer as if the dead Vietnamese might spring up on those ragged stubs and attack, or as if the death that filled those filmy eyes was contagious.

His mind swam with the heat, the smell of death, and the sound of the flies. What if the docs could have sewn Donovan's legs onto . . . Then he snapped out of it, horrified by the foolish, gruesome musing.

For the longest time, the school principal's son from South Dakota stood, fixated with an intense mix of morbid curiosity and hot shame.

Call out! a voice inside said. No, don't, another voice argued. It's your body, your find. At least take his rifle, the darker voice whispered.

"Hey, over here! I found a body!" he finally called out, lifting the Chinese bolt-action rifle from the edge of the sandy hole. His eyes were relieved to be staring at something as simple as the worn wooden stock of the primitive weapon.

Soon the bomb-ruined body was the object of great curiosity and discussion. "They're not very big, are they?" Private Simmonds said, betraying his cherry status.

"No, but these slant-eyed bastards don't care about size. They probably think us Americans make nice big targets," a man named Murphy said, his black face glowering as he kicked the fly-ridden head. "That's for Donovan!"

Dale stood at a distance, amazed that someone would kick a dead body, at the same time understanding Murphy's great need to strike out. He'd probably been in country with Donovan since the beginning of his tour.

Then Simmonds's small blue eyes lit up. "Hey, Sarge, I hear that sometimes they use ears for a body count. Maybe we should cut both this asshole's ears off and tell 'em we found two gooks!" He fished in his fatigues for his folding Camillus.

Unfolding the blade, Simmonds bent down close to the horrid corpse. Dale froze. He tried to say, I'm in charge here. Don't be doing that. But no sound came out.

Then, with a grin that exposed snoose-stained teeth, Simmonds looked up at Dale as he began to slice at the cartilage.

It was either a sudden attack of humanity, or the shocked look on the sergeant's face, but Simmonds stood up. "Naw, them ears is too fuckin small. Even if I wore them on my hat, nobody would hardly see them, especially after they dry up and get all crinkly."

Even Dale laughed nervously with the assembled curiosity-seekers, relieved that for now the horror had been contained. For a long time they stood staring and smoking, releasing hatred on a man who was beyond caring.

Later, Dale carefully stored the old Chinese rifle deep in the track, somewhere between the ammo cans and the C-rations. He never saw his souvenir again.

42

THE UNMISTAKABLE SOUND OF A HUEY WHOPPING IN OVER THE MOUNTAINS to the south of LZ Baldy brought Lieutenant Chellis stumbling from his bunker. Up all of this dark February night, the weary lieutenant had been filled with an overwhelming sense of expectation that was like waiting for his own birth. The growing light of dawn found him bleary-eyed, stubble-faced, and a little drunk.

Silent, emerging like a phantom from the heavy morning mist, Frank walked up behind the officer. "Freedom Bird, sir?" he said loud enough to startle the man.

"Ah yeah," Chellis turned and grinned, "in from Da Nang and it sure sounds pretty, Chief."

Moments later, amid a tornado of dust and pebbles, the helicopter sat down. Frank watched as from the open bay door stepped a large sandy-haired officer who looked as handsome and fresh pressed as a recruiting poster. Without ceremony, carrying his duffel and his ruck, Chellis appeared before the stranger. Setting down his gear, he held out his roughened hand: "Lieutenant Robert Chellis."

"Lieutenant Albert Farinelli, sir, glad to make your acquaintance," the newcomer said, extending his own large right hand.

"Lieutenant Farinelli, you're in for one hell of a tour!" Then glancing around said, "Chief, come over here for a minute."

Frank looked around sheepishly, then walked over. "Yes, sir?"

"Farinelli, this is E-4 Frank William Jealous Of Him. He is a full-blood Sioux Indian and the main reason I am about to step on the Freedom Bird. If you want to make it to the Freedom Bird yourself, I strongly suggest that you listen to him. The worst thing that can happen is to get lost out there." He pointed down past the booby-trapped perimeter to the thick jungle. "Let Frank teach you the ropes, although he can read 'em just fine; he doesn't even need a fuckin map."

Frank's rib cage swelled a little while a tear formed in his eye. This was good-bye, not only for Chellis but for him, good-bye to the first person that had made him feel like a man. Frank stuck out his hand and the new man gripped it and pumped.

"I hear you, sir," Farinelli said, saluting. Without further words Lieutenant Chellis hugged Frank, grabbed his gear, and disappeared inside the helicopter.

It didn't take Frank long to like the new man. Farinelli, who was nearly six two and built like a football player, stood and walked erect, like an officer. He had a clear voice, a slight southern drawl, and intelligent hazel eyes, eyes that while they did not seem to judge, somehow made Frank feel as if they saw right into him.

Walking around that evening, drinking a warm beer, Farinelli sauntered over toward Frank. "I want you to know that I heard what your former LT said this morning," he said, handing Frank a warm one. "I know I'm the cherry, the shake-and-bake fresh from studying accounting at college. But if you're a good teacher, I can be a quick study. I'll let you know I'm plenty scared, but I'm no chicken. I can only promise you one thing: I'll do the best I can and I'll never send you guys where I won't go."

Frank popped open the beer and took a long swallow, then nodded toward the officer, acknowledging what he knew already to be the truth.

On February 12, Farinelli was out on patrol with two of the four squads that made up his platoon. They had just set up their day laager when his RTO got a desperate call from the leader of the fourth platoon. The RTO covered the mouthpiece and whispered, "They lost, sir, and spooked real bad."

Farinelli listened intently to the headset, then called Frank forward. "The two squads from Fourth Platoon are lost and the sergeant is pretty upset, wants us to come and get 'em. What do you think?"

Smiling a little, yet in a serious tone, Frank said, "I think it's time for one of those lessons we were talking about, sir. If we go and get them, sure enough Charley will just wait for us, listen to our radio communication, and set an ambush. Could be real bad, real bad, sir."

Shaking his head, Farinelli said, "You're probably right. What do you think we should do? We can't just leave them out there tramping around the jungle till they starve or get killed."

"No sir, we can't," Frank said, pulling out a map. "Let me see that radio."

Calmly Frank proceeded to ask the lost platoon leader what the country around them looked like, what kind of trees there were, where the ravines were, how far back they had passed a stream. Carefully, so as not to reveal a map coordinate, Frank began to lead them in. Farinelli watched as the Indian would stare at the map, wait for another transmission, listen, look at his map, then give them a new compass bearing.

After an anxious, sweaty hour the lieutenant could hear the lost men. He was amazed, but the other soldiers only smiled and sat smoking and bullshitting quietly.

Moments later the lost squads came in looking tired and sheepish, but relieved. Farinelli offered Frank a cigarette. "What the fuck, man, are you some kind of good luck charm or what?"

"Just for others, sir," Frank said, laughing humorlessly. "Just for others and not even . . . for all of them."

43

IT WAS MID-FEBRUARY 1969, A MONTH SINCE DONOVAN'S DEATH. WITH THE superstitious respect shown a true short-timer, Big Red had been sent to the rear area for supplies. Dale Nielsen, no longer a cherry, sat concentrating on the idle task before him. The world behind his APC was an orange and red inferno of C-4 and Rome-plowed jungle. Increasingly, he believed if someone were to be shot, if someone were going to die, it would be someone else.

Months earlier this part of the jungle had been cleared by the large Cats. In teams of two, Seabees had pulled huge anchor chains, toppling the trees and shrubs. Despite this deforestation, the enemy had returned to their well-camouflaged bunkers and tunnel systems. Now it was time for the United States cavalry to burn the tangled jungle floor to ashes, exposing the enemy positions.

In six days of light duty they had only occasionally made contact, and that had been random AK fire, rockets, and RPGs. It seemed to him that these were aimed at the row of huge D-7 Caterpillars as they further reduced what was left of the dead, dried jungle to knee-high mulch and stumps.

"Those guys are nuts!" Dale yelled over the roar of the slow-moving track. He pointed to the man in the wire cage atop the Cat.

"Yeah! These Seabees don't seem to know there's a war going on. They take an RPG and don't even slow up!" Behind him Specialist 4th Class Edward Grubouski, a big, gangly blond from Cicero, Illinois, screamed as he tore off two-inch chunks of plastic explosive. He lit them and tossed them into the broken trees. "They must recruit guys who are totally numb for this gig!" Grubouski turned back toward the towering flames.

Enjoying his adventure, Dale sat atop an ammo can beside the new fifty-caliber gunner. He liked this seat; it went with being squad leader. He hadn't minded a bit when Dan Miller showed up to replace Donovan.

He sat there thinking about how good life was right now. Before him was a primitive stove made from a C-ration can, fueled with small bits of plastic explosive supplied by Grubouski. On the thick aluminum deck sat a bag of caramels from the accessory packs dropped in the day before.

Beside him, looking red and beautiful against the chipped green paint, smoke, and destruction, sat two large Delicious apples carefully buffed to a brilliant luster. "Hey, Miller! These are going to be pretty nice!" Dale poked the gunner in the ribs.

The baby-faced blond turned and forced a grin. Dale had taken to making candied apples since he had realized what the caramels in the Aid-Packs might be good for. The men laughed about it, even the short-timers like Sergeant Hau. Dale had even gotten a big grin out of Captain Crocker when he formally presented him with his first candied apple.

Just the sight of a man making caramel apples atop a whining APC seemed to break the monotony and constant, dull ache of tension. He'd sit up there polishing the apples with the care of a skilled craftsman, the men on the next track turning frequently to check on the progress. The young sergeant would hold them up for the men to see, turning them, examining them in the sunlight. For a moment the war was gone and the small, tracked vehicle a stage for a frustrated pantomime artist. The noise and flames provided a magnificent if exotic set for Sergeant Nielsen's performance.

Next came the caramels. Each was carefully unwrapped and examined for color, consistency, and exact squareness, or some such criteria only guessed at by the men on the next track. Whatever it was, every so often a rejected caramel would be flung disdainfully into the roaring flames, or simply tossed to one of the men.

Soon everybody within eyesight was caught up in the drama of the selection process. Dale would hold the candy up, on the flat of his right palm, then turn it over until he would either nod favorably and drop it into the boiling goo or shake his head and, pinky finger held high, toss it away.

One caramel seemed to be of marginal quality; so Dale nudged the machine gunner, indicating he should render his opinion on the brown chunk. Miller took the candy and, with a growing blush on his hairless face, proceeded to give it a going-over. Finally he nodded his head and handed it carefully back to the sergeant who dropped it into the mix. The men roared with laughter.

The performance ended when hot candy hung in perfect brown sheets on the apple. Then, fork-speared apple in hand, the chef would sit with a look of total consternation. Who should receive the prize? What might be this judge's secret criteria? Would it be a gift for a man whose deeds had earned him this exaggerated favor? Should it be given to someone who had screwed up, as one last dig, or to some lonely newcomer who hung on the edges of the squad, waiting for acceptance.

Today Chef Nielsen stood exposed to gunfire, making a mockery of Dante's empire. Holding the glorious apple aloft, he stood, defying the enemy, waving the glistening prize like a monarch in sleeveless Olive Drab, fixing his gaze solemnly on one gangly kid after another, until he spun and presented it with a bow to his accomplice. The new gunner stood in his hatch beaming. With his first bite, Miller signaled the end of the performance.

44

FEBRUARY 23, 1969, LZ BALDY

THE MOONLESS NIGHT WAS THICK WITH HEAT AND HUMIDITY. CARL SCHOFER lay in the bunker snoring loudly while Frank Jealous Of Him peered into the impenetrable gloom. He had been on watch for two hours and would soon be turning it over to Steimsha.

The complete blackness was shattered by occasional H&I fire. The mortar crew lit the landscape every twenty minutes or so, creating in the clearing around the firebase a surreal ghostly flickering of burning phosphorus.

With the latest volley Frank looked long and hard at a shrub that stood near the edge of the clearing three hundred meters out. He imagined that the shrub had moved. He rubbed his eyes, upset that his mind was wandering. Seeing danger where obviously all was quiet was something a cherry might do, he scolded himself.

When the next volley of H&I went off, that bush and two others now stood in the fire zone. Heart pounding, Frank reached over and punched James Esch on the leg. "Hey, Esch man," he whispered. "We got some walking shrubs. Get over to the command bunker and tell them." Esch had not completely crawled from his poncho when the ground near the command post shook with incoming rockets. Within an instant, men were awake and throwing thousands of rounds into the tree line.

Down below, a man screamed something in Vietnamese, and the tree line came alive with a wave of Vietcong sappers, each carrying a suicide charge of explosives in toward the American command area.

Stark fear raced up Frank's spine. He snapped in a fresh clip and waited for the next flare to go up. Shimmering phosphorus yellow soon lit the landscape. Men were now clearly visible clipping the first row of wire. Frank squeezed violently on the plastic handles that led outward to his forward Claymores. The world exploded with the screams of wounded men, but the assault wave only intensified.

LZ Baldy was wide-awake now. Dazed men stumbled from sleep toward foxholes while trying to dodge incoming mortar and rocket fire. Some men shouted orders, others yelled oaths, a few screamed in agony as rockets exploded into the defensive perimeter, spewing death. Frank stood his position, peering into the killing zone. He aimed and squeezed off a barrage at a man creeping under the wire. In a brilliant flash, the sapper simply evaporated.

Carl slid into the foxhole beside him. They could hear Farinelli shouting for the men to lay down suppressive fire.

At 0347 the earth shook as Bunker 9 in B Company's sector received a direct hit. It was so close that Frank, Schofer, and Esch were pounded with debris and dirt.

Farinelli grabbed his radioman, Charlie Brown, and headed for the bunker, where in the light of illumination flares he could make out two of his men squirming in anguish. He reached for the radio headset. "This is Blue Leader at LZ Baldy requesting Charger dustoff! Over."

Artillery shells with bright red tracers roared out from the LZ in the supposed direction of the incoming shells.

"How's it looking?" Farinelli called to his company medic who had now reached the devastated bunker.

"Not good, sir. Two of the guys can wait for morning; they're dead, sir! Two others need immediate medevac."

"It's already done! Just see what you can do for them until dustoff arrives."

Another volley of mortars slammed into the perimeter, spraying red dirt and shrapnel in all directions.

Farinelli slapped his radioman on the back, handed him the headset, and climbed out of the carnage back toward his point man.

"What's the situation, Frank?"

"Pretty wild, sir. Keep your head down 'cause it's still coming in!" AK fire slammed into the earth-filled bags.

"Looks like it's a general, coordinated assault. LZ Cork's been hit. They got dead sappers on the wire, and I've been hearing MACVs calling in since the shit started. How's it look down there?" Farinelli nodded toward the concertina wire.

Sergeant Schofer responded. "I think we got a few of them, sir. We had two or three get to the second wire; maybe two penetrate."

"*We*, Kimosabe?" Frank barked at him. An old Browning thirty caliber opened up on them from the tree line, ending the conversation.

At 0400 the lieutenant was back on the radio, asking why medevac had not come in. "We got some guys hurt bad up here! Where the hell is that chopper?!"

The radio popped. "They're busy, sir. It's been a wild night. Just got word they'll be heading back out now, sir! Over."

By 0420 the medevac chopper landed amid occasional incoming shells. Incoming small-arms fire popped and zinged everywhere. At 0503 Schofer yelled, "Al! Looks like we got someone moving one hundred fifty meters out!" Farinelli radioed for illumination, but when the sky lit up the wire was vacant.

Frank looked out. "You're starting to see things, Carl. I think you need some sleep!" He slumped to the bottom of the shallow hole. "What you got for C-rats?" he asked, grinning at Schofer who sat shaking his head.

"Chief, you're always hungry!" Schofer laughed, tossing Frank a candy bar.

At 0700, weary from the night, Frank headed slowly back down the exposed slope, followed in a long line by his squad. At 0735 Frank pointed to a cache of Chicom grenades and unused M-79s wrapped in leaves at the base of a mangrove. The lieutenant radioed in. "Blue Raven, we've got some Chicoms here and some rockets. Should we blow them in place?"

At 0835 there was a loud explosion.

• • •

On March 6 the 146th received orders that would transfer them to LZ Professional near Chu Lai. LZ Baldy became just another memory.

45

BLUE LIGHT ERUPTED SPORADICALLY FROM UNDER THE HUGE ROME PLOWS, as it had every night. A helio-arch glow illuminated a dozen welders' masks. In the center of the firebase they worked, dwarfed by the machines they tended, constantly cursing as they welded patches of new skin onto the sleeping brutes.

"These guy are nuts!" Hau said to the night, offering Sergeant Nielsen a cigarette.

Dale slouched behind the fifty caliber; he patted the gun handles nervously. "It's like no one told these combat engineers what nice targets they are for a rocket attack, and they haven't looked up long enough to have figured it out." His eyes scanned the perimeter. His ears, which in the past months had become batlike, focused on the world beyond the RPG screen of concertina wire.

"I'll let you in on a little secret, Henry; nothing scares me as much as the idea of being attacked and overrun at night." He paused. "Now, going out on night ambush isn't exactly my idea of a relaxing evening either. Actually I don't know how I'd actually rank them." Dale stopped long enough to hear Hau's deep chuckle. "So even though this is the slackest thing I've done in country during the day, the nights are as long as . . . well as long as the hair in a wild turkey's beard!" Dale slipped into a little Walter Brennan.

Hau strained to keep from laughing out loud. "Do you folks from the country really talk like that? 'Long as a turkey's beard'?"

"Well, actually, no. I just come up with them for you. You always seem to appreciate my weak humor."

Again Hau chuckled softly, and then fell silent.

"Well, if you're going to miss sleep and keep me company, you've got to talk too, honey," Dale said, not wanting Hau to leave. "I just told you what I'm most scared of here. Now you tell me."

After a long silence. "Drowning! Mostly I'm afraid of drowning."

Dale laughed. "Drowning? Here we are in the geographical center of Tay Ninh Province, guarding a dust patch, in the middle of the dry season, sitting on top of this fine amphibious craft, and you're afraid of drowning?"

"Yup." Hau smiled into the gathering darkness. "Back in Maui, when I was a boy, we'd swim and play on the water for hours everyday. It's the one thing we could do on the island, so we did a lot of it. Some days the surf would be gentle, and some days it would be wild.

"I had this pal, his name was Paué. His dad worked as a foreman for Dole Pineapple.

"Well, the surf was real big one day, I'm talking huge. I think I was about six. I think Paué was seven. We made a bet that we could handle the surf; he went first." Hau fell silent.

"That was the first time I saw a dead body up close. Paué lying all twisted and bent on the beach. I used to have awful dreams after that, and in these dreams I'd be caught in an undertow. I'd be struggling toward the sunlight, but the surface would move away. My heart would be racing when I woke up.

I guess from that I developed this fear of drowning. I guess because of that I thought that if I died it would be from drowning . . . and besides, it's a real handy superstition for this point in my life." Silhouetted by the blue arc light, Hau pointed out across the ruined jungle into the darkness.

It was Dale's turn for a quiet chuckle.

46

FEBRUARY 25, 1969, LZ PROFESSIONAL

DEAR DAD & BERNICE,

A few weeks ago we were on stand-down in Danang when they told us we were being reassigned to the 101st Airborne. They told us that they sent our folks a letter so you would know how to reach us, but I'm writing just in case they didn't contact you. Without the new address letters from home would never reach me.

Now they sent us up here to a place called LZ Professional. It's near a town called Chu Lai. It's bigger than LZ Baldy and been here quite a while by the looks of things. It is basically a hilltop fortress maybe two hundred yards across in sort of a circle on this mountaintop. The China Sea is only a few klicks from here. The lightning storms and showers that blow in off the ocean make the new Lieutenant real nervous. He studied weather in college and he says this lightning is real dangerous cause we're so exposed. Said it could kill you if it hit.

The lightning is amazing; it reminds me of the summer heat lightning over the hills at home, but some of the guys say they never saw anything like it cause there is so many strikes that it lights up the whole sky.

Right in the middle of the perimeter is a helicopter pad. Near that is a heavily bunkered command area. The walls are probably seven or eight sandbags thick, reinforced with empty shell boxes from 105 shells and surrounded by a big tunnel system that leads into it.

On this LZ we got a 4.2 mortar platoon and a battery of 105's. All around the edges are two man bunkers that are reinforced with sandbags and empty wooden shell boxes. I share mine with Carl Schofer, the guy I sometimes write you about. In front of that is a row of concertina wire. Further out are booby traps and foo-gas.

From where I'm sitting is three hundred yards of clearing before the jungle starts. That's a good thing because the jungle here is so thick you wouldn't believe it and the mountains are even bigger than around LZ Baldy. I don't know how long this place has been here but from the looks of things, a long time.

There is no kitchen here, but the Artillery set up some showers made out of airplane wing tip tanks. They're painted black, so they fill them with water and wait till the sun heats the water up. It's really good since we been hanging around a lot and it's getting really warm here.

I got a stripe last month. I was promoted to E-5, but we had a stand-down in Chu Lai. We had grilled steaks and all the beer we could drink. I got pretty wasted and got into a fight with a mouthy guy who turned out to be a rear area master sergeant. So I only had that stripe for a short time. Farinelli was pretty upset with me, but he hasn't been here as long as I have. This place is really getting to me. Besides, he got pretty wasted too.

When we're out here not on patrol all the guys seem to do is argue. I think it's the strain, but I'm real tired of it.

When we're on stand-down it's like one big party. They got a quarter master there in Chu Lai and a big PX so you can go out and buy stuff. The South Koreans kind of run the show, so you can buy stereos and watches. I bought a nice watch I'm gonna bring home for Congo. It's a city a little smaller than Rapid. You can buy silk shirts and suits, anything you want.

Everyday it rains here. Farinelli says first you get the buildup of clouds that drift in from the ocean. The mountaintops like LZ Professional get all socked in. Then the static electricity builds up with the cooler air off the water hitting the warm air of the land. Farinelli says the worst place to be in a lightning storm is standing around on a rain soaked mountain top with no trees around. It sounds like incoming fire when it hits. So much for now. Tomorrow we're heading out on patrol for a week or so. I'll write more later. See you in the funny papers.

Frank

At 0700 Frank was leading Farinelli and half the company down the steep, muddy mountainside into the thick trees outside the perimeter. Instinctively Frank kept high up on the slopes in the rocky area above the trees. If they were exposed in a clearing there would be little chance of being ambushed from above. This patrol, Farinelli had told them before dusk, would take them fifteen klicks from LZ Professional.

For two tiring days they humped the steamy mountainsides and saw frequent signs, but not the enemy. At 1000 on the third day Frank signaled the men to crouch and then made the motion for Farinelli to come up.

"Sir, a lot of these footprints aren't gook sandal tracks. There's been a whole battalion through here in the last few days. Looks like they use this pretty frequent."

"Thanks Frank. I'll radio in the coordinates and they can bomb the shit out of it." He patted Frank on the back and moved toward his RTO. The word of massive enemy troop movements passed like electricity among the troops. The afternoon wore on, miserable and hot until a torrential mountain shower soaked the patrol to their skin and turned the trail into a slurry of mud and crushed plants. Slowly the patrol descended, using the trees and the storm to cover its movement toward the valley floor.

The clouds had been replaced by hot sun when Frank stopped in a thinly wooded area and motioned for the patrol to crouch. The jungle floor was speckled with shafts of white light that penetrated the thin cover overhead. Alert to Frank's movements, Farinelli signaled the men to blend into the trees. Up ahead Farinelli could see the Chief's head nose up, sniffing the air. The air was filled with a sticky-sweet putrid odor.

Farinelli crept forward. "What is it, Chief?"

"Smell that?" Frank indicated an area off to the left.

"Yeah, guess I do. What the fuck is it?"

Frank shook his head. "Don't know, sir, but it smells like something died."

Frank crouched and crept forward following his nose. He was back in moments, ashen faced and obviously shaken. "Sir, I think you better come with me."

Signaling the patrol to stay put, Farinelli disappeared with his point man. At first the lieutenant could only smell the increasingly obvious and over-powering smell of putrefying flesh. In the distance were rows of what looked like large sacks made from black rubber. The two men moved silently forward; the sound of a thousand blowflies buzzed loudly in the thick air.

To his horror the lieutenant could now see that some of these black sacks had blond hair. The dog tag chains were stretched tight, separating the dead soldiers' swollen, naked torsos from their balloonlike heads. Frank looked over to see Farinelli repeatedly retch, fighting with all his soul not to vomit himself.

"Poor bastards," was all the lieutenant could manage to say as he stepped back from the grim discovery.

"Think we ought to tell the others?" Frank asked, voice shaking.

"See what you mean . . . You and I better take a look around and see what there is to see before we call in the medevac. Don't want the boys hanging around the dead too long—morale is bad enough."

Not far from the collection of decaying American soldiers Frank stopped and looked curiously at something protruding slightly above the forest floor. What at first looked like two swollen black footballs turned out to be the decomposing buttocks of another casualty bent in half and stuffed head and feet down into the opening of a tunnel. Frank felt lightheaded, sick, weak-kneed. He turned, looked at the lieutenant, shook his head in despair, and started to cry.

Farinelli radioed for twelve body bags and a Charger dustoff. It wasn't that there was any need to hurry for the dead platoon; it was the living he was now worried about. He had never seen Frank crack and it unnerved him. He knew the whole scene had been left by the enemy to intimidate him and his men, and it had.

The area was secured, and soon the men were gingerly helping the helicopter crew slide the dead into body bags. Moving the bodies only made the smell worse, causing many of the men to vomit. Farinelli looked over at his point man. The distant, stricken look on Frank's face could not be hidden from the men. Under the OD towel he wore as a poncho, Frank stood anxiously fingering a pearl-inlaid crucifix.

47

THE SUN STIRRED THE HOT MORNING AIR IN A CLOUDLESS BLUE CAULDRON. Sergeant Dale Nielsen sat in the shade of the track picking through piles of C-rations. "Don't give me this 'I ain't hungry' bullshit! What'll it be, Miller? I do a mean ham and motherfuckers thing." Dale tossed the can over his shoulder. Miller caught it.

"You're kidding, Sarge, this stuff sucks!" Miller flipped the tin over in his hand.

"Now, that's what some folks in these here parts will tell you, son, but don't you be fooled. They're just saving them for when no one's around." The sergeant affected a fatherly tone.

"What you do is ask one of the Mama-sans for one of these." Like a magician pulling a rabbit from a hat, Dale produced an onion from his fatigues. "Don't just sit there. Open up a few of these cans and put the contents gently into this!" He tossed the smiling blond a small aluminum pot.

"Miller, you want to chop the onion small enough so that it cooks real quick and gets absorbed into all those natural lima bean juices." He licked his lips. "Next you take a little piece of C-4 and light your stove . . . Pay attention, Private. You put a little sugar in, a little salt . . . maybe a dash of pepper, and you've got some mighty fine eatin'."

Minutes later Dale served the steaming concoction. "This stuff isn't half bad, Sarge," the baby-faced blond said between bites.

When they had eaten most of the stew, Dale pushed the boy to talk. "How you doing, now that you've had breakfast?"

"Oh, okay, I guess," the private said staring at his lima beans.

"You guess? What does that mean?"

His voice quavered slightly. "I hate this place, Sarge. Guys like you do real well here, but I hate it here. I mean, I guess that I'm scared."

"Well, join the crowd, Mr. Miller. Some of us are just better actors than others. I went to NCO school to perfect my acting lessons. So don't feel like you're in that part of it alone." Dale spooned out the rest of breakfast onto Miller's plate. He was not being entirely honest with the frightened gunner.

"It's not like that for me, sir. I mean, I'm sure you guys are scared, but for me it's like a heavy overcoat that I live in all day and all night, every day since I got here. I think someone gave it to me when I got off the plane." The boy grinned at his own metaphor.

Dale smiled at Miller and nodded. "That's better, Dan. A little humor now and then always helps."

Miller's sunburned face went somber. "It's like it's weighing me down, tiring me out."

Clearing his throat, Dale said, "I don't know what to tell you, Dan, but you've got to do something about it. I think you've got to believe you're going to make it.

"It's not real good to think this way either, but you've got to believe it's not going to happen to you. That's how I feel. The more shit we see, the more I feel like I'm watching. The guy beside you may get hit but not you—you're invisible. Maybe it's like I'm inside of an invisible shield. You know, like on those old toothpaste commercials.

"You need to learn some mental tricks, so you can deal with this place and make it out of here." Dale's voice was low. Miller didn't know if all this talk about invisible shields was to protect his confidence, or the sarge's.

• • •

Days later, like giant combines in a Dakota wheat field, the Rome plows went round and round, shattering the thick wall of jungle before them. On either flank, the APCs stood guard.

They had taken fire from the northern section of the quadrant about noon. The platoon had assaulted the hedgerow and found nothing.

By 1500 they were swinging back north for another pass. Boredom had replaced tension, until Sergeant Nielsen pulled an apple from his fatigue pocket.

The Caterpillars churned slowly clockwise, moving in practiced unison around a six-kilometer circle sluggishly toward the center. A metal object clinked under the track.

Dale sat polishing his apple when *Whoom*, he was thrown high into the air.

On the way up he saw the track settling slowly back to earth. Men were flying everywhere, some were whole, others were missing parts. From his vantage point Dale could see the smoke coming out of the hatches of the demolished APC. In slow motion the men on the other tracks dropped off into defensive positions. He wondered why the world was so quiet. He thought he had died, his soul instantly risen. No, I don't see myself on the ground, he reasoned. No, I'm not on the track either.

Away and to the left toward the jungle he flew, like a cat out the window, his flailing legs and arms proving useless in affecting his direction. Slowly back toward the earth he floated, landing squarely on both feet among flattened trees, some thirty feet from the track.

Instinctively, he ran directly toward the cover of the jungle. In his shell-shocked confusion curious bursts of light twinkled toward him from the silent trees, teasing him closer. He got so close to the stand of trees he thought he could see a man making those yellow lights with a gun!

A wild screaming started in his ears. Terror gripped him as his long legs sprinted back toward the ruined track. Stumbling over knee-high stumps, he tripped and in the process dove as far as he could.

Ten fifty calibers and M-60s blazed from the row of tracks, over Dale's head. They raked the jungle until Crocker signaled guns down.

Hands over his ears, head pounding, ears screaming, Dale lay there until the corpsman rolled him over. Why doesn't he make any noise, he just keeps moving his lips, Dale thought. "Fuck, I can't even hear myself!" Dale screamed at the corpsman. Pointing toward something, the man moved off.

First Dale found his knees, then stood on shaky legs. He wobbled a bit, then inspected himself. He was still in one piece. A high-pitched whining sounded in his head.

Over the whine he could hear the clamor of men screaming, yelling to each other. People were running everywhere. Men were down, some not moving. What had been his track only an instant before sat a ruined hulk, billowing pungent black smoke and orange flames into the hot air.

To his left Dale noticed a small group of men standing above someone in the broken trees and shattered undergrowth. Dazed, ears squealing, he stumbled over wild-eyed to see what was going on.

A small man lay there writhing, all but the top of his blond head covered in blood. Crimson oozed from his ears. His eyes stared wildly, begging. He was obviously slowly choking on a thick flow of vomit and blood.

Dale stood there amazed that a man whose intestines lay in a pool beside him would still have his eyes open, could still move his arms. "Fuck, it's Miller!" he muttered in horror.

The corpsman ran up, a look of complete desperation twisting his features. He screamed at Dale. Above the whirring in his head he heard something about "Not breathing!" and "CPR!"

As in a dream, Dale bent down, calmly trying to remember how to perform mouth to mouth. While Dale was thinking about basic training and what he had been told, Private Miller retched violently. A new flow of darker liquid slid out of his mouth.

Dale's head began to clear. "No fuckin way!" he said, looking up at the other men. Eyes wide, none of them moved a muscle.

For eternal seconds, the men stood staring. Miller's movements ebbed, the jagged stumps of his legs twitched, and he was gone.

An hour later Dale sat beside the ravaged track, amazed that he was in one piece. He contemplated the sight of Miller all smashed and gutted, and how well his Colgate Invisible Shield had once again protected him.

He heard Crocker call one of the engineers over for a conference. "So what do you think? I mean, that was one hell of an explosion!"

"No mine could do that," the engineer said. "Those gooks found one of our five-hundred-pound bombs and rigged it for when you guys came by again."

By 1600 the dustoff choppers retreated into a brilliant sunset. They took out five critically wounded and two dead.

48

EARLY APRIL RAIN PELTED THE BROAD TOPS OF RUBBER TREES, SOAKING THE ground, making it impossible to find a dry cigarette or a place on yourself to keep them dry. Dale Nielsen smiled as he watched Spec Four Nickels go from man to man looking for a fresh smoke.

They had moved to an old Michelin plantation. A large set of war-torn, French-style chateaus lay just in sight to the north. In the deep gray, under the canopy of the largest rubber trees, Dale felt strangely calm, at home. It was not just the trees but the fact they had been planted in straight rows and tended. The whole area around the rubber plantation was one of order in chaos.

Like phantoms, the Vietcong would sneak back into the area that had been their home and covertly harvest the precious latex. They were like shadows among the trees, moving silently, delivering the raw rubber to the north for absentee French owners. The little people were constantly at the edges of sight and in the fringes of the troopers' minds.

Dale sat on his helmet trying to raise himself up off the wet forest floor. His eyes were fixed on the command area. There, E-7 Sergeant Hau sat bull-shitting with Crocker. They had grown casual with each other. Dale rationalized it was because Hau was a model soldier and literally old enough to be any of the enlisted men's father. They were talking about their kids.

"These are mine," Crocker said, flashing the picture of a two-year-old holding a baby. "It's been almost six months since I saw them. They probably don't look anything like the photo. Married their mom straight out of West Point. Had our fifth anniversary last week." Smiling broadly, he handed Hau a picture of a pretty brunette. "Won't be long now, Sergeant. Thirty-five days and a wake-up and you'll be seeing your kids."

Hau's teeth flashed against his dark skin. "This is my wife and three kids," he said, carefully unwrapping a small bundle of letters and photos and handing them to Crocker. "Looks like I got you beat on one count. I married their mom right out of high school. Been married forever!" he laughed. "Fantastic woman."

Dale sat there studying the two men. Beside him Edward Grubouski pulled a dry pack of three cigarettes from a foil utility pouch. "Nothing like a smoke after a particularly lovely fuckin lunch," he belched, offering a cigarette to Dale.

"Ed, you have the most controlled, most precise, and unusual sense for the 'f' word I have ever heard," Dale observed.

"Yeah? Well, thank you! But I must humbly admit I had a tremendous amount of practice before I ever got here. My mom is a lovely Polish woman, a large woman with naturally rosy cheeks and big calves. Her dad was a long-shoreman. I think she learned the finer points from him."

"She sounds lovely." Growing serious, he asked, "What do you think of those two?" nodding toward the command track.

"The best," Grubouski said, shaking his head. "You just don't find company commanders who will go into the fighting with their men. I heard, when I was first in country, what it was like before Crocker came on board. I guess the outfit had the most incredibly stupid fuckin dickhead this man's army has ever stumbled across. I think they found him in some shake-and-bake ROTC reject program! In the fuckin trash can! But I've been pretty fuckin lucky, compared to some of the guys I trained with. And then there's you!" Grubouski laughed.

"And Hau, he's probably the reason half these guys are still alive. He's one incredible fuckin Hawaiian! It's going to get rough when they leave." His voice dropped.

At 1100, the company was moving slowly forward through endless rows of rain-drenched trees. Evenly spaced and abreast, the APCs ground to the north, dismounts out ahead.

Dale's new driver was a veteran named Dickerson. He sat in the hatch smoking Winstons. Captain Crocker had teamed them up. Every time Dale turned to look back, the black man was grinning. An older reservist from Washington, D.C., Dickerson was considered the best. Dale felt lucky this day. All seemed right with the world.

"Ahhgg!" An ear-piercing scream startled the men. Dale fell to his chest. Crocker signaled the line to halt. First Platoon dismounts scrambled toward a man rolling on the ground. "Punji stake!" the medic shouted to Crocker.

Dale had never seen a punji stake except the mock ones in advanced infantry training. He moved closer to get a look. In the middle of his squad, the man lay on the wet ground moaning loudly. To the wounded man's right was a small hole in the flat earth.

Dale stooped and pulled at the thin layer of vines and humus that had concealed it. His nose wrinkled from the strong smell of human feces. Fascinated, he pulled more of the matted dirt away and looked inside. At the bottom of the knee-deep hole were three diagonally cut, razor-sharp bamboo splints, each smeared with molding, maggot-covered shit.

"You're going to be OK, man! Calm down." The medic tried to soothe the man on the ground.

"Am I going to lose my foot?" the man cried.

"Naw, but it's probably just bad enough to buy you a plane ticket to the real world!"

"No shit?" the man questioned.

"Well, actually the shit was on the stick!" the medic joked.

The man on the ground tried to grin.

Medevac showed up at 1135 and flew the man to the surgical unit in Cu Chi.

· · ·

All afternoon the drizzle continued, making the company miserable. Under the rubber trees, daylight was now like late dusk. The air was cool and smelled of rich red soil. By 1230, Alpha Company was moving toward a set of old plantation outbuildings. Intelligence from Command and Control had reported NVA activity in the area.

Despite the sightings, the only thing that had changed the monotony of this morning's patrol from yesterday's was that now the men in front watched the ground more closely.

From on top of the command track, Crocker signaled the men to a halt. He strained to see into the gloom, then motioned the dismounts to a crouch. Next he fired his weapon into the air. The men on the ground still saw nothing.

One hundred meters ahead, gunfire erupted from the stuccoed buildings. *Bkow, Bkow, Bkow!* An old Chinese single shot shattered the silence.

Under the cover of murky light, three people slipped from the furthest building toward a grove of trees and then into a clearing. As they sprinted over the open ground, *Va-troom!* the entire company, fifteen fifty calibers, the same number of M-60s, and sixty-plus M-16s on auto-fire shredded the silence.

Astonished by the magnitude of the volley, Dale stood shooting from the hip, his rifle on full auto-fire. Never had he seen anything like it! A cloud of cordite smoke lifted from the company. A thousand red tracers spread out across the land like horizontal fireworks.

The noise was deafening, the smell of spent gunpowder exhilarating.

The earth, where the fleeing men had last been seen, exploded in a spray of dirt and dead leaves that lifted high into the misty air. The running men seemed to evaporate.

Crocker signaled guns down. Nobody paid attention. He waved again and the guns finally sputtered to a stop. Then he signaled the men to move up.

With the confidence of excited hounds, the platoon sprang forward to search the area.

Ten minutes later Crocker stood on his track scratching his thick head of sopping blond hair. A thorough search had turned up nothing. There was not so much as a drop of blood. It was as if the enemy had ascended to heaven. Fifty meters to the east the men found a shallow depression in the flat floor of the plantation. It led east and connected with another. Eighty soaking wet men stood staring at nothing!

Dumbfounded, Crocker said the absurdly obvious: "They must have gotten away." Then he began to laugh. It was a deep infectious laugh. "What a bunch of killers! Did anybody think to aim?" Usually aloof, he giggled like a kid on the playground. It spread from man to man, squad to squad, until the entire company stood wiping their eyes.

Dale stood closely watching his captain. A warm sensation spread from his chest, engulfing him. He looked at the tall officer bent with laughter and felt a powerful admiration.

Grubouski poked him, bringing him back from his thoughts. "It doesn't get much better than this, does it?!"

Slapping a new clip into his rifle, Dale fairly beamed. "No, it fuckin doesn't!"

Grubouski's eyebrows went up.

49

MUSIC PLAYED SOFTLY FROM A LITTLE PANASONIC RADIO ON THE WOODEN floor. Dale had slept through his first night on stand-down, while most of the others had gotten blind drunk. He was getting ready for delicious sleep on the second when Grubouski descended into the bunker.

"Come on, Nielsen! What's wrong with you? Don't chicken out on me. You gotta come meet these guys. They're fuckin nuts, you'll love 'em." Grubouski had showered and shaved and stood there looking like a college freshman eager for a hangover. Only the uniform and sandbags ruined the illusion.

Arms behind his head, Dale lay on a cot with real sheets and blankets, grinning at his friend. "Really, I just want to sleep!" His voice softened. "But if you're going to stand there feeling sorry for yourself with those big blue Pol-lock eyes of yours, I'll go with you. You know what it does to me, Ed."

Grubouski's eyes blinked in uncertainty. Then a slow blush reddened his smooth cheeks. "Well, get going then. You think they're going to wait for you?"

. . .

The air escaping from the bunker reeked of juniper and pot. In the dimmed light of candles, The Doors blared from a recorder. Conversation ceased as men scrambled to hide the liquor and pot. "Shit!"

"Calm down. It's only me, and Nielsen here!" Grubouski introduced Dale to men sprawled on cots or hanging from the roof in hammocks.

A lanky soldier stood. "You can call me Short Stuff, because I'm too short to see!" he chuckled, slapping Dale on the back. "You guys have to be inducted into the order." He held up a near-full bottle of Jack Daniel's and passed it to Grubouski, who took a long pull. He passed it to Dale whose eyes glazed then watered as he lowered the bottle.

Producing a perfect joint, Short stuck it in Grubouski's mouth. Some of the men began to laugh when they saw Dale's innocent expression. Grubouski took a drag, held it briefly, then coughed hoarsely, "Shi-I-t." He passed the smoldering dope to Dale. At first he was hesitant. Then he smiled, shrugged his shoulders, closed his eyes, placed the joint to his lips, and inhaled deeply. All those assembled broke into a cheer. Now Mr. Short Stuff held forth two paper cups. "Gentlemen! Well now, Mr. Ed and Mr. Nielsen, by the powers invested in me by Jack Daniel's and the United States Government, I declare in order this meeting of the Freedom Bird Worship Society." A cacophony of grotesque birdcalls rose into the smoky air.

By midnight, with the help of Jack Daniel's and the marijuana smoke, Dale was animated, staggering a little, but well able to defend his position that war was a part of man's nature. "Toy guns and war movies have nothing to do with it! Why did humans fight when they didn't have television? I mean, David slew Goliath and he never saw a football game!" He jabbed at the air, making his point seem even sillier.

He stood there waiting for someone to respond or for the next profound thought to burst into his well-oiled consciousness. He was thrilled at how the smoke was helping him see connections. Brain swimming in his cranium, he studied this guy called Short Stuff, waiting for a response.

After the fourth joint he'd also acquired the strangest feeling. It was as if his mind was sliding downward, unable to stand up fully in his brain case. Despite this, each thought came quickly, crowding out the one before.

He wanted to express them, to hear how fine they sounded when they came out. "Men have been fighting since the beginning of time; well, not the beginning of time, but man's time. Men have been fighting over all kinds of things. It's never stopped with all the treaties and treatises ever written."

Wow, that sounded good! he thought. Only it looked like Shorty's attention was gone and would not return for many hours.

Dale stood there feeling deserted in this his hour of revelation.

Lying on his back, propped against the wall, Grubouski stared glassy-eyed at his sergeant. "Better check his breathing, man, I think you bored him to death."

"So what do you think, Mr. Ed? Do you think war is an unnatural act?!" Dale grinned, then giggled stupidly as his vision cleared and blurred.

Grubouski pulled himself carefully to his feet, balancing himself against the wall as he stood. "Come on, old buddy, you lost your fuckin audience." He helped Dale out of the sandbagged hut, up the earthen slope, and into the muggy night.

In the dark bosom of the Alpha Company bunker, while the first soft light of day crept over the firebase, Grubouski snored obscenely.

Dale couldn't hear it. Where he lay, it was soft and warm, and wet! His mind pounded, his gut cramped before he was awake enough to force open his eyes. First the right eye, then the left snapped open. Everything looked large, looming up above him. Rubbing his burning eyes with his hand only managed to cover his face with mud. He stared at his hand in a sort of detached way as if the mud couldn't possibly be real.

Rolling to his back, he sat up. Almost puking, he realized he was lying in a shallow mortar crater completely soaked with water and red mud. By the way the water smelled, he was sure some of it was his own. The whiskey had become poison in his cramping gut, the pot had left him confused. He stood up very slowly, looking at the shallow pool beneath him. He couldn't manage any profound insight. He only hoped nobody had seen him.

50

MARCH 9, 1969, LZ PROFESSIONAL

THE FIRST OF THE 46TH WAS BACK IN THE FIELD ON AN EXTENDED SEARCH-and-destroy mission. Sunlight glinted off a narrow streambed as Frank Jealous Of Him signaled the column to halt. "Tell Farinelli there is a small village up ahead." The word filtered nervously back through the loose line of men.

Within minutes the two platoon leaders conferred out of earshot. Carl Schofer moved closer to Frank. "What do you think, Chief? They gonna give us trouble?"

"I don't know, man . . . If they're out here, they aren't farming for the south!"

Schofer shook his head. "The only thing we got going for us is that it's a small village, only four or five hootches."

"Why? You got a feeling?" Frank asked.

"Shit, bro, I always got the feeling. Like right now I feel like I gotta piss real bad, but nothing comes out. Like there's a bunch of butterflies in my gut, but if I don't pinch my ass cheeks together I'm gonna shit buckets!"

"Yeah, I know!" was all the Indian said.

Squatting amid his men, Farinelli's boyish, Italian face looked older, more solemn than usual. "Well boys, we're going in. We will move in and form a line, and try to walk through the village. When we've secured it, First Platoon will come in to reinforce. When we have a perimeter, we'll interrogate and then evac the villagers. Just routine, but keep your butts down. You never know!"

The squad crept north, on the east side of the river. "Better run through the jungle, and don't look back." Lyrics by CCR played through Frank's head.

As usual the acrid smell of dung cooking fires wafted from village. On point, Frank, followed by Schofer, split off toward the east and the far end of the village. Up the streambed, they stopped at a spot that afforded cover. Other men crept to the west around the village until the First Platoon began to move up for the walk-through. Nothing indicated that any resistance might be forthcoming. The rest of the company moved up behind Frank, flanking the streambed.

Spec Five David Ostner from First Platoon came into Frank's view. He stood midstream, crouched low, M-16 across his chest. Ears straining, he moved slowly forward.

One hundred meters north, barely visible in the upstream glare, three tiny men splashed into the creek bottom. Frank tapped Schofer on the shoulder, but before they could sight in, the NVA were raking the streambed with a lethal torrent of AK fire. Frank and Schofer went prone. Ostner screamed loudly, then went down into the knee-deep water with a loud splash. "Fucker's hit bad!" Schofer yelled.

 Frantic screams came from the village. Sunlight blazed off the rippling water, obliterating the horizon. Men from Second Platoon tried to take aim. They blindly fired hundreds of rounds upstream. Arms flaying wildly, one of the escaping Vietnamese went down. Friendly fire created a spray that destroyed what little vision Frank had.

The Second Platoon medic was already moving up on Ostner as he slowly rose from the water. To horrified onlookers, it appeared as if a dead man had resurrected and was trying to fire his weapon.

Within seconds the firing was over. Moments later Frank and Schofer were standing in the tall grass of a clearing where the enemy had disappeared. Leading away from the stream was a jellylike crimson trail that led from the bank into the forest, but no body parts were found, nothing that would count for anything.

The platoon narrowed the perimeter, moving in quickly toward the village. The brief firefight had broken the tension. Ostner sat on dry ground examining his weapon. A round from an AK-47 had destroyed the chamber and had ricocheted harmlessly away from the sergeant. Word spread quickly. Frank looked at Carl Schofer and shook his head. "He's got to be thinking some weird thoughts!" His friend also shook his head, and said, "Must have been taking his shit pills!"

The village contained only five hootches, none more than a few weeks old. Rice shoots still remained in the seed paddies. Schofer and Frank helped round up the frightened women and children. There was a pretty young woman that stared defiantly at Frank. It did not seem to him that she looked at Schofer or any of the other men, just him. It was as if his black Mongolian eyes and hair made him a traitor. Her eyes seemed to question what he was and why he was here, piercing him, making his very soul heavy with their hatred. Under his makeshift poncho, made from a split OD towel, he nervously fingered the pearl cross on his smooth chest.

A sense of foreboding began to form in his gut; a feeling that he was an Indian, fighting, harassing, and destroying his own kind. A sense that he might be punished by some unseen power larger than the war itself settled in his soul. "I'm an Indian like you, Frank, ain't nothing going to change that. Fighting in a white man's war don't change that." He could almost hear Garfford High Pipe's words, see his sarcastic face.

He drove the guilty thoughts from his mind, then searched the village systematically. Ever since discovering the dead platoon two weeks earlier, a growing sense of dread made him more cautious. He looked carefully at each hootch to make sure it wasn't occupied before he entered it. His eyes strained to see a wire or booby trap, any detail that was misplaced. The search produced nothing but rice and clothing.

Farinelli had each of the villagers' hands bound behind their backs. All were older men, well past the age of soldiering.

"What are you doing here?" The captain grabbed the hair of one squatting man and snapped it back, pulling him to his feet. A woman began to moan. "Where are your IDs?" He tugged on the man's hair, shoving him back against a small tree, his head striking the trunk. Still the man only shook his head.

The captain bent down and grabbed the next tiny man, jerking him violently to his feet. "Why are you here? This is a free-fire zone. You guys are Vietcong! Vietcong, you understand?" A small tear formed in the man's right eye but he would not look at the captain, who threw him down in disgust. "Fuckers! They never do talk. Never know English. Never have proper identification. We're going to burn this place, then just waste the VC goddamn lot of them!"

Frank overheard the oath and looked nervously at Carl Schofer. "Shit! You think they'll do it, Chief?" Schofer asked, lighting the grass hootch with his Zippo lighter.

"Don't know what he'll do. These people are just doing what they are told . . . just like us guys. Only they got to pretend they're just farmers. They know that we know why they're here. They're growing rice for the Vietcong. It's like my ancestors hunting buffalo to feed their warriors."

Schofer looked at the Chief with wrinkled brow, then walked on toward the next grass shack and lit it.

At 1600 the evac Chinook lifted off, carrying the prisoners from the smoldering ruins of the village, and the men of Company B filtered back into the mangrove forest headed for their night laager.

• • •

Frank sang along with the opening lines of CCR's "Midnight Special" as it played from a tiny transistor radio. His improved spirits had Schofer and Farinelli grinning as they sipped on coffee. It was three days later and the First of the 46th was jittery from rumor of a large NVA force heading their way.

At 0830, First Platoon of Company B gathered around their young lieutenant, who sat near the base of a large and gnarled mangrove tree. "We got a potential situation brewing. Company Command has intelligence that a fairly large assault is being planned. Down near Hau Duc they're seeing a lot of movement. These are NVA regulars. The Higher Higher has been seeing a lot of movement. We're going to move out and form a blocking action along this valley." He indicated where they were on the map. "That means we'll be on an assault line. Old Chief here, well he's gettin' shorter . . . and therefore will not always be out on point protecting your buns. So you will have to keep your eyes open. You got any words of advice, Chief?"

Surprised, Frank stood there thinking for a minute of how to explain what for him had become instinct. Lundren, Lewis, Esch, every eye in the platoon was on him. Men from the other platoons moved in for a listen. The cherries stared at the dark-skinned man with the towel split like a poncho over his neck. This Indian kid had quite a reputation and soon a large number of men were gathered.

"Well, you got to use your feelings, your intuition, not be distracted for a minute. Chances of hitting a booby trap are greater than seeing any NVA. They'll probably stick to trails. So watch the ground, then before you step look up." He thought for moment. "You men got to do your own thinking today. You lose your concentration and you could be a dead pack. There could be wires along the ground," he indicated his knee, near the large K-bar knife strapped to his calf, "or chest high," indicating the area near his bright red neckerchief. "Really look at the trees. If there is a cluster of leaves, or a dark spot that shouldn't be there, it could be a sniper or a wired shell. The wires are small, so move slow, keep an eye on the men to your flanks so we move at the same speed.

"If you see any disturbance on the ground, turned leaves or loose dirt, be extra careful, and move around it. If you hear anything, stop and check it out. You guys that are smoking all the time, be careful you watch the jungle and not your smoke, or it could all be over in a second. If the enemy is downwind, that smoke lets them know you're there before you get there. You got to become one of them." He pointed outward with his chin.

Farinelli tapped Frank on the leg. "That's good advice, Chief. Take your shit pills, boys, and let's move out."

Moments later the hot jungle closed in silence around the nervous men. The battalion commander's helicopter could be heard whomping high overhead, breaking the menacing quiet.

At 1100 the radio clicked with an evac order for six men with fevers from A Company. Farinelli shook his head and plodded forward. Frank kept his eye on Schofer. Sweat soaked his OD towel. He moved evenly, almost flowing through the foliage. "Carl!" Frank whispered loudly, signaling with his hand for his buddy to slow down. "Watch it, man, this ain't no race!"

At 1750 an explosion rocked the air on the left flank, followed by a volley of American gunfire and muffled screams. The men in First Platoon planted their faces in the earth. It was over in an instant. At 1800 the radio crackled with a cryptic message: "Four men at Bravo-Tango One-Five-Two-Zero-Nine-Eight with shrapnel wounds from a booby trap. Need immediate medevac." Within twenty minutes an LZ was chosen, hacked clear, then purple smoke popped for the incoming Huey.

At 2000, Charlie Brown's black face looked grim. The RTO told Farinelli that Hau Duc was being probed by a large force. "Better them than us!" was the lieutenant's only comment. Both squads of First Platoon made their night laager at location BT 2019 without further incident.

The next morning Frank was up early, writing a letter.

> Dear Clynda and Family,
>
> It isn't long now that I might be leaving this place. I got word from home two days ago that Darlene Ghost attempted suicide. I don't know why none of you could have told me I'm going to be a Dad. I am not a child. In fact, I am not even the person you knew before I left. No one can come here and stay the same.
>
> The other day I helped evacuate a village. There was a woman in that village who reminded me of home. I could feel her eyes on me. She looked like she could be from Wounded Knee. She stared at me.

I think she wondered why a man who looks like me was here fighting with white soldiers.

These things slowly build up and they change you. I guess you have to deal with them or go crazy.

Bernice, I want you to get Darlene and keep her at the house for a while. Even though I probably don't love her, I will do the right thing by her and marry her. This place gets me more scared by the day. I'm thinking of trying to talk the Lieutenant into letting me out of the field a little early. He's a real good guy.

I have a bad feeling. Still, I know these guys really count on me to get them through. They call me Chief, and they think I got something special. I wish I could tell them I'm just like them, scared, but it wouldn't help.

He let the letter rest in his lap. When Carl Schofer woke, he studied his friend, noticing the moisture in his eyes. Frank felt his gaze and shoved the unfinished letter in his pack.

It was 0830 when Frank set out again volunteering at point. Farinelli turned to Schofer. "He sure makes my life easier, and like Chellis said, he doesn't even seem to need a map. He's almost spooky." Schofer only nodded and slipped into the underbrush.

51

IT WAS A BLISTERING NOON HOUR WHEN ALPHA COMPANY TOOK ITS FIRST casualty of the day. McPhereson from First Platoon had been shot, most of his right shoulder torn away. He was too far out in front, too aggressive.

At least that's what Dale reasoned, now advancing in a low crouch on the suspected location of the sniper. The whole Michelin plantation had been an exaggerated cat-and-mouse game in which the dismounts were used as bait.

Sometimes exciting, other times boring, it was a game in which a tacit agreement between sides had been reached. As long as you knew and followed the rules, he felt, your chances were pretty good.

With each death he calculated, rationalized, the mistakes that were made. With each nameless casualty he became more assured he was learning the rules of survival. Hau served as the assistant professor of war, Crocker the full professor.

Two hundred meters from the tree line, Crocker signaled the dismounts to a squat. The fifty-caliber gunners slammed a round into the chamber. Now in the scorching sun, out from under the exquisite coolness of the rubber trees, Dale's squad moved on line toward a quiet row of trees and shrubs.

Unlike others, Dale felt strangely indifferent to the brief discussions of death that broke out in the night perimeter among men cursed with fear. He didn't feel what they did. It made him feel at once lonely and superior. These were the ordinary thoughts he was having this scalding day. There had been little but McPhereson's "accident" to disturb his reflections. From his position he could make out potential openings in the foliage, almost see the barrels protruding from the bunkers. The sun baked his bare arms. The sleeves of his fatigue shirt had been sacrificed to wear, rot, and disdain for the very idea of uniforms. Besides, Crocker didn't seem to notice or care. Pants rolled up just below the knees, the bottoms long since shredded by saw grass and shrubs, he was evolving slowly, hour by hour, day by day, into a seasoned veteran.

McPhereson, he reasoned, was his own problem. The tall blond had been a recent replacement, had not lasted long enough to become a veteran, to learn the rules. Now the trees were one hundred meters away. The tracks halted, motors idling.

Fifty meters away, Crocker, advancing in line with Dale and the other dismounts, dropped to his stomach. His uniform, by contrast, was intact, even polished. He was a powerful image to the young sergeant, a master of cat and mouse, and he looked the part.

Usually the cat would strike and then run away. Today they had decided to stay. The trees erupted with the staccato of AK fire, then the bark of thirty-caliber machine guns. Green tracers flew out toward the crouched men. The fifty-caliber gunners on the tracks opened up with suppressive fire. The men on the ground moved up in standard operational procedure.

The NVA, deep in their bunkers, didn't seem to mind the incredible firepower of the APCs. They didn't decrease their firing. Clipped grass and pulverized dirt walked toward Dale as he lay firing into the trees.

With detached calm he watched the enemy fire adjust toward him, now only ten meters and closing. "Come on you fuckers, *di di mau!* Run you sons of bitches!" he muttered as he snapped in a new magazine. Only the enemy aiming the gun didn't hear, didn't care if the American knew the rules.

"Fuck!" Dale rolled to his left to evade the marching rounds that sprayed dirt ever closer to his position. They merely adjusted, following his movement. Should I leave things to them or . . . his legs pumped up under him, raised him into clear sight of the bunkers! His quads burned as he exploded forward, toward the deadly trees, toward anything that looked like cover.

Ten meters from the blazing hedgerow he could hear the bullets tearing the air near his head, see the tracers flying toward him. Instinctively he dove, flying over the ground, smacking his head hard against a sapling. He could hear the bullets impact, splattering destruction. He felt a wet spray but no pain. He buried his face into the dirt of the shallow bomb crater, heart pounding, lungs sucking air like a galloping racehorse.

He lay there for what his brain took as an eternity. Hours seemed to pass before Dickerson moved up, track blazing at the trees, before Dale pulled his wild-eyed face from the dirt.

When he looked up, thirty inches above his head the small tree was gone! It was sheared in a ragged pulp where Dale's waist had been before his dive. A fleeting image of his legs separating from his upper body in a bloody spray, running blindly, his upper torso and arms collapsing conscious, helpless, terrorized him. Then was gone. He scrambled to a safe position behind the track.

The company had pulled back only three hundred meters from the hedgerow when the air force screamed in, spewing napalm on the stubborn soldiers in the bunker system. The cavalry men cheered loudly. Crocker then ordered them to move back up for a final sweep.

As he walked, Dale could not shake the grizzly image of his helpless, legless body struggling on the bloody grass.

The trees, once green and lush, were now devoid of leaves, all life baked from them by the sticky jell of napalm. Mini-guns had perforated the remaining trunks like a thousand deadly woodpeckers.

Moving slowly, as if life might have somehow survived the inferno, Alpha Company closed on the bunkers. Grubouski was the first to find them. "Will you fuckin look at this!" he said slowly, stunned. "Talk about your fuckin weenie roast!"

When Dale moved in, to the left, he saw what Grubouski had seen, and stood frozen, sickened by the sight. In the roofless hole stood three blackened men. He stared at their white teeth, locked in a charbroiled grimaces on lipless, noseless faces. The baked skin on their arms was strangely cracked with pink lines and huge blisters.

Transfixed by morbid wonder, he stared at the North Vietnamese stripped naked by the fiery death. The seared men leaned against the narrow walls of their earthen oven. Beneath their thin, roasted legs were the remnants of puddles of urine and strings of burnt shit.

Dale stood for the longest time, an involuntary camera, his mind clicking away. When he stepped back he was no longer thinking of his own body. Grubouski puked. Dale found it contagious.

52

AFTER A LONG TURN ON THE PERIMETER DALE FELL INTO A FITFUL NAP. Horrible images intruded on his dreamscape, shattered his sleep, woke him with a replay of the day's mental photographs until he lay covered with sweat.

At 0800, Hau made the circuit like a village crier. "We're staying put today. There's going to be Catholic mass at ten hundred. All men, regardless of denomination, are encouraged by Captain Crocker to attend."

Dale sat in a shallow foxhole chewing on a tasteless slice of pork. He wiped some sauce off his stubbled chin with his arm and turned to Grubouski. "You going?"

"If I do it'll only be so I can write my fuckin sainted mother and tell her about it. Somehow this seems like a fuckin weird place for religion!"

At 0930 a command and control Huey landed outside the small perimeter. Out jumped a major in pressed fatigues. Two orderlies accompanied him to the center of the circled tracks, dragging large wooden cases.

At 1000 on the button, mass started. In the Our Lady of the Rubber Tree Chapel, most of the men of Alpha Company sat, leaned, or stood. In front of them, in stark contrast to the dirt, grease, and Olive Drab, was a silver-haired priest magically transformed in brilliant, flowing robes of purple and gold. Before him stood an altar covered with a starched blinding white cloth. The orderlies now played altar boys. Their vestments, trimmed with lace, fell on combat boots.

"In the name of the Father and the Son and the Holy Ghost." The Catholic boys' arms moved in reflexive unison, touching their sunburned foreheads and bare shoulders.

The mass proceeded by rote until the sermon. Dale stood leaning against the track, trying to reconcile childhood memories with this odd setting.

"You know, my sons, there is a scene in the Old Testament where David stands in the Vale of Elah, a mere human, shaking before God, his people, and the mighty Philistine, Goliath. Goliath was no average foe. He was in fact a giant among men. In his day he had slain hundreds of Israelites.

"God had spoken to David, told him if only he had faith in himself, he could slay the mighty Goliath. And he strode forward, wrapped in the power of the Lord, and slew that terrible giant." The priest's arms became animated, his robes fluttered like wings in the still air. "And that, my children, is what you have done here in this lonely corner of God's Kingdom. Now you may say the Vietnamese are not giants!" He managed a smile. "But the threat of Godless Communism stands as a giant before us this day, far mightier than mere Goliath. Truly you are the Davids."

Dale's mind flashed for a second on the three lipless, grinning men in the scorched pit. He tried to shake it away.

"You have made the army proud. Each enemy casualty sends a clear message to the Communist masters that their mindless servants cannot triumph. I am reminded, my children, of our Blessed Savior as he strode in righteous anger into the temple in Jerusalem. He tossed the money changers from the door, sent the sacrificial animals scurrying from that sacred place. And that is what you have done in this faraway place. You have been God's servants, God's messengers, dispelling the evil of totalitarianism from this troubled land. I want you to know how proud we are of your sacrifice." He paused, gathering momentum. "Each of you has suffered here, seen things . . ."

Again Dale's mind flashed back, this time on the smoking, singed hair of the dead soldiers. Before him the voice of the priest droned on.

". . . things that have made your soul feel empty of Christ's healing grace. That's why we have gathered here today, my sons. Whether you are Catholic or Protestant, I want you to come forward at Communion and receive the Body of Christ. Come forward and feel our Savior's infinite power restore your souls, that you might once again vanquish the enemy and restore God's glory to Vietnam. So sayeth the Lord."

The priest knelt and kissed the Bible on the folding wood lectern and returned to the altar. Dale turned and whispered to Grubouski. "Doesn't he think those men we cooked yesterday were human beings, had families, wives, and children, or were they just soulless puppets? I'm leaving! I know he's trying to be useful, sincere and all that, but this is a little more than I can handle."

Grubouski gave his buddy a confused look, shrugged his shoulders, and turned back toward the service. Dale went out from the circle and sat beneath a tree, alone with his thoughts.

53

THE PLAIN WAS FLAT AND DRY. THE RED DIRT HAD ONCE BEEN A FLOODED paddy producing rice for hungry civilians. Now it was an overgrown card table on which a deadly game played out. Dale couldn't help but get flashbacks to White River, South Dakota. To his summer job as a cowboy and how he loved that land.

Like this it had broad stretches of grass flats, here and there broken with lines of trees. In prairie country one might be watchful of the ground, careful for cactus, varmint holes, or snakes. This wasn't South Dakota. Here in the open, on this horizontal savanna, the company was badly exposed to the enemy.

No longer a rookie, Dale studied the ground for anything that might be used for cover. It was not that they expected to be hit; this area was devoid of peasants and relatively secure. Out on its cracked mud surface, in front of the tracks, the platoon advanced smoothly at about two klicks an hour.

Dale could almost feel his track behind him. Dickerson, sitting behind the periscope, tossed a cigarette out of the hatch. The machine gunner adjusted his ammo belt. Overhead the sun sent down a blistering shock wave. Dale's mood was calm. It seemed to the young soldier that he was fated to watch this war, be brushed by it, but that he would return home unscathed. After all, he reasoned, I should have been killed twice. Twice, I haven't gotten a scratch. Where some of the men shook harder with every step, he felt only excitement.

· · ·

Crocker had pulled the platoon leaders in at dawn. Around him the men drank coffee and cocoa. "This is a pretty straightforward mission. We're leaving here at oh-six-thirty and move to this coordinate. Battalion commander wants us to assault a long hedgerow here. Intelligence . . .," Crocker paused for the routine chuckle, "intelligence has it that there are NVA tunnels intersecting that row of trees." He pointed to the hand-drawn map next to the topo. "We are to move up to within five hundred meters, dismount, then move forward on a search-and-destroy mission.

"I want you to put your men on alert. The way this map looks, we'll be exposed the last four hundred meters. They'll be able to see us. We won't be able to see them. Tell your dismounts not to get more than one hundred meters out in front. That's all. Now let's go out and have some fun."

Dale walked in a crouch, now sweating heavily. On the smooth dirt he noticed a small anthill. Its red occupants scurried about, oblivious to Dale and the war. He mentally measured the hill, then dismissed it as possible cover.

The three platoons were now spread abreast one hundred meters from the trees. It was a classic mechanized infantry advance. The vegetation on the far side of the abandoned paddy was getting thicker.

Crouched with his RTO twenty-five meters behind Third Squad, Crocker did not like where he was. Intelligence had not described the area accurately. It was not a single row of trees and undergrowth but a large line of trees flanked by low-lying mulch and bombed-out stumps. "They were right about one thing," he whispered to his radio man. "It is flat."

The cat-and-mouse game had taken an hour since the dismounts jumped from the tracks. To make an ambush like this work, the enemy had to lie low, be patient fishers of men. They could wait until all the Americans were close to their invisible bunkers to spring their L-shaped trap.

The APCs were now back one hundred meters. Dale's mouth was cotton dry as he strained to see into the cover. Fifty meters behind, Crocker swore into the hot air. "Fuck, I don't like this. Don't like this at all."

Fifty meters to the tree line and still dead silence. Dale thought, if there was to be an ambush it would be now.

Captain Crocker swallowed bile. He'd seen this before. He knew too well why they called this last fifty meters the kill zone.

Dale looked to his left at the wavy line of men. Then his vision began to swing to the right. *Whoomph!* Out of the corner of his eye Third Platoon evaporated in a cloud of black smoke.

The spray of metal fragments spread, felling one man from First Platoon, two from Third. Before the smoke had cleared, men lay screaming and dying. NVA opened up with small-arms cross fire. Confusion broke the remaining line.

Dale and the man beside him turned in unison, scanning for milliseconds the pan-flat terrain for cover. The world was a blur of acrid smoke, screaming men, and machine-gun bullets. Dale leapt into an uncontrolled sprint, the tendons in his legs snapping loudly from the acceleration. His eyes moved mechanically, flashing from side to side, scanning the ground for anything that he might dive behind. For fifty meters his heart pounded wildly, his breath came in gasps, his throat thick with dust, cordite, and adrenaline.

It was then, when the slow-motion computations of a panicked mind begin to acknowledge death, that he felt the bullets landing around him. In that moment, he saw it. Twenty meters away was an anthill. It was the only thing that altered the stubbled flatness of the ambush site.

He launched himself, flying the last five meters, arms extending his lean body outward, toward the ants and cover.

He rolled to his back, looked at the blue sky, acknowledged his body parts, then rolled back to his chest. By now Dickerson had pulled forward thirty meters. The track's fifty-caliber gunners lay down a steady stream of fire.

Coming up on his elbows, ears pounding, eyes wild, Dale fired into the tree, dropped the expended clip, snapped in another, then fired madly.

It seemed minutes passed before the tracks moved up to his position. The gunfire from the tree line continued sporadically, tearing bloody chunks of meat from the dead and dying men of Third Platoon. Dale heard Crocker shout, "Pull back!"

The men dove instinctively behind the advancing APCs, firing from behind them toward the deadly tree line. Dale picked up his downed M-60 gunner, hoisting him over his shoulder. Then, under the cover of the massive firepower, carried him to safety behind the track.

"Pull back, for a medevac!" Crocker spoke into the headset. All fourteen tracks reversed, bullets zinging off the aluminum until they were out of range.

Crocker surveyed the situation, and keyed the handset to C&C. "We've got nine men down, two dead, four serious, and three in fair condition." The radio transmission continued, Crocker calling in a litany of air strike and artillery coordinates.

. . .

Drinking a warm Coke, Dale leaned against his track, reconstructing his actions. A smile crept over his face. He wasn't scratched. Other men lay dead, dying, and maimed. He had been as close to death as they, seen the carnage erupt, and had reacted well. He thought of the ants and silently thanked them.

By the time medevac helicopters descended, there were three bodies covered with ponchos. A collective anger now spread from man to man, officer to officer, until the darkening mood was visible on their sunburned faces.

From the two choppers scurried a medevac team that took over from the company medics. With them was a man with a camera, his hair too long for military. What remained of First and Second Platoon stood by in horror as he flipped back the ponchos, photographing the staring, distorted, ruptured faces of their fallen friends. *Snap.* He took a close-up of Johnson's missing face. *Click.* He took a long shot of Doolittle, careful to include the bloody remains of his legs.

It was when he pulled the poncho from Schwartz that Dickerson reacted. "What the fuck you think you doin', asshole?" He moved quickly toward the photographer, others following. The man with the camera made the mistake of ignoring them.

Crocker watched the men pounce on the photographer. He grinned openly when the man's camera flew through the air. He yelled "Enough!" when they threw the struggling newsman onto the Huey. "Fucker better think twice, man!" Dickerson let go of the man's throat. "Fucker better think twice."

Dale stood chuckling to himself, grateful the photographer had broken the tension, proud to have Dickerson for a driver and a friend.

Twenty minutes later, in a splendid show of technology, the fallow paddy shook with incoming artillery. When that ceased, the air force moved in, sending four jets to napalm and strafe the tree line. The Second of the 22nd sat or stood on the tracks, taking in the show.

54

April, LZ Professional

LIFE ON STAND-DOWN AT LZ PROFESSIONAL TOOK ON A FESTIVE NATURE when a patrol came back in. B Company's first sergeant had somehow procured steaks, potatoes, and beer and rigged a homemade grill out of an old fuel drum. By 1000 hours he had made the rounds of the jungle-weary men, announcing his impending feast. A Huey landed at 1030 and kicked out a load of supplies and mail. The minute the pilot stepped back to help the door gunner unload, Jim Esch crept around the canopy and in an instant the pilots' LRP rations of freeze-dried fruit were stolen.

At mail call that morning, Frank received a letter from Billy Hollow Horn and shoved it in his pocket. Carl Schofer had received a package from home. It was the usual package from his sweetheart and the platoon's veterans knew what would be in it. He carried it with a look of triumph back to the bunker where Frank and the other men of the squad stood by.

"Hey Frank, I got a treat for you!" he yelled to his buddy. Frank flashed a smile and walked over to the crude table that stood under a shade made from old shell casings and tarpaulin.

Some boys had received packages of their own; others read letters, lost in thought. A few just looked on.

Carl tore at the string and brown paper. As usual it contained two-quart Ball jars of the finest homemade spaghetti sauce the men had ever tasted. There were two pounds of pasta, and a package of grated Parmesan, all of it packed tightly in salted popcorn.

Lewis jammed his hand into the popcorn only to have it slapped by Carl. "Hey man, this popcorn is for the Chief. It's tradition!" he grinned. "If he wants to share it, that's up to him. As for the rest of you fuckers," he paused, eyeing them with exaggerated suspicion. "It's real Italian spaghetti and meatballs at twelve-hundred!" A cheer went up that made Lieutenant Farinelli look up from his letter.

Moments later Frank sat with his box of popcorn on a rocky outcrop that overlooked the concertina wire and jungle. He pulled the letter from his clean fatigue blouse and tore open the envelope.

Dear Brother,

I know that I should not be telling you things that might affect your morale. I wish like hell I could be there with you. It is tough to know what to do, sitting back here in Wounded Knee. I know your family will probably keep this from you, but we are like brothers, so I'm writing anyway. Last month Darlene Ghost was killed in a car accident.

Frank's hands began to shake, his throat tightened.

She had been down to your mom's place, and I guess something was said because she went straight home and took a bunch of pills. Her brothers had been giving her a hard time about how she was ready to have a kid by you and how you didn't even care, calling her stupid and things like that. Guess that's been going on for a while. You know how they are.

Well I guess they came home and found her on the floor. Maybe they had been drinking but they threw her in that old Plymouth and headed out for Pine Ridge. They hadn't made it to Wounded Knee when the car flipped and she was killed.

I know this is really bad news, but I thought it would be better coming from a friend. Mary misses you very badly, and speaks of you every day. You must stay well, Bro, and come home. We all miss you and send you our prayers.

Your Brother,

Billy Hollow Horn

Frank sat stunned, empty, condemned to hell.

Later Carl Schofer walked over. Frank was standing, looking down at the valley. "How's the popcorn?" he called out.

Frank turned around, red-eyed, fingering his crucifix. Clearing his throat, he said, "It's, ah, great man. Tell that old lady of yours it needs a little butter though."

Schofer studied his friend for a moment, shook his head sadly, said "Spaghetti is almost done," then walked away.

Slowly Frank slipped the cross from his neck, thinking of Darlene and the baby. He kissed it, and then hung it over a tree limb.

55

IN THE BLUE-GRAY, PERFECT STILLNESS BEFORE DAWN, TWO MEN IN BLACK silk peasant dress moved swiftly through a strip of standing jungle. Like panthers they crept without sound, quickly, efficiently. One man stood watch holding an AK-47, while the other climbed a tree.

Silently he rigged a homemade booby trap, constructed from a spring-loaded firing device and an unexploded 105-millimeter howitzer shell, to a tree branch over a gravel road, then concealed it with leaves. Next he stretched a fine wire over toward the edge of the forest. Then he and the armed man vanished.

• • •

At 0600, atop a heavily sandbagged bunker, Dale Nielsen snored. It was early April and Alpha Company had been temporarily reassigned to Fire Base Three Wood for road security.

By the time the Michelin rubber plantation reconnaissance-in-force missions were completed in late March, constant casualties had reduced Dale's command to a squad of three. The remaining men spent large segments of each night on perimeter guard. No one had slept a full night in weeks. Dale had acquired the precious skill of catnapping the minute he found a flat spot.

Alpha Company's time in the area around the plantation had included no major battles, but day by day, one casualty at a time, war had taken its toll. Now it was time to rest, rebuild the squads, and repair the tracks.

Mail call was at 0800. Dale got two letters, one from his folks, the other from Gail. He shoved the one from his folks into his fatigue pants and ripped open the one from his wife.

Crocker had spent the early morning hours making his rounds chatting with his men. Finally he sat next to Dale. "So you got a letter from that wife of yours? Gail, isn't it?"

"Why yes, sir. It is. I mean I did," Dale sputtered from nervousness.

"I got one from my wife, too." The captain pulled the letter out and began silently reading it. Dale looked at the letter in front of him and tried to read, but the presence of the company CO was too distracting.

He studied the captain without being obvious. Twenty-four, Dale figured, probably an athlete at the academy. The man's face was smooth, deeply tanned, with slight creases at the eyes.

"So what she saying?" Crocker broke the silence.

"Ah, nothing, sir, at least I, ah, I haven't read it yet, sir."

"Well, mine says she'll be waiting for me wearing nothing but Saran wrap, and that sounds real good to me!" Crocker smiled. "I'm down to twenty-five days and a wake-up."

"What then, sir?" Dale asked.

"To tell you the truth, I hope I get assigned to an army recruiting center in an old-age home!" he smiled.

Dale laughed. "No, really, you're so good at this. I mean, you must like it."

"I liked my first tour until the first kid got killed. Since then I've come to hate it. I do my job but I'm scared every day. Maybe having two kids at home, and a wife," he nudged Dale, "maybe it does something to you . . . makes a man cautious, scared."

"Not that I ever noticed, sir."

"I'm no different from any of you guys; just got the opportunity to go to West Point is all."

"No!" Dale insisted. "You are different. We pretty much look out for ourselves out there. You look out for everyone but yourself. Like remembering my wife's name. You're the reason Alpha is so good." Dale blushed slightly.

"Well, thank you. I need to hear things like that, but you are the reason Alpha is feared. Each one of you guys, with a few exceptions." Dale noticed Grubouski's eyes dropping and grinned.

"Each man makes this outfit work. Look at Mike Saranov over there. He's a damn conscientious objector, but he's the best radioman I've ever had. He doesn't even carry a gun, but when I turn around, he's right there." The captain fell silent, then stood, tapping Dale on the shoulder. "I just came by to tell you that you're becoming a fine squad leader."

When the captain had moved away, Grubouski whistled between his teeth.

At 0900 Third Platoon passed the eastern listening post and headed up Road L1. Crocker's track was on drag. Five klicks out they dismounted, left the road, and assumed a sweep pattern heading across a section of fresh rice paddies.

On either side of the highway, men melted into the foliage taking flank. Crocker, Saranov, and Loudner's squad took point.

The sun was unforgiving; it heated the air until it was suffocating. At 1215 Crocker called an all clear to the firebase, then indicated a lunch break. During the break he called the platoon and squad leaders to his position for a conference.

He produced a hand-drawn map. "We're going to mount up, then proceed five K's east, past this village, then north, past this village, back to the road. There's a large stand of trees here that Battalion Command wants us to sweep through. Finish this one quickly and we can all get some extra sleep."

56

BACK AT FIRE BASE THREE WOOD, DALE PULLED A WORN DRIVE SPROCKET from the front of his track. He held it up, examined it, then tossed it into a growing pile of expended parts. He was basking in what Crocker had said about him, "becoming a fine squad leader," and thinking how he'd put it in a letter to Gail.

Inside the command bunker, Spec Four Lawrence Pratt monitored the radio transmissions from Third Platoon. At 1305 he heard an all-clear report from Crocker, noted it on a pad, then lit a Pall Mall.

In line, the four tracks from Third Platoon moved across an open section of land. In the center was a tiny village, ten hootches in all. The air was filled with the stink of dung-fueled cooking fires. A few of the older children ran out, carrying the smaller ones to look at the tracks.

In two of the paddies men were plowing with water buffalo. One waved, then stood watching as the men rode by. As soon as the small column was out of sight, he secured the buffalo and ran into the jungle.

Two klicks from the village the platoon came upon the wooded section shown on the hand-drawn map. The men dismounted and prepared to assault, with the tracks providing support.

Out of sight, two ears strained the air for vibrations like a spider feeling its web. On line, Holland at point, Crocker and his two RTOs on drag, they began the slow assault through the trees.

No fire was received before the men crept into the patch of jungle. They were tense, although Crocker seemed relaxed as if he knew the RIF would be fruitless.

Fifty meters in, the lead squad found rusting food tins with Chinese markings. Twenty meters further, Lieutenant Holland on point, they came across an abandoned bunker system. He radioed Crocker. "Red Dog Two we've got some old bunkers up here. By the looks of things they've been abandoned for some time. Over."

In the command bunker, the next thing Pratt heard was a negative situation report from Crocker. "Have rendezvoused with advance squad. Nothing to report." Pratt jotted it down, logged the time, then stood to stretch.

In the thick trees to the right of the bunkers a small, nervous hand held a thin wire. The arm muscles going to the hand tensed, and began to take in slack, then stopped.

What he saw gave him pause. Walking through the trees was a man with two RTOs, sure sign of a company-level officer. He would wait a moment longer.

"You've secured the area?" Crocker looked up at Holland.

"Yes, sir, made a thorough search." He pointed to the decaying bunkers and looked directly at the invisible trip wire.

"That's good, Dennis. Have your tracks pull up and we'll head back to the road from here. This is the only kind of ambush I like!"

The unseen hand pulled the wire tight, then stopped again. His prey had just moved out of range.

Holland's four tracks, with the command track behind, crashed into the jungle.

Back at the firebase, Dale torque-wrenched the shaft bolt, then put in the heavy cotter pin. In the command bunker, Pratt drank a cold beer.

The APCs could now be seen in the trees. Crocker and his RTOs stood on top of an old bunker talking and laughing. The lone man moved back to his wire. Hidden in a grove of teak, the hand tugged hard on the deadly wire. A barrage of shrapnel shredded the air. Men screamed in agony. Crocker and the closer RTO crumpled to the gravel, their helmets and shoulders turned crimson.

Pratt sat startled at the next communication. A shaking voice came over the air. "Four men down, including Crocker and Saranov. Urgent dustoff at location Two-One-Zero-Zero-Three-Zero." It was Holland's voice! Pratt keyed his radio, but there was no response.

Rumors flew in the firebase. "Crocker was hit, but not bad." "No, Crocker wasn't hit at all." And worst, "Crocker was down and dead."

Within moments Dale sat outside the command bunker with a dozen other men, waiting. Seconds seemed like hours. He turned toward Albert Denning, who sat silently beside him. "It's bullshit! I'm sure guys like Crocker don't go down like that! Maybe average guys get popped but not men like Crocker. He'll be back, I know it!"

Denning just stared off, then said softly, his voice cracking. "There is no such thing as 'guys like him.' You are a stupid fucker! Don't you know it fuckin don't mean nothin'!"

A sinking feeling slid down Dale's spine. Sweat sprang from every pore. He slowly got up and walked back toward his track.

He didn't know what time Crocker's death was confirmed. He spent the afternoon alone, sitting outside his APC, feeling strangely disillusioned and, even worse, abandoned.

57

HOT HUMID AIR HUNG OVER THE JUNGLE. ON THE COAST A LIGHT INLAND breeze began to stir. By noon it was steady and at least twenty degrees cooler than the air it slammed into.

Frank Jealous Of Him, who always took point now, stopped and made a circling gesture with his hand. Lieutenant Farinelli moved up and, like a reflex, pulled a map from his fatigues. He pointed to a concentric set of wavy lines, then to a small rise to the left. Frank nodded and looked up at the sky. Huge black thunderheads made the jungle dark.

At 1830, ten men in Second Platoon had found and secured the night laager. "Shit! Would you look at those fuckin clouds. It's going to fuckin rain all night," a tall man said, emptying his ruck.

Frank, in a voice just loud enough for the others to hear, said, "Humpty, there's a reason the brass call this area LZ Professional. It stands for Lightning Zone Professional. Besides, you have to learn to look at the bright side . . . you'll probably smell better if it does rain." Frank flashed a sarcastic grin, indicating how tired he was of the war and Humphrey's constant complaining.

Humphrey dropped to the ground on his helmet. "Maybe you like this stinkin' jungle, Chief, but I don't. As far as I'm concerned, turning eighteen in America is a fuckin prison sentence. No, it's worse. In prison they at least send you a little note telling you when you're going to get popped. Here you never know."

"Fuck you, Humphrey!" Downey shot from across the tiny clearing.

"Articulate fucker, aren't you!" the angry soldier shot back. "Downey, you're so stupid, you don't get any of this, do you?" Farinelli winked at Downey, then went back to his maps. "Every other fuckin day somebody gets hurt or killed and you don't get the point. It's the fuckin law of averages, man. At the rate we're going, we'll all be staring up at red plastic."

Lieutenant Farinelli looked up and folded the maps. "That's about enough of your bullshit, Humphrey." The sky lit up, then the ground shook with thunder. Some of the men stretched their hammocks between trees. Others sat trying to heat coffee.

Farinelli strung his poncho between two trees at the center of the laager. Frank picked some trees ten meters to the south. "No offense, LT," he said, smiling at Farinelli, "but you know I got a nose like a bloodhound. I'll camp upwind." The lieutenant grinned back. *Crack!* The sky slit open, releasing a steady downpour. Pat Downey was the second man to sit on his helmet to raise himself from the muddy jungle floor.

Within seconds the mush of rotten leaves on the hilltop turned to soup. Albittron was the last of the group to pick up his helmet and place it under his butt to get out of the water.

Standing next to Frank, Humphrey tied up his poncho. "You guys all think because I'm scared that I'm crazy. It's you fuckers that are crazy."

"You think I'm not scared?" Frank snapped angrily. "I'm scared crazy, man, and being around dudes like you makes it worse. We're all scared. If you don't believe me, take a poll, asshole."

Humphrey turned to face Frank. "Man, you have got to know you're just a warm body waiting to be a cold one. You're fighting for the government that fucked your people, Chief, and I'm an asshole?"

"No, you're a honky asshole to me. Whether I'm fighting for you whites, or whether I'm just trying to get home alive, I'm not even sure. You white boys got a world to go back to. If I make it back home it will be to poverty and racial bullshit. Most of you white guys think you're over here protecting the Constitution. I don't. I may look like a dumb Indian, but I came over here on my own, knowing better than any of you what the Constitution is sup-posed to do, and what it really does. And now I'm just beggin' God to forgive me, let me get home alive." He thought again of how he'd killed Darlene and his baby. "I'm a short-timer and just being with you long-timers is a drag."

Boom!! Farinelli's hammock tore from the tree, throwing him into the jungle. Dazed but still conscious, Frank rolled over to look where the mortar hit. He heard men screaming. He saw others lying perfectly still. Panic ensued, each man running toward the jungle for cover. Only the medic moved toward the wounded, and what he saw confused him. The men lay there unconscious, but there was no blood, no shrapnel holes.

"Lightning, we got hit by lightning!" Frank called out, running toward the still figures. Pat Downey lay there, breathing, but unconscious. Eddie Miller moaned, rolling violently, his back turning crimson. Steimsha was awake but stunned. The pungent smell of burned skin hung in the air. Two other men were found at the edge of the perimeter, one burned badly, the other unconscious.

Of the four men standing, three ran to the wounded. Humphrey stood by, stunned. Carl Schofer grabbed his carbine and ran for the edge of the jungle.

Within seconds Frank stood over one of the stricken men yelling for Humphrey. "Humpty! Get over here, I'm going to breathe for this guy. You work his chest."

Humphrey looked around, then ran toward the Indian. "God, this is bad! God, he shit in his pants!" His voice shook. "Gooks shooting at us, children trying to kill us, and now this. This is fuckin incredible!" he chattered. "Fuckin incredible . . ." He pumped on the man's chest. The sweat of fear dripped down his face.

Farinelli called in. "Location Two-Zero-Eight-Zero-Six-Eight requests immediate dustoff after a lightning strike. We got five men down. No, wait, that's four fair, two critical, ah, one missing. Other platoons should be in any minute. Over."

Schofer walked following his nose. Twenty feet into the jungle, he saw a man lying face down, his butt a pulp of flesh and feces. He smelled like burnt shit. Schofer rolled the man over gently, only to see a cruel burn on Gerald Albittron's boyish face. "Shi-it!" He waved to Farinelli, then picked the man up, gagging on the smell. "Fuck!" he grunted. Albittron's head hung limply down.

Charlie Brown, the RTO, handed the headset back to the lieutenant. "We got an addition. Make that three critical, four fair."

Slowly the other platoons came in, at first amazed and then glad to relieve the other men. Schofer turned Albittron over to the medic from Third Platoon. He couldn't get him to breathe, but as long as there was the slightest pulse he kept trying.

Steimsha was the first to recover enough to feel the burns on his ass. Soon it was discovered that all four of the conscious men had burns on their asses.

"Dear Mom, I fried my butt in Vietnam," Frank said, starting to laugh. Pretty soon just about everybody was laughing. Some laughed until their eyes streaked the dirt on their faces. Others like Schofer only laughed till they puked.

58

ON THE FOURTH DAY OF JUNE 1969, ONLY FIVE MEN REMAINED OF THE eleven who had made up Second Platoon. Enough for one squad. Farinelli said, "The captain wants us to join the First Platoon until we have replacements. We're taking point, so get with it."

Carl Schofer moaned and then asked Frank what he had for breakfast. Frank searched through his ruck. "Looks like chipped beef, if you want it."

To their right, Ronald Humphrey lay perfectly still in the shallow foxhole. He had been last on guard. By dawn the expression on the man's face had permanently changed. Eyes that had darted about nervously the day before were now fixed, staring at some unknown place. Frank noticed it first. "Have you seen Ronnie, this morning?" he asked the lieutenant in a whisper.

"No, Chief, what's up?" Farinelli asked, folding a tiny compass.

"If he were an Indian I guess you would say he looks like he's seen a ghost. I don't know what you white folks would call it." Frank snickered nervously. "I think he snapped, sir."

• • •

The day laager was a medium-sized village that had recently sprung from the jungle, right in the middle of a free-fire zone. From the tree line, it looked like the village was trying to reclaim some rice paddies that had been neglected. There were two middle-aged men tending a small herd of water buffalo. Some of the women were washing clothes; others transplanted rice.

"There seems to be a large number of women and children," Schofer said to the lieutenant.

"What do you say, Chief?" Farinelli nodded toward the village.

"It's getting to me, man; they're beginning to look like Indians." Frank managed a weak grin. "It looks like they're just trying to make a living, sir. Still, I would wait till the other platoons come up." Farinelli nodded and looked at his watch. He ordered the men back twenty meters, then signaled them to lie low.

When First Platoon had positioned itself to the right flank of the village and the Third Platoon to the left, the signal was given to move in. Sergeant

Lewis had to pull the ashen-faced Humphrey to his feet and push him ahead. "You fuckin asshole, better get your shit together, my man, or you'll be dead before sundown!" It was 1055.

Hearts pounded loudly. Mouths went dry. Sweat dripped profusely as the ragged remnant of two platoons walked forward. Soon they would be seen from the village and, as the veterans understood, from any machine-gun bunker hidden in the village.

"Remember, if these people are here in the middle of a free-fire zone, they're probably farming for the NVA. Stay on your toes."

Frank's heart pounded. "I hate this part more than the rest," he called to Jimmy Esch. Esch nodded in response, fixing his gun on the men with the buffalo.

When the first soldier appeared at the edge of the village, the smaller children swarmed, eyes wide, toward the hootches. The women stood stock-still. One of the men with the buffalo walked toward Farinelli, spewing a long blast of Vietnamese. Farinelli signaled for the men to proceed into the village. Some of the women began to cry as the men approached. "Let's keep this to the point!" the captain yelled between radio transmissions.

After a hurried search of the village, all they had found was a U.S. Army fatigue shirt and a rusty U.S. helmet. Captain Thomas grabbed the graying man and spoke slowly. "We are going to burn your village. Where do you want to go?" The old man said something in Vietnamese and some of the women began to sob. Then he turned to the captain and started to jabber. All the men could understand was "Hau Duc."

"Sir, none of your people will be hurt if you cooperate . . .," he tipped his helmet and smiled at the villagers, "but if you don't, you will feel the wrath of the U.S. Army."

By 1100 the radio at battalion headquarters crackled with Lieutenant Farinelli's report. "This is Blue Leader. Company B has secured our day laager. We've got thirty Vietnamese who request urgent evac to Hau Duc. Over." A short chuckle went up from the men.

"Standard procedure!" the captain barked.

With that all the women and children were herded into a circle and forced to sit. Those who resisted were shoved at gunpoint. The Kit Carson and the captain were interrogating the men. "They say they're just out here farming!" the captain said in disgust. "You tell them they're fuckin liars. Tell them they're farming for the NVA, and we know it!"

Farinelli shouted, "Humphrey, Schofer, Chief, continue searching the hootches." The lieutenant from First Platoon took charge of destroying the water buffalo.

"This is fuckin nuts." Barely audible, Humphrey broke his silence. His eyes were still glassy.

Frank bent to enter the first hootch. "Just stay out of the way, Humpty."

"There's nothing in this place except clothes and some kitchen stuff," Schofer said.

"Yeah and these hootches look new," Frank added. "I hate this! Man, I hate this. These people are just here to harvest that rice crop." He tore up the matting on the floor, "Nothing here!" He backed out of the hut. Behind a rag something metallic caught his eye. He reached up and pushed the rag aside. "It's a tag. A fuckin dog tag. Some folks named Gleason are going to be getting a letter."

"What do you suppose happened to the poor, fuckin bastard?" Schofer fingered the tag.

"You know, they probably ate him!" he answered himself. Laughing loudly, he showed the tag to Ron Humphrey, dangling on its chain like a shrunken head.

Humphrey sat down hard on a pushcart, staring at nothing. Schofer took the tag to Captain Thomas and returned to the search. They could hear the Kit Carson shouting in high-pitched Vietnamese. The old man then screamed an unintelligible oath back.

Every time a buffalo was shot, Humphrey's whole body would jolt. Some of the animals bellowed their agony as they went down; others simply splashed silently into the bloody water of the paddy.

"It's a shame to kill all that buffalo and not have a big feast back at the old teepee, eh Chief!" Schofer teased Frank.

Already edgy, Frank was annoyed by the banter. "Sure is, bro. I'd cook up the best part for you."

"Yeah, sure. What's that?" Schofer said as he entered the next hootch.

"I'd make you a big bowl of *taniga*. Just thinking of it makes me hungry, man." Frank struck the floor with the butt plate of his M-16.

"Fuckin *onega*! I don't eat that shit. What the fuck is *onega*, anyway?" The idle chatter made his fear and queasiness more tolerable. Outside Humphrey sat staring at his rifle. *Crack, Crack!* A buffalo screamed in pain. *Crack!* There was silence except for the whimpering of children.

"*Taniga* is prepared only on special occasions, for special people. It's considered a delicacy."

Schofer tossed a sack of rice out of the hootch. "That does not tell me a fuckin thing, man. It's a delicacy. So what is it, raw liver? I hear Indians liked the raw shit, like liver." He poked the roof and ceiling with his bayonet.

Frank looked over at Humphrey who now sat shaking, his skin pale and dry, then back at Schofer. "You're getting closer, my white-boy *kola.*"

Carl stepped out of the hootch. "You mean it's raw liver?"

"No, the shit part." Frank flashed a grin.

"For Christ sakes, man, you're going to feed your good buddy shit? Well, I don't want any of your fuckin toneeger, or whatever the fuck you call it. You take the next hootch." He punctuated it by lighting up a smoke. He, too, began to wonder why Humpty sat there shaking.

Crack! Crack! Crack! A cheer went up from the buffalo detail. Unnoticed, tears formed in Humphrey's eyes. Frank tossed two bags of rice out of the house. "If I didn't know better, I'd say Ronnie looks like he's praying to his gun. Something you white folks probably do?" he needled Carl.

At 1545 a large C&C Huey landed, and they loaded up the civilians. Accessory packs and rations were tossed on the ground. Soon the sound of the big chopper faded. In the quiet of the abandoned village Captain Thomas yelled, "Burn it!"

Crack! "Ahhh!" An agonizing scream sent the men to their chests. Like a cat Frank scanned the clearing. To his left, he could see Humphrey lying on his side. "Humphrey's been hit!" he yelled out.

The medic from Second Platoon was the first to the writhing man. "It went off! Ahhh! It just fuckin went off in my hands!" Humphrey screamed through clenched teeth. He clutched the remains of his left hand, now a horror of bone, tendon, and blood. "My rifle just fuckin went off!"

Black thunderheads gathered above the burning village.

59

RAINY SEASON IN TAY NINH PROVINCE HAD TEMPORARILY BROUGHT AN END to firefights and ambushes. A two-month sojourn to the south of Dau Tieng had been a relief from the near constant action of the first three months. Now the men in Dale Nielsen's platoon were itching to get back up north where they could do some good.

Since Crocker's death, a long string of temporary commanders had come and gone. The Second of the 22nd, Alpha Company had a reputation for being combat veterans who showed little respect for uniforms or military protocol. They had thus been posted by themselves, where their "attitude" wouldn't affect others.

It was from this temporary campsite that they had left that morning, their mission to sweep a section of road between Dau Tieng and Saigon.

The lead track ground forward at a snail's pace. From its deck came the sound of Armed Forces Radio. Fifty meters ahead on the narrow road was Sergeant Dale Nielsen. Just to the rear of him were men in the woods, one hundred meters on either side of the road, as flankers.

Working point, Dale studied the damp ground for the slightest disturbance. He liked walking point better than riding on the track, or merely walking beside it. The cautious walking stirred his imagination with childhood images of soldiers fighting their way up Normandy Beach, firing from the hip. Or he might be the Rifleman, twirling the lever on his thirty-thirty while surgically mowing down bad guys.

When the sweep formation required him to be in the woods, he'd often hoped, without fulfillment, that he might run into a NVA squad at rest and obliterate them with a few blasts of his M-16.

Concentration was difficult. The rainy season had seen a sharp decrease in action until the only casualties Alpha suffered were from homemade Vietcong mines and booby traps. They hadn't seen the enemy in weeks. Every day seemed a repeat of the day before. Boredom and lack of concentration had become the deadliest enemy. The local VC had only to be patient hunters and they could take their quota of American casualties.

Dickerson sat in the track, head and shoulders out, controlling the lead vehicle effortlessly with the extension arms. His uniform and appearance, generally impeccable, were now actually crisp. He held a civilian Pall Mall between his smiling lips. Life in the field in Vietnam didn't get any more slack than this, and his expression showed his appreciation.

In contrast, Dale walked ahead without benefit of pant legs, sleeves, underwear, or socks. His image was partly contrived, partly accidental, and partly the result of the wet conditions and the effort to prevent foot and crotch rot. He had not shaved since his first firefight, so his upper lip sported a thin line of light brown hair.

Dickerson was the first to hear, but thought nothing of it. So what if the Higher Higher came down for an inspection. They were out on patrol where they were supposed to be, doing what they were supposed to be doing. As far as Alpha was concerned, that was all that mattered.

The helicopter landed next to the road in a dry paddy. A young colonel stepped from the C&C Huey and approached Dickerson, who was continuing forward. Dale, engrossed in his fantasies, didn't notice.

"Soldier, who's in charge here?" the colonel asked impatiently. Dickerson responded: "Sergeant Nielsen is up on point. Should I get him for you?"

"That's what I requested, wasn't it?"

Dickerson signaled the platoon to a halt and sped his track forward. "The colonel wants to see you," he shouted to Dale. Don't know what it's about."

Dale turned around and saw the angry officer. He walked quickly back toward the stalled platoon. "Sergeant Nielsen, sir! How may I help you?"

"Soldier, you could help me very much by telling me what the hell you think you're doing out of uniform?" The man's face reddened as he took in the other men. "Son, you are a disgrace to the United States Army!" He moved up close to Dale, his eyes burning in their sockets. "I have a report that Alpha is the worst-looking, worst-behaving bunch of misfits this man's army has ever seen. Why, according to the information I have, you guys have to camp by yourselves outside a defensive perimeter because nobody will have you. Is this true?!" He turned to look at the rest of the outfit. The scruffy platoon only increased his rage.

"Why, I don't know, sir," Dale finally managed to respond.

"Don't know? Well, as of this minute you're relieved of your platoon. Is that clear, sergeant?"

"Yes, sir." Dale was mildly irritated.

"I'll be back in a week! If by then you have shaved, cut your hair, and have a proper uniform, I will return your platoon. If not, I'll make you wish you were never in the recruiter's office. Is that clear?"

"Yes, sir." Dale's voice was barely audible above the idling chopper.

Behind the colonel's back, Dickerson stood on his track grinning from ear to ear.

The colonel searched the men. Finally his eyes came to rest on the grinning Dickerson, who stopped smiling. "Now there is a soldier who looks like a professional. Soldier, what's your name?"

"Dickerson, sir, Spec Four Ralph Dickerson." His combat boots fairly glistened.

"Dickerson, you are the only man in this platoon who deserves this command. You are the new platoon sergeant and will be until I return. Is that clear?"

Dickerson smiled, enjoying the attention and Dale's embarrassment. "Yes, sir. It is."

Without further word, the young battalion commander walked back toward his helicopter and was gone.

Dickerson broke into a loud gravelly laugh, all the time pointing his index finger at Dale. "I told you, my man, clothes is what makes you! You are a slob." Tears rolled down his dark face. "You're a disgrace!"

The whole platoon broke into laughter. Dale's face burned at the very idea that this was any of the colonel's business. It was nothing short of harassment. But then he too broke into a grin.

He walked over to the track and climbed aboard. He handed the puzzled Dickerson his rifle and slid into the driver's position.

"What the fuck you doing, man? This is my track!" Dickerson was suddenly in no mood for laughter.

"No, Platoon Sergeant Dickerson. With all due respect, you have orders from the colonel. You're walking point today and I'm driving. On road patrol, platoon leaders never drive. They walk. Besides, I've always wanted to be a driver. It's the best part of this war. I might even grow a beard!"

Dickerson stood there, sweat glistening on his forehead beneath his tight Afro.

"You lousy mothah-fuckah! You're actually going to listen to that colonel, and make me hoof it?"

Dale shifted the vehicle into drive and waited for Dickerson to dismount.

Dickerson scowled. "I'm going to shave that stupid mustache off and get your sorry ass into a uniform if it's the last goddamned thing I do."

Dale lit up a cigarette and steered the vehicle forward.

60

THE NIGHT OF JUNE 8 HAD BEEN EXCRUCIATINGLY LONG. THICK CLOUDS threatened rain, but produced only a fine drizzle and inky blackness. Even pulling early guard and hitting the sack by 2400 hadn't helped Frank Jealous Of Him sleep. At 0400 he sat up grunting in disgust.

Toward the center of the laager, only barely visible from his hole, Frank noticed the command area stirring. At 0500 Lieutenant Farinelli tapped one of the sleeping men on the shoulder and pointed toward the next poncho-covered hammock.

• • •

Outside Wounded Knee, at the Body of Christ Church near Grass Creek, tambourines and guitar music could be heard floating from the open windows. In the trailer house, Matthew turned toward the window, looking out through the dusty glass at a sea of stars. Sitting up, he grabbed a half-empty pack, shook a cigarette out, placed it between his lips, and lit it. Then he stood and walked outside.

In the cool air, Julie stood under the pine-bough shade dumping coffee grounds into a large porcelain cauldron. Matthew leaned against the trailer watching the little girl wrestle the pan onto the wood stove. "I can't sleep, I'm going to take in the show. You want to come?" he called to his sister.

"No. I'm supposed to have coffee for when they come out." She nodded toward the church.

Tossing his spent cigarette aside, Matthew crossed the little compound to the church and pushed open the door. He stood in back of the tiny chapel adjusting his eyes and ears to the building spiritual ecstasy. Mazy Little Dog noticed him first and, grinning with divine joy, nudged Bernice.

• • •

In the cool, damp gloom of a June dawn, Sergeant Carl Schofer rose to a sitting position, looked at his watch, then gasped in a low growl, "Fuckin five o'clock."

The sound of C-ration cans sliding out of a ruck elicited Schofer's ritual question. "Chief, what you got for C-rats?" he called from his hole. "I had a real nice dream about my girl last night, and you know that makes me hungry."

"I had a dream about your girl, so I'm starving too. Guess you're out of luck, Sarge," Frank said flatly. Banter, however foolish, seemed to ease the awful strain of a patrol already twenty-one days out. Before Schofer could respond, Frank said, "You're in for a treat, Carl, my *kola;* I've got some of that Breakfast of Champions you're always hitting me up for." A can arched the narrow distance from one hole to the next.

"That's terrific, Chief, ham and eggs, just great! I suppose you eat that shit. That's what you got left 'cause you won't eat it and now you want me, your pal in arms, to eat it. Probably so you can tell Esch and have a laugh about it."

Another can arched over the mounded dirt, hitting Schofer in the shoulder. He fingered the can till its label showed in the growing light. "Chief, you are a saint," he said, opening the sliced pork.

"Now, what do I get out of the deal?" Frank asked.

"Shit, you know I'd share whatever I fuckin got with you," the other man defended himself.

Frank whistled quietly through his teeth. "Yeah, you're true on that one. You get dysentery; you give it to me. You get foot rot; you make sure I get it. I know it's 'cause you want me to have what you have. You're true as shit on that, brother. You're always looking out for my welfare." Frank chuckled.

"Just want to make sure that scrawny brown butt of yours makes it home. You know me, pal!" Schofer was laughing too.

At 0600, Lieutenant Farinelli ended breakfast when he signaled Sergeant Lewis to come to the center of the perimeter. All eyes followed. "Bob, I want you to take your squad and do your regular sweep. Make sure the perimeter is secure and come back in. The captain here wants to make an early start." Lewis looked over to see Captain Thomas light up a heat tab and drop it into his stove.

Signaling his squad to pack their things, Lewis folded a map and shoved it in his ruck. Short moments passed before he looked at his watch. His eyes grew wide against his dark face; then he circled his hand above him.

Frank was the first to join him at the opening to a narrow trail, followed closely by Don Lundren, Schofer, Esch, and the new radioman. At 0610 Frank pushed up from a squat to a crouch, then led slowly down the trail.

The radio crackled at rear area: "Company B, Second Platoon departs night laager on patrol." Under a hot blue sky, the last man melted into the dripping leaves.

· · ·

Guitar and tambourine music filled the little church. For all his effort, Matthew had not seen who it was that had gone down to the floor, shaking in a faint. It was later, sipping sweetened coffee, just outside the green pine boughs of the shade, that he overheard Bernice's voice in the darkness.

"And she said it would be a test of the church?" Bernice asked in a low tone.

The other woman's voice was louder. "I'm sure that's what she said, just after that part about men who are cheating on their wives. I thought some of the men looked a little quieter after that," she chuckled.

· · ·

A third of the way around the base of the night laager, Lewis wiped his face with his towel, then signaled the radioman. He clicked the key twice, indicating the trail was secure. Frank was twenty meters ahead, followed by Schofer to his right and Esch to his left. Next came Lundren and Lewis in the trees to the right and left of the trail. The dead silence of the forest floor gave the patrol a weary, endless quality.

As usual Frank set the pace. It seemed to Schofer that he moved more slowly than usual. In over an hour the Sioux scout had seen nothing.

The jungle air was now beginning its long torturous climb toward a noonday boil. Sweat stung the eyes of the Indian, exaggerating what, over the last few weeks, had become a permanent bloodshot red. At 0830 a brief "All clear at position Bravo-Tango Two-One-Two-One-Zero-Two" crackled out of the radio in the laager. Farinelli sipped on his first cup of coffee while he and the captain made small talk.

Frank called softly to his right. "If anything bothers me, it's that either there's really no one out here, or they know we're here." Schofer did not answer. The longer the patrol went without a sign, the more frightening it became. Long, heart-pounding minutes passed until Frank recognized the trail they had left two hours before and signaled a halt.

Lewis came up to Frank, face drenched, sweat running from his lips into his mouth. "Well done, my man," he slapped the Indian's hands. "Well done."

The black man pulled the map from his pack, studied it for a minute, and said, "I need some volunteers to go fill our canteens. That small creek we crossed earlier is as good a place as any."

Parched with thirst, Schofer whispered, "I'll go." The all-encompassing quiet was disturbed only by the soft noise of water bladders and canteens being passed forward.

"Hey, bastard, that means I got to go," Frank said, shaking his head at his friend. "You know I got to have what you got." His big teeth shone brightly against the cinnamon face.

"Well fine, be that way, asshole!" the other said, gathering the containers.

• • •

Cool spring air blew through a worn screen into the crowded bedroom. Clayton Jealous Of Him stared up at the ceiling. Bernice slept soundly beside him, her rhythmic breathing almost taunting. He turned his face away, looking past the cot Julie and Carol slept on, out the open window, toward the western sky. Seconds later a dying star slid from beneath the cloud cover toward the prairie.

Turned back toward the ceiling, his eyes could see the face of the woman on the floor of his church, her rounded features filled with the spirit.

• • •

On the way toward the water, Frank noticed two places where the thin cover exposed them to shafts of bright light. He communicated this to Schofer by exaggerating his crouch down behind the first layer of vegetation. His companion mimicked him.

At water's edge he sat behind a thick palmetto sapling as he slowly filled each canteen. Sunlight flickered down through gaps in the canopy, creating pockets of brightness on the decay of the jungle floor. To fill the canteens, all that he exposed to the narrow clearing was his arms. From behind a stand of tall grasses, Schofer filled the bladders.

One by one the containers were filled, some twelve in all. The sluggish flow of water into the canteens only made their temporary isolation that much more terrifying. When all the lids were in place, Schofer signaled Frank that he would lead the way back. Frank nodded. It was 0850.

Amid the rustle and slosh of six water bags, Schofer swiftly approached the first thin spot. There was a distinct click off to the right. Frank heard it clearly, loudly, as if played over an amplifier. Carl did not.

Crack!! Carl Schofer screamed as a section of his back sprayed across the trail. He fell in a heap. Back in the laager, Farinelli spilled his coffee and stood.

Crack, Crackety, Crack. The staccato of AK fire threw Frank to the dirt, his heart in his throat. He looked at his squirming friend. "Fuck, fuck!" he muttered to himself.

"I'm hi-I-I-t. Fuckin God Damn, I'm hit," Carl gurgled.

After tossing off the bandolier of canteens, Frank unloaded a clip into the jungle, snapped in another, then dove for Carl. His naked shoulder plowed into the ground as he landed. "I'm here, man. I'm here for you, white boy," Frank screamed. "Hang on to me, I'm going to get you out."

By now the squad had moved, trying to take cover below a decaying, vine-covered stone wall. They too were pinned by an unseen sniper. Sergeant Esch fired a clip in the direction he thought the shots were from, then sprawled, moaning, into the undergrowth with a head wound. Frank could see Lewis trying to create suppressive fire.

"We've got trouble!" the radioman screamed into the set. "Two men down. We're under sniper fire. Help us, man!"

Chaos broke out in the laager. Farinelli moved toward his boots, stalled, then picked up his bandolier, rifle, and steel pot. Crashing barefoot down the trail, the squad ran headlong toward their buddies.

Lewis could see Frank move to the front of Schofer, who was now shaking uncontrollably. Frank's mind flashed on basic training and Nielsen's silly grin. "Huun!" The Indian pulled him up, straining to lift Carl high enough to get under him. "He's got him!" Lewis screamed impulsively. "Fucker's got him."

Frank turned. The world was a blur of noise and pain. Then he spotted Lewis. He couldn't hear the voice, but he could see the teeth, just the lips and teeth moving like he was looking through a tunnel.

He pushed up hard under Carl, straining to get the weight of the man into the right direction. He was moving now, gaining speed, when he came into the second clearing. He saw Carl's head explode, then blue sky.

He heard Farinelli yell, "Frank! Just lie there! Don't move. I'm coming."

He never saw Albert Farinelli crawl up the old stone wall, because he couldn't move his head. He was still looking at the deepening blue, up through the jagged canopy, when Farinelli crested the wall just meters from Carl. He could hear Farinelli, "I've got you, man. Just hang on!" but he couldn't turn to see where it came from. He couldn't turn to see Farinelli's hips ripped open with gunfire. He didn't see or hear Farinelli struggle to crawl forward with useless legs, because the sky overhead had shifted from powder blue to cobalt then to black.

• • •

On the worn stoop, out in the growing wind, Clayton stood waiting or watching. He had risen, afraid that his tossing might disturb Bernice. He had left her lying there with her pregnant belly and her rhythmic sighs.

It seemed a night to be alone. Or maybe he felt alone even lying beside her. As he lit his third smoke, he felt the air change. He noticed a difference in its odor as well. It seemed strange that sage should give way to prairie rose.

61

CLYNDA PATTED THE VOLLEYBALL UP AGAINST THE TINY HOUSE, MAKING A relentless banging inside. Matthew had asked her to stop three times, but either she was entranced by the rhythm or her thoughts were far away. So he'd gone for a walk. About eleven a tribal police car, lights flashing, siren off, pulled up the dirt lane and swung off toward their yard.

The officer beeped the horn, startling the girl out of her thoughts. "Your mother or father home?" The man's face looked grave. Something in his voice and manner made Clynda's heart pound with fear.

"No, they're in Pine Ridge. Mom's at a bake sale at Billy Mill's Hall and Dad is with Grandma at the BIA, waiting for a lease check. Why? Is something the matter?"

The officer answered her question with a blank look, then said "Thanks." He reversed the car and sped off toward the gate. Matt saw the car's whirling lights from the distance and jogged back toward the house.

Panting, he ran up to Clynda. "What did he want?"

A worried look clouded her young face. "He didn't say, just something about finding Mom and Dad."

A sinking feeling now pulled at Matthew's heart. "Maybe it's something about Billy," he said, hating the sound of the words.

"Don't say that! You don't know!" She threw the ball away. "You shouldn't say things like that. Something bad could happen!"

At the store in Wounded Knee the police car stopped for a moment beside a U.S. government vehicle. Inside a uniformed white man leaned out the window. "Did you find them?"

"No, but I think I know where they are. The other kids were home but I didn't say anything to them. I thought their folks should tell them. I should be back with Clayton and Bernice in a hour."

The man began to roll up his window. "I hate this job . . . I'll just wait here, I guess."

The tribal policeman gunned his Chevy toward the highway, past the Sun Dance ground, and sped off toward Pine Ridge.

He found Clayton and Bernice waiting patiently with a long line of people in front of the treasurer's office. Beside them sat Bernice's mother and the younger kids. The officer walked past the others, and seemed to hesitate in front of Clayton.

Clayton looked up at the officer and smiled. "What's up, Ben?" he asked.

"Can I speak with you outside for a moment?" The young officer looked upset.

"Sure," Clayton said, then stood and moved toward the exit.

Outside the day was gray, a cold mist materializing out of the June overcast.

"Clayton, there's a fellow with the army, at the store in Wounded Knee, says he needs to see you."

"About what?" He studied the policeman's face.

"I can't say, but you should get over there right away." He put his hand on Clayton's shoulder.

"I don't even have enough money for gas to get back there. Bernice's mom's going to get her lease check today and then I can go. Bernice and her mom are supposed to help with a Head Start bake sale over at Mill's Hall."

The officer reached into his pants pocket and pulled out some bills. "Here's five. Put gas in your tank and go talk to him. You can always come back." Something in his voice told Clayton he already knew what the army man wanted.

He walked back into the office. In Lakota he told Bernice, "Tell your mom we'll be right back. We're supposed to see a man at Gildersleeve's, right away."

He put gas in the car and turned back toward Wounded Knee.

At Grass Creek, Matthew and Clynda sat in the tiny house, waiting for the other shoe to drop. Something in their subconscious already knew what the news would be. They didn't say it to each other, but they knew, and they were sure about it in a way only a brother and sister could be. It made their stomachs sick, their ribs heavy with horrible anticipation.

In the car, Clayton told Bernice what the officer had told him. "He's from the army, maybe they are going to bring Billy home early, maybe he's going to get a medal, maybe . . ." Bernice reached over, and touched him on the leg. She didn't want to consider any more maybe's.

In the trading post Mrs. Sozinski peeked out, and motioned to one of the women who had brought moccasins to trade. "That government car's been there for hours. A police car met him, then went up toward Grass Creek. He came back right away so he must have gone to Jealous's. I hope it's not something about Billy."

With that, rumors flew among everyone who came into shop or to pick up mail. Nobody who came in left, until a small crowd had gathered, buzzing among themselves in Lakota.

It wasn't long before Clayton's old car pulled up, and the crowd moved out onto the porch looking on in hushed silence.

The uniformed man stepped from his car and walked toward the couple. In his right hand he carried a small envelope.

He managed a weak smile. "Are you Clayton and Bernice Jealous Of Him?"

Clayton extended his badly shaking hand toward the tall recruiter. "Yes, we are."

The sergeant handed Clayton the envelope. "Sir, on behalf of the United States Army, it is my sad duty to inform you that your son Frank has been killed."

Bernice gasped "Billy!" then collapsed against Clayton, almost knocking him down. The small crowd rushed from the trading post. The women sent a loud, mournful keening into the cold air while the men carried Bernice, large with child, back toward the car.

Clayton, his usual dark complexion now a pasty blue, stood shaking his head, mouth open, staring with teary eyes at the military man. He wanted to ask if a mistake had been made, wanted to know how this white man knew about Billy, but no sound came from his lips.

Knees weak, Clayton took a moment to find his voice. "Will we see that it's Billy? Will they let us look at his face?"

"Certainly" was all the man could think to say.

"Billy's got a brother and four sisters . . . could you help me tell them." He wept openly now.

The man took Clayton's hands. "Certainly."

At eleven o'clock a growing caravan left the village of Wounded Knee. Under a gray, rain-spattering sky, they drove slowly toward the Body of Christ Church and two solemn teenagers who did not want them to come.

Now it was Clynda who had gone for a long walk. She stayed out on the cold prairie, hoping that so long as she did not go home, what she most feared would not come true.

62

CARS STARTED TO ARRIVE AT THE GRASS CREEK HOME WITHIN HOURS OF THE news. People pitched small canvas tents in the churchyard. Some were relatives of Bernice or Clayton. Many were just friends or church members who, stunned by the news, could not stay away.

With each day the number of campers grew. As was customary, men hauled firewood and water. A few families donated beef for the big cooking pots. Some women cooked; others served. A community was founded in grief.

A field nurse traveled from the Agency and gave Clynda and Matthew some sedatives for Bernice and their dad. Each day that week, for a brief time, Clayton would emerge from the little house and in a fog wander among the tents smoking donated cigarettes, drinking coffee, taking hugs.

His eyes were red-rimmed, glassy pools against his gray skin. His hands shook as he extended them to people who spoke to him of Jesus, heaven, and eternal rest. No matter how many hugged him, spoke to him, turned their sad eyes toward him, it did no good. His heart had died within his living breast. As in a cold empty room, he felt no relief, no warmth.

Bernice, whose baby innocently defied everyone and everything, continued to feel it kick her in the ribs. She received visitors in the house, often lying in her bed, seldom venturing outside.

Matthew at sixteen was resolute. "Until I see his body for myself, I won't believe it," he told everyone. "You don't know Billy like I do! He'll come home, I know it!" he would say over and over to anyone who would listen. His eyes remained dry; his heart, though, was wild with fright.

Clynda felt abandoned. Her cherished brother would not return. Life hurt; just breathing hurt. Food had no taste or smell. A part of her hated the people in the yard, even her mother and father.

Two-year-old Verla went from camp to camp, sometimes feeling the sadness, other times glad for the visitors' attention. Carol at nine was all the help she could be. Sometimes the death of her brother settled on her like the weight of the world; at other times she helped Clynda look after the little ones.

At fourteen, Clynda had to manage the situation, make sure that her folks ate and took their pills, and show newcomers where they might camp. She felt no solace in the relatives, their kind words; nor could she bring herself to take the sleeping pills.

Sleep eluded the girl for days. Her eyes sank deep in their sockets. Weight seemed to melt from her hips until by the fifth day she felt an anger stir within. The building rage extended to everyone: the folks, Matthew, the army, even Billy. They were all to blame for how she felt. The anger replaced the emptiness, gave her the strength to eat, and finally on the seventh day, like the Old Testament God who had abandoned them, she rested.

On June 19, the camp, now swelled to sixty tents, received word that the body was on its way from Washington, D.C. to Rapid City. With the news, Matthew's panic grew within him like a cornered animal. What if his faith was in vain? What if it was Billy in the metal box and not a stranger's face?

"If it is Billy, I'm going to leave after the funeral. I can't bear it, to look at her. If it wasn't for Bernice, he wouldn't have left for the army!" he told Billy Hollow Horn. Billy only stared at the ground.

"I want to tell her how much I hate her. I feel like getting a gun and killing her. And Dad, I hate him too!" His voice shook. "He could have done something, could have kept Billy from going." His mind raced with hatred and pain. "I don't want to look at them. If it is Billy, I'm going to leave and never come back."

63

FROM RAPID CITY, ACROSS THE OPEN STRETCHES OF GREEN JUNE PRAIRIE, the funeral procession seemed to float south in the shimmering heat. At Caputa, people came out of the trading post to stare.

In the lead were two highway patrolmen on motorcycles, red lights spinning. Behind them was the hearse, two more patrolmen, a military jeep carrying the honor guard, and a truck carrying thirty U.S. airmen. They led slowly, cognizant of the 150 cars that followed.

It happened just past the hardscrabble border town of Scenic, where South Dakota gives way to the northern reaches of the Pine Ridge Reservation and the raw beauty of the jagged Badlands. As if by some unseen hand, the broken body in the flag-draped coffin transcended its green uniform, changing from a soldier named Jealous-Of-Him, Frank W., U.S. 56565568, to Billy, brother, cousin, lover, friend, son.

At Rockyford School, the flag flew at half-mast. From the long caravan dust boiled into the air as far north as the eye could see. In Sharp's Corner, the people had come from Medicine Root district to stand along the road, some one hundred strong, giving silent welcome.

In Porcupine, the scene was chaotic. Oglalas lined the road. Crying violent tears, the women, arms raised high, waved their handkerchiefs like scalps. "Lee-lee-lee." A soft victory trill rose and built, frightening the state police, rising ever louder as every woman, young and old, added her voice. The men and boys stood by dabbing shyly at eyes brimming with tears.

Later the captain of the guard would say, "It was in Wounded Knee that the world seemed to turn upside down." Along the highway, men and women cried openly. Parked cars bleated their horns, flashed their lights. In the little village, women ran from their homes; some screamed and fainted. Billy Jealous was home.

Near the Gildersleeve Trading Post, a lone car swung out to lead the procession. The motorcycles swung off toward the east and the tiny Body of Christ Church. In the yard was a menagerie of tents. Many had been there since the ninth of June, their boarders camped close by to comfort the family and share in their grief.

In contrast to the awful wailing in the village, the yard was eerily hushed. From the tiny house came Clayton supported by Matthew. Behind them came

Bernice supported by Clynda and Mary Hollow Horn.

Out from the jeep came the honor guard, their crisp uniforms brilliant in the sun. The airmen filed from the canopied truck forming a pathway to the church. *Click!* The captain of the guard opened the door of the hearse. From the church came the first strains of "Branded Man."

When the casket was slid from the hearse, a terrible keening went up. "I-eee! I-eee!" Some of those gathered surged forward and hugged the flag-draped casket, almost knocking it from the hands of the soldiers. Others dropped to their knees. A few women fainted with the growing hysteria.

"Billy! Billy, my boy, my son!" Bernice sobbed loudly. Thirty airmen formed a quick corridor to the church through the crowd of mourners or Billy would have remained outdoors. Inside stood the remaining members of the Sioux Playboys. When they had finished their song, Roger Running Bear stood at the front of the little church and, while Billy was carried slowly up the narrow aisle, sang "Precious Memories."

The flag-draped gray metal casket was lowered to a funeral bier, covered with a bright star quilt. The front door was closed, and all but the honor guard and the immediate family were escorted from the chapel. Virgil Little Dog, who represented the army, had accompanied Billy from Vietnam. He now stood with a representative of each military branch at parade rest beside the casket. The funeral director arranged the flowers, then set up a table next to the casket.

Clayton and Bernice stood by Clynda and Matthew. Two-year-old Verla now peeked from behind Clynda and Carol, not old enough to fully perceive the idea of death, or that the box contained their big brother. Julie stood by fighting tears.

It was Matthew that broke the silence. "I want to see his face!" he said coldly in Lakota. "I've been waiting since the ninth of June, and I want to see his face." His body was tense with purpose. No one responded.

"I'm going to see the body in that casket! I don't care what the rest of them think!" He swung his arm violently toward his family. "I know it's not Billy!" He was now yelling in Lakota at Virgil Little Dog. Of those on the honor guard, only Little Dog understood what was happening.

"You tell me you're his brother . . . well, if you are his brother, you will open that box and show us it's Billy!" Matthew lunged toward the casket knocking it off the bier. Stunned, the white soldiers shrank back for a moment while Little Dog grabbed for the crazed boy. Matthew fell over the bier, straining at the bolted lid, trying to force open the sealed box.

The Marine Corps guard was the first to reach him. Pounding the frenzied teenager in the back with his fist, he knocked the air from Matthew's thick body. Then the air force guard grabbed him from behind and lifted him to his feet, holding him fast.

"Congo, I know it's your brother! I was there when they put his body in the casket!" Virgil Little Dog yelled in English while the boy tried to squirm free.

"How do you know?!" Tears came to Matthew's eyes. "Tell us! Tell us how you know he's not still over there somewhere!" he screamed.

Little Dog stepped toward Matthew, his face soft with compassion. "Little brother had a scar on his wrist." He pointed to his own arm. "Do you remember?" Matthew twisted less forcefully but did not respond. "Well, when the casket got to the States I made them open it again, and I looked for that scar. It was there, and I have not left Billy since. I wish to hell I could tell all of you maybe it's not Billy, but it is. You have to believe me. I loved him too!"

With that Matthew stopped struggling, and the guard let him go. While they lifted the casket back onto the bier, Matthew left the church. It was Mary that caught him near the trailer house, hugged him, and then walked him inside.

• • •

That night the military casket stood in the tiny sanctuary surrounded by flowers. On the wall behind it were two star blankets. One was a broken star, quilted in the sacred Lakota colors of red, blue, yellow, and white, the other a closed star pattern in red, white, and blue. To the right an American flag hung limply from a hardwood staff. In front of the casket was a folding table covered with pictures of Billy. Among them was the one of him and his smiling brother and sisters taken before he left for Vietnam. Beside it was a black-and-white photograph of him with his father taken when he was five. The largest was a color photo of him in his dress uniform sent home from basic training.

Some three hundred mourners filed one by one past the photos. They would pause to kneel by the casket. Some tried to embrace its cold, metallic bulk. Others merely touched it or placed flowers on it.

The photos cracked the resolve of even the most reserved, and they began to cry. Some moaned with soft sounds of resignation; others howled in anguish and had to be supported. But it was Mary Hollow Horn that caught the family's attention and temporarily hushed the murmuring in the little church. Cloaked in widow's black, her sixteen-year-old beauty radiated through her grief, like a deep red rose veiled in a smoky haze. Straight and proud she walked patiently, waiting her turn. Under her small arm she carried a quilt.

When it was her turn to pass by the pictures, Mary began to shake ever so slightly, but she would not let Billy's spirit see her break down. Picking up the army picture, she gently embraced it. Matthew, Clynda, and Julie stood and walked forward to wait quietly by the casket. Before Mary knelt, they took the star blanket from her and spread it before the congregation, then draped it over the casket. Done in the long days since the awful news, it was of tiniest patchwork, of finest embroidery, in warm roses, pinks, and scarlet, a lover's robe.

Hours later the procession had passed, and gray-haired Enos Poor Bear stood before the congregation. He had boys that had been close to Billy, and a son still somewhere in Vietnam. "Tonight in honor of these white honor guards, I will speak in English. As chairman of this tribe, I have had to attend too many of these wakes. We have already lost Daniel Stands, Jr., and Blair Two Crow. It is still hard." He dabbed at his eye.

"My boy, Webster, is still over there. I pray to the Lord Jesus for his safe return." A murmur of affirmation went up from the congregation, rippling through those standing outside at the doors and windows.

"It seems that it is our best men who are called upon to defend the flag. It is our best families that are crushed with grief when those boys come home wrapped in that same flag. I knew Billy from the time he was this high." He held his hand at his thigh.

"I have known Clayton since we were boys at the boarding school. All of this makes it hard to do this. To come here and lay one of our bravest Oglala warriors to rest!" A short trill "Lee-lee-lee-lee!" rose inside the church, passed to those standing outside.

"Billy has made us proud with his music many times. He has represented our people to the youth of the white nation, and that is why they honored him at the School of Mines last evening. Many of you were there to witness the young white people honor our son. This has never happened before!" Again a loud murmuring filled the little church. His eulogy went on with the eloquence of an old-time chief. As is the custom, others followed, some brief and emotional, others remembering Billy's humor and pranks.

At midnight, the cousins, aunts, and uncles, some close, others distant, fed the mourners fry bread, beef soup, cakes, and pies, which they had brought. By one o'clock, the honor guard had saluted their fallen comrade, eaten with the mourners, and retired to cots in the air force tent.

The mourners who had tired left, replaced by those who waited outdoors. Some children slept in their mothers' arms; others made a place to sleep under the church pews. For the Lakota, it was a sign of respect that the church should stay full throughout the three-day wake.

At one-thirty, Clayton came back in. Less than forty years old, yet like a man suddenly aged, he moved haltingly toward the front of his church. He sat with his thin face buried in his hands. At two-thirty Clynda took him back to the house.

• • •

The air force men were up at dawn working noisily in their field kitchen. Between the busy Oglala women and the soldiers, some five hundred people were fed by 9 A.M. More than that number were fed at noon and again at 6 P.M.

For hours the mourners filed by, and like the night before, some women wept loudly in the traditional way, sending up a loud wailing; others stopped to look at the photos, dropped a sympathy card on the table, and knelt by the coffin. Toward the end of the procession, a mixed-blood girl named Marlene Turich stood in line with her mother. Between them they held seven star quilts. Quietly, without disturbing the quilt Mary had donated, they stacked them on the coffin and left. People whispered among themselves asking who this mysterious girl was.

When the long line had passed, Mr. Albert, the high school basketball coach, stood in the front of the congregation and spoke of Billy's skill. "Which despite his lack of height made him an asset to the team. And I'll never forget his spirit, because that is what sports is about. Not giving up. Hanging in there when everyone else has given up! This is how he lived and died." His voice cracked. "I never thought I would see this day, stand here speaking at Billy's funeral, because of all the students I have had in class or coached on the basketball court, none had an ounce more life than this young man."

It wasn't long after his comments that the congregation heard screaming outside. "He never did give a damn about you! He told me so!" Pauline Lone Elk's voice yelled angrily.

"We'll see who he loved and who's a big liar!" Linda Black Bear shouted back in Lakota. Mourners seated in church craned their necks, while those outside jockeyed for position to see. Cheryl Red Cuff pushed through the crowd. "Don't you have no shame!" she yelled. "Billy didn't care about either one of you. It was me he said he would marry!"

Inside the church Mary Hollow Horn began to rise. Clynda, much taller and stronger, reached over and forced her back into the bench. It seemed to

Clynda that half the teenage girls on the Pine Ridge Reservation had a claim on Billy.

Mary had never even slept with him, and she hated these girls for disturbing the wake, fighting over a dead man. Again she tried to rise; again a hand pushed her back onto the bench. This time it was her brother.

From outside came the sound of punches being thrown. Pulling hair, kicking and screaming, all three girls tangled in a flurry of jealous violence. Mary could take no more. She stood up and bolted through the crowd.

By the time she got outside, men held the screaming girls apart from each other. Mary leaped at Linda Black Bear. "Can't you see! He's dead!" she screamed, and landed a punch squarely on Linda's nose. Then some of the men grabbed her and pulled her away from the other girls. She twisted and strained to break away before she could calm herself.

A soft sputter of laughter went up from the congregation, but it was brief. Soon the high school track coach rose, walked by the honor guard and toward the front to speak. For a time everything returned to normal.

Pedor Sharp Face, a young member of the Body of Christ Church, led prayers, and then there was a short lull before another speaker. It was during this lull that Joanne Tall came in. She walked directly to the front of the church, threw all of the quilts on the floor including Mary's, and stomped angrily on them. "I want to put this one on him!" she said, spreading her own star blanket on the casket. Virgil Little Dog walked up to her and quietly asked her to leave. There were no more incidents that night.

While mourners filed by during the third night, the band played a few songs with Delores Hollow Horn singing lead. A small woman with a baby stood in the back of the church. Billy's aunt whispered to a lady beside her, "That's Colleen Kills Well, and that little girl is Billy Jo. That's Billy's little girl. He wanted to marry her and give that girl his name. Now it's too late, but at least there's the little girl."

Colleen quietly walked up to the picture and held it in front of the two-year-old. Then she walked over to the casket and placed the baby's chubby hand on it. She stood for a moment, then with every eye on her walked toward the back of the chapel. She spoke with Clynda for a moment, shook her hand, and was gone.

During the long evening, each of the band members took turns speaking of their friend. First it was James Hollow Horn the lead guitarist, then Bill Hollow Horn the base player, then their drummer Thomas Harvey, and finally his friend Gerald Ice.

The morning of June 24 spread like a turquoise dome across the cloudless horizon. At 6 A.M. the air force kitchen clanged with activity. Soon the honor guard entered the church dressed in fresh splendor. Cars waiting for the funeral service started to arrive by eight.

In the tiny bedroom of the two-room house, Clynda helped dress her sedated father in his best clothes. As he stood stiffly, like a display window mannequin, she buttoned his shirt and straightened his tie. Bernice moved slowly, trying on one maternity dress and then another, each time standing for long moments before the mirror as if time had no meaning.

Little Verla scampered in and out of the house, unaware that this day was to be any different than the next. In fact, she liked the big camp and all the attention that it brought her. Soon she and some little friends stood in the back of the half-empty church, giggling and pointing at the soldiers.

One by one the elders and leaders of the Body of Christ Church assembled. There was Bishop Ed Ridge who had been a preacher back when they were still called Holy Rollers. Calvin Pino and Wayne Whiting from Kyle and Clifford Sitting Cloud joined him. They huddled together shaking their heads and speaking in hushed tones, discussing which hymn should be used and how the service would be conducted.

Cars lined the narrow lane clear into Wounded Knee. Mourners continued filing by the casket, some as they had done each day, others for the first time. Members of the American Legion and VFW assembled at the side of the church, straightening their uniforms and filling their carbines with blanks.

At nine the little brass church bell clanged, signaling the mourners to move quickly past the casket, but it was to no avail. From Porcupine, Allen, Pine Ridge, and Manderson they came, hundreds strong. Finally, Ed Ridge, wearing his best black suit, looked at his watch, frowned, and signaled the congregation to order. It was almost eleven.

The cards and photos were gathered from the folding table, and it was replaced by chairs upon which the other preachers waited patiently. In the front two rows sat the immediate family, uncles, aunts, first cousins. Behind them sat the men from the legion.

In the narrow aisle on either side of the flag-wrapped coffin stood the honor guard at attention. People outside strained to see in through the windows and door. Many more paid their respects from the front seats of pickup trucks and cars that spread to the ridge top across the greening prairie.

From inside the church came the first strains of Merle Haggard's "Branded Man," sung by Delores Hollow Horn. The funeral service had begun.

When the song ended, the bishop rose holding his Bible. He walked to the center of the sanctuary and began the sermon. "Friends, we are gathered here on this sad but heavenly day to bid a joyous farewell to our brother in Christ, Frank William Jealous Of Him. His body is with us here today, but as we all know his soul has risen up!"

"Yeah!" rang through the congregation.

"Risen to another plane, to a better place, to be with the Father of us all!"

"Praise God!" rang out.

"He has laid down his life willingly that we may live in freedom!"

A resounding "Yeah!" filled the air.

"So even though it is sad for those of us left behind, it is a joyous day for Billy because he is in Heaven with our Savior Jesus Christ! He's not suffering now. His pain is lifted! His soul is standing in the brilliant light of Heaven! We know that if we die in faith, we will see him there one day: happy and smiling, laughing as he always did while he was with us on this earthly plane of sorrow." His voice rose and sank, sweeping the congregation into a rhythmic rapture.

When he was finished the church burst forth with a resounding "Praise God!" Then at the direction of Delores, the mourners burst forth with "Precious Memories."

One by one, the preachers rose and gave testimony. At noon, not familiar with Indian time, five air force jets streaked in perfect formation out of the northwestern sky. As was tradition, there was one plane missing. They flew over Porcupine, cracking the morning air like rolls of thunder. Rocking their wings they flew off, each in a different arc.

As if they could not let him go, the service continued for hours. It was well past one o'clock when Delores began singing "White Cross on Okinawa," signaling the end of the church service. At a command from the captain of the guard, the coffin was lifted by the soldiers and marched to the door of the church. They halted until the legion guard and family had assembled behind them.

"Bil-ly! Billy boy!" Bernice moaned over and over. Clayton walked stone-faced and glassy-eyed beside her. The children followed crying openly. Then they all moved forward in cadence under a perfect sky. Out through the crowd, the honor guard carried him to the waiting hearse.

Cars lined up behind the long black Cadillac, creating a continuous line from Grass Creek to Wounded Knee, from Wounded Knee to Porcupine, and up the dirt road to the cemetery. At two o'clock, cars were still driving slowly past Gildersleeve's store.

At the grave everyone sobbed as Bernice was handed the flag from the casket. Three salvos of seven shots rumbled into the air. Then in a quavering tone, taps blew. As male relatives took turns, Billy was laid to rest one shovelful at a time.

64

SEPTEMBER BROUGHT A CESSATION OF THE DAILY MONSOON RAINS THAT had sidelined the Second of the 22nd to an unguarded encampment south of Cu Chi. Two months late for R&R, Dale Nielsen squatted next to a can of boiling coffee reading the printed order.

"So where you headed, Hawaii or Thailand?" Ed Grubouski quizzed his buddy over a breakfast of steak slices.

"I wanted to go to Hawaii, thought I might even check out Hau, but I guess it's Australia. I thought it might be nice to see some civilization. Besides some officer got my slot for Hawaii. I've got five days to get arrangements made."

"Jeeze, man, the only guys who opt for Australia are looking for some white pussy! I thought you were married." Grubouski grinned broadly.

"God, you've got a one-track mind! I'm meeting Gail there. Since I kept getting canceled for Hawaii, I thought Sydney might be the next best thing. The Red Cross is helping her with flight arrangements and a passport."

"Bet you're pretty excited about seeing her?"

"Of course, Grub, she's my wife, and I'll get out of this armpit!" He tried to communicate excitement, but over the months in country an emotional numbness had grown toward everything in the real world. He wasn't sure if it included Gail.

• • •

A week later and two thousand miles away, a set of stairs was rolled into place and the door of a Qantas jet swung open. Dale sat waiting for the aisle to clear of its steady line of Aussie and U.S. servicemen headed for holiday. It was the smell of the perfumed stewardess that began the strange flood of thoughts an hour before. As he stood in the doorway, he could see the tall buildings, elevated highways, and sprawling suburbs, stretching like an American city in every direction.

His reaction was unanticipated, visceral, as if a veil of Olive Drab gauze had been lifted from his soul. As he slowly descended the ramp, behind the long line of noisy soldiers, his legs felt queer, foreign. With each footfall, his vision cleared and his heart began to pound more wildly; his lungs seemed tight. He became aware of a combat-acquired heaviness of heart and mind only in its lifting.

With each descending step, he felt noticeably different, but he could not identify the specifics of it. Certainly part of it was that Gail waited for him at the hotel. It was as if the imaginary bullet-proof, Plexiglas shield, acquired in the first days of combat, was suddenly dissolving. It left him vulnerable to feelings and sensations he'd almost forgotten. When his right foot hit the paved runway, his attention shifted to finding his wife.

In typical military fashion, all of the American men were herded onto a bus and driven downtown to the Three Kings Inn. It was a ten-story structure reminiscent of an American Sheraton.

At the front desk he was directed to room 301. He only hoped she was in and not out looking for him. His heart beat violently as the elevator carried him upward. He felt good, even aroused.

When he unlocked the door she jumped from the bed and grabbed him violently, kissed him, holding him long and hard. Moisture flowed freely down her freckled cheeks. He held her, at once profoundly happy and yet strangely ill at ease from the eight-month absence, the deaths, and the unrecognized, unresolved changes within.

After long moments she released him from the anxious embrace and leaned back a few inches, looking at him, noticing the tiny lines in his face. Though her husband had always been slender, Gail's hands now felt his ribs through his shirt. She did not mention it.

When their lovemaking was over, Dale felt weak and defenseless rather than warm and tired. He was possessed by an uncomfortable guilt, as if he shouldn't allow himself to feel good.

"If we get moving we can check out and find a motel on the beach," Gail said, breaking the silence. "I checked it out this morning, and there's a nice place right by the water."

Not wanting to think or be in charge, Dale smiled. "That sounds good to me. This place must be a fortune."

"Forty dollars a night!" Gail said, throwing her underwear into a bag. She slid on a pair of wide bells and a T-shirt and was ready.

The effect of her nipples floating beneath the thin cotton amused Dale. "I like the way you look in that T-shirt!"

"Oh, that's the way it is at home now. Women are liberating themselves!" She winked and led him out the door.

The little seaside motel was all that Gail had promised in her letter, sea breezes and the smell of salt drifting in the sliding glass door.

By four o'clock Dale was lying on the bed, hair wet with seawater and sand, sleeping deeply. Gail smiled at her husband, then pulled a romance novel from her bag.

That night, in a small café on the beach, they watched the sun turn the western sky ablaze in reds and pinks. "It's been a long time since I've thought of life after Vietnam," Dale said. "I guess there's a part of you that doesn't allow those kinds of thoughts. Like, if you think about it, maybe you're going to get scared, slow yourself down, react poorly, and lessen your chances."

Gail looked at him, popped a raw oyster in her mouth, and refilled his wineglass. That was the only thing he said about the war, and she didn't push him. "Mark is going to go to Black Hills State next year; major in theater. I guess he's pretty excited about it. But you know Papa Al; he wants Mark to go to a prestigious college. He thinks Black Hills is a waste of time and talent."

"That's Papa Al. Always lets us know when we've disappointed him!" Dale sighed.

They spent that evening strolling on the endless stretch of beach. The soothing and cleansing sea breeze blew gently as the two walked in an embrace. It was now the war that seemed distant and surreal.

. . .

The golden Sidney sun was high in an azure sky when they spread their towels near the shore. Tidepools and little creatures brought alive the biologist that had traded his microscope for an M-16. As when Dale was a boy, tiny animals moving beneath inches of perfectly clear water, going about their life's imperatives, scurrying between clumps of seaweed and anemones, totally captured his attention.

He watched a smaller male crab clinging tenaciously to the shell of its larger female companion. It all seemed so simple. His eyes moved over to Gail nestled on a towel between two large rocks. Her bikini top removed, resting peacefully in the warm sand, she reached up to brush a strand of brilliant auburn hair from her forehead.

He pulled a pack of cigarettes from his jeans and walked toward the water, the cool wetness splashing against his thin ankles. He felt the sand pull from between his toes, out from under his feet, like life itself. Life isn't forever, he thought. One moment you're standing on a boy's feet; the next, you're a man and the sand you stand on can be gone in an instant.

Thinking of Crocker, he stood watching the waves crash one by one, endlessly rolling up on the shore and then rushing back toward the ocean. In time he pushed the war away and thought about his own life, and how he would fill his days, if only he made it back home.

That night they made the mandatory journey to Grubouski's mecca of bars and clubs in downtown Sydney. Dale would not be able to face Grubouski, and the others, if he did not have tall tales to tell.

Whiskey A Go Go was legendary among the men in Vietnam. To them it was of purest adolescent fantasy. Rumor had it that it was filled with gorgeous, horny Aussie women looking for handsome, sex-starved American boys. Dale and Gail sat drinking gin and tonic water, watching the crowded dance floor, feeling the rhythm transferred from records through a sound system that vibrated the walls. All the while, perfectly shaped, half-naked girls gyrated in gilded cages high above the dance floor. Relieved that they would not have to participate in the silent sexual auction, the reunited couple enjoyed it for what it was and wasn't.

Sitting on the bed at 2 A.M., Dale watched the silver waves of high tide crashing against the rocks, refilling the tidepools with fresh seawater, nutrients, and oxygen. Tomorrow he would see what new secrets they held.

Gail touched him on the shoulder. "Honey, there's something I've been keeping for you. I think you should see it."

He turned to face her as she slid a frail newspaper clipping from her wallet and handed it to him.

He took it and held it near the lamp. His heart stopped. It was a picture of Frank, under the headline "Fallen Hero Returns To South Dakota For Burial."

> On June 9, 1969, Frank William Jealous Of Him was killed while trying to rescue a fallen comrade. Awarded the Silver Star posthumously, his body has been returned to Rapid City where it will be waked June 21 at the South Dakota School of Mines.
>
> He was a popular local musician preceding his induction into the United States Army and had often played for the students there. By special request of the college president and student body, a memorial service will be held there before his remains are delivered to Wounded Knee, his home community on the Pine Ridge reservation.

The article went on, but Dale's eyes had clouded up. He turned away, suddenly chilled by the offshore breeze. His throat gagging, guts cramping, he rolled over and pulled himself up into a fetal position. Gail covered him and switched off the light. It was a full half hour before the tears came.

65

TWO DAYS LATER THEY WALKED TOWARD THE PARK IN DOWNTOWN SYDNEY. It was noon, and businessmen were coming there to eat their sack lunches. Beneath a towering eucalyptus, Gail spoke of school, and Jean, and how the snow would fall in a few months. She could see that her man had much to say, but knew he found it hard, so she desperately tried to fill the gaps. There was a quality in Dale that had always kept her at arm's length, and now the distance seemed like a mile.

The Australian men in suits, who had left the world of banks and offices, picked out a favorite tree and sat. Some watched the rugby game now in full chaos; others moved a little further into the park to view the more orderly movement of a soccer match.

When they had picked out their vantage points, these businessmen and barristers removed their shoes and socks and rolled up their pants, as if in silent reverence for their ancestors who came to these shores in chains, barefoot and hungry. Allowing the cool, lush grass to fill the spaces between the toes, eyes closed for a moment, they leaned against the smooth gum trees, feeling the tropical breeze against the skin of their shins.

It was here that Dale found his voice. "I know I haven't said much . . . I know you've been patient . . ." He turned to face Gail, who now seemed embarrassed that Dale could read her thoughts. "I just haven't known what to say or what I have been feeling. Something happened when I got off that plane." Gail reached over and took his hand.

"I mean, it's like you're in a world of mud and grease and death one minute. There's a part of you that says, This is the way it is, like some weird, extended camping trip. The real world of clean clothes, and wives, and perfume is so far away. I guess I developed this attitude like I couldn't get killed.

"We had this captain . . . I wrote to you about him. His name was Crocker. He was like an officer in a movie, calm and brave and handsome. When he got his body bag, instead of getting more scared, I slowly adjusted to it . . . I guess I got the notion that the war had already taken him, and that it only wanted a few men like him. This sounds stupid." He blushed.

Gail squeezed his hand; her deep brown eyes studied him. "No, it doesn't. Please talk to me."

"Well, the war is like a starving monster. It eats men's lives to keep itself going, and, well, I figured if it got Crocker, maybe it would leave me alone." He dropped his head. A tear trickled down his bronzed cheek. "I guess I really believed that.

"I wasn't scared, never really scared like some of the guys, because I believed the war only wanted a few men like me. I tried to be like Crocker, calm and brave. It was as if I was only watching the war. Other men would tell me how scared they were, some would even cry, and then they would get blown away. I thought if I didn't allow myself to be scared, if I didn't allow myself the idea that I might get wasted, the war wouldn't see me. War would pass me over, like a hungry man at a buffet who quickly skips over the things he doesn't like." His voice cracked.

Gail withdrew her hand as if she feared what he might say next. She fumbled nervously through her purse for a cigarette.

Pulling a single blade of grass he ran his fingers over its green skin. "Getting off the plane the other day, something left me. I think it was my myth about the war, and my ego about men like me. There are no men like me. I'm only a man like Frank, and damn it . . . I want to go home." His voice now openly shook; tears ran down his gaunt face.

His wife had never seen him like this, and a familiar sensation sprang from the pit of her stomach, a foreboding she'd had for eight months, maybe longer. She'd dutifully kept it inside, at times wrestling it back; at other moments, exhausted by the effort, she had taken to drinking for comfort.

Dale cleared his throat. "Well, this morning, looking at the little crabs and shrimp in the tidepool, it hit me. Their lives are short. They are born, grow, reproduce, and then they die. They don't know a damned thing about years, or time, or the future. Young people are like that, stupid about life and death. But you can't always be like a snail or a fish! I know now that life is short. I want to go home and live it. I don't want to belong to . . . to live for the army or my dad. I want to live for me."

Gail felt a cold wind at her spine.

66

MATTHEW JEALOUS OF HIM SAT IN THE WARM TRAILER LISTENING TO THE radio. "San Francisco" crackled from the tiny speaker. He tried to think of what San Francisco might be like; he visualized friendly hippies. When the song said, "flowers in their hair," he could almost smell them. They would be dressed like gypsies, and the sun would be warm and feel good on his skin.

When the song ended, he stepped outside. The moon looked far away. It seemed to Matthew that it sat over a distant place, where it would be easier to think of the future instead of the past. Here the past held everyone fast in its bearlike grip.

• • •

The July day was hot before it began. In the yard sat a brand-new 1969 Chevrolet station wagon, its options sticker still emblazoning a window. Beside it sat a newly purchased year-old Ford pickup, its powder blue finish still shiny.

At breakfast Clayton studied his son, then handed him the steak and eggs. "So what do you think, Matt?! I got them to throw in plastic seat covers so we can keep the seats nice, till the kids are bigger. It even has electric windows and air-conditioning." He spoke in English between bites.

"It's nice, Dad, real nice," Matthew answered softly in Lakota.

"Oh, wait till you ride in it, it's so smooth." Bernice grinned at the thought. "They practically gave me the pickup. That salesman was thanking us, and telling us how much he appreciated our business!" Bernice went on as she sawed at the overcooked steak before her.

Clynda perceived Matthew's mood and remained silent.

"We're going to Rosebud Fair, aren't we, Clayton?" Bernice said, taking a bite. "We bought buckskin dresses for Clynda and Mom."

"We're leaving this afternoon. We'd like you to come with us and the little ones," said Clayton, still searching Matthew's face.

"No, I'm going into Wounded Knee and spend the weekend with Jim Hollow Horn. They're trying to teach me how to sing," he grinned. "They're not doing very well at it."

• • •

That night he stood with the band in Jim's house. Matthew had smelled of alcohol when he got there, and it created a tension.

"You ready, Congo?" said Jim. "One more time from the beginning. And one and two and three and . . ." The band smashed into the long, opening bars of "Proud Mary."

"When I get down to da river, gonna find a place where we can go."

At Matthew's every sharp and flat, Jim grimaced. By ten they sat outside drinking a bootleg beer. Matthew broke the silence. "You guys don't have to say nothing; I know I'm not Billy. It's you guys that wanted me to learn his songs, and I been trying." He looked downcast. "But I'm not Billy, even though I appreciate the chance."

He grabbed another beer and stood. "No hard feelings," he said, shaking Jim's large hand. He walked out into the darkness between the little frame houses, log cabins, and tarpaper shacks that were Wounded Knee.

67

RAIN SPLATTERED AGAINST THE THICK ALUMINUM DECKING OF THE APC. IT was steady, unrelenting. Inside Dale Nielsen slept fitfully. Dark images of men creeping in the darkness, of dead boys screaming from inside their poncho liners, all manner of horror invaded his sleep, snapped him awake.

The day had been one of the worst. In a world where "Don't mean nothin'" and "Press on" were gospel, Grubouski had said something that had registered. Try as he might, Dale's mind kept returning to that conversation. "They're fuckin with us, man. Fuckin with our heads!"

Dale's stomach had been upset that morning. He dismissed it as a flu bug or bad water, but it was persistent, weakening. At 1100 he sat next to Grubouski. "What do you mean fuckin with us?"

"It's like they know Crocker is dead, and we got an asshole running this outfit," Grubouski said, head down. "Or maybe they're getting revenge. Look at how many guys got dusted off just since you been back. That's more casualties than we had the whole time Crocker was in command."

Dale tried to shake Grubouski out of his funk. "Come on, Grub, you're letting this get to you. What am I gonna do if one of our best guys starts getting nervous."

Grubouski looked at Dale. "You got the second part right. I'm nervous, but I've been nervous before. I'm telling you it's all different now. Guys are coming and goin' so fast that I don't even get to know their names. I mean, that's fuckin nuts, man. Even the CO knows it. You ever see us using tanks before?"

Now at 0100 Dale lay wide-awake. Again he replayed the day. Three fire-fights in one day; all of them produced casualties. Two boys in Fourth Platoon had been decapitated. Late that afternoon they had all tucked in their tails and withdrawn.

. . .

By 1600 they had parked beside a tank. It dwarfed the APCs. At first the tank had made Dale feel secure; now Ed Grubouski had ruined that.

All the usual defensive activities had crowded the night. RPG screens were deployed, listening posts dug, and Claymores set. One thing was different: there had been none of the usual banter among the men. Besides, Dale thought, Grubouski's not a real complainer, not one to ignore.

He lay there hearing his Spec Four, "They're fuckin with us man!" while another part of his mind counted the wounded. Ten wounded, two dead. An increase in acid burned his stomach lining. "Fuck," he whispered. "Fuck!" He had never been this nervous before, certainly not at night. He couldn't shake it.

By 0220 he fell asleep again.

Fifty meters beyond the perimeter, the rain created a curtain of noise that in different circumstances would have been soothing. In the listening post out in front of the temporary firebase, it tortured Jackson's ears as he strained to hear into the blackness of the Rome-plowed jungle beyond the Claymores. He hated the moonless night. The loud rain forced him to use his eyes until they burned. No loud snaps would come from the soggy jungle tonight. No voices, or whispers, or footfalls could compete with the downpour.

Eyes wide, the black man moved his head back and forth until 0240 when he woke Private Stensen. "Man, you sleeping like a baby. The only thing louder than this fuckin rain is your snoring, man."

Stensen smiled. "I was having a good dream," he said, suddenly aware of how wet he was. "I was at home, and my mother was screaming at me about some socks. It was great," he whispered.

Jackson slid to the soggy bottom of the shallow pit. "Better key in so the boys don't get nervous." Stensen hit the key twice, then he crawled to the top of the muddy foxhole.

At 0257 an RPG slammed into the screen next to Dale's. His eyes flashed open. *Boom-Boom-Boom!* In rapid succession more RPGs blasted into the perimeter. Men began to scream.

A second barrage of incoming rockets arced over the screens and slammed into the command area. The new CO frantically pulled the radio from the wounded RTO. He keyed the listening post, keyed it again, then screamed,

"Come-on bo-oys! Give us a report!"

Boom-Boom-Boom! Rockets hit men in the mortar platoon as they tried to react. Dale's brain searched for a response. Why hadn't he woke when the first mortar tube popped? "Fuck!" He banged his head on the decking overhead. These things are loud . . . because they're not mortars. They're RPGs! Suddenly he was more than awake. Electricity shot through his groin. He fought the powerful urge to piss in his pants.

Images of little men overrunning the tiny perimeter flooded his mind as he crawled in the darkness of the track's belly. He tried to think of what to do, how to react, but drew a blank. They're fuckin with us, man! he almost cried.

There was a sensation in his brain he couldn't identify. It took hold of him, shoved him forward, moved his feet and hands. It lacked coherent thought; it drowned out the inner voice.

Up through the fifty-caliber hatch he forced his quivering torso. His hands leapt for the paddles of the gun. Directly ahead of Dale's position, bright flashes erupted in the jungle. Death rained in on them. Two rockets hit the track to his right. Men screamed short, gurgled cries.

Usually he would have remembered the men in the listening post, waited for them to call in that they were down, out of the path of fire. Tonight thoughts of other men never entered the orange-red fire that seared the insides of his skull, forcing him to flip off the safety. He fired madly into the jungle toward the source of the rockets. Hot casings cascaded through the hatch, burning his insteps, sending him into a mad dance.

"Fire at will!" he screamed to his squad. "Wake up! Fuckers, wake up!" A steady stream of red tracers flew from his fingers toward the flattened jungle. The shower of spent brass casings grew into a red-hot, slippery pile under Dale's bare feet, exaggerating his torturous jig, building the craziness in his cranium.

The tank beside him came to life, roaring out a torrent of beehive fléchettes that turned the invisible trees into a mulch.

More rockets poured in. In the brief white-hot flashes, the CO had seen at least six men get hit. He radioed in for an air strike. More flashes. Except for the awful wailing of their wounded and dying men, two more tracks from Alpha fell silent.

Even the newest of the men knew what this kind of accuracy meant. They were close and getting closer.

A volley of 4.2 mortar flares went up, illuminating the carnage and making visible the sappers running toward the perimeter. Dale screamed, "They're gonna overrun us! Fire! Fuckin fire!" as he fired volley after volley toward the running Vietcong.

Friendly shells exploded beyond the listening posts. In the command area the RTO was dying, the captain lay badly wounded but still functioning. When the last sapper lay crumpled over broken trees, the guns felt silent.

"What the fuck you yelling about?" Grubouski asked from the rifle pit. Dale focused on the words, the voice. What had been a raging brilliance of terror went dark as an old Zenith.

Dale noticed a numbness in his arms, felt the blisters rising on his naked feet and shins.

His first thought was to respond, to yell at his corporal, but his mind cleared, and he stood there dumbfounded. From the distance, Puff the Magic Dragon growled with revenge in the dark sky.

"I mean, forget those fuckers in the listening post! They're history, but you were drawing fire like arrows at a bull's-eye. What were you fuckin thinking about?" Grubouski asked angrily.

The words hit Dale's mind like a fragmentation grenade. He hadn't thought! He had not been coherent since he sat up in the track fifteen minutes before. He began to sweat, not the sweat of exhaustion, but the sweat of remorse, of guilt and embarrassment, of stark fear. He believed he had seen Jackson and Stensen shredded with fire from his fifty. Probably killed those men, he thought. He could not say it.

"Man, you're the one always telling us to wait, not to make a target of ourselves, and here you are, laying out a steady stream of tracers. I thought your barrel was going to melt." Grubouski was angry. "Coulda got your fuckin ass killed."

When the last dustoff helicopter pulled up at 0400, the area was quiet once again. The last thing the CO did before they loaded him was order the men to stay on alert that night. It was unnecessary.

Standing in the darkness at the fifty caliber, Staff Sergeant Dale Nielsen was in agony. The world was a new and frightening place. He crouched over the gun, reliving those fifteen minutes, horrified by the panic he had reacted to. Scared to death by the thought that he had killed two of his men.

At first light, the newly initiated shook himself from his private hell and volunteered to go out to the listening post. The lieutenant looked glum. "I know what you're thinking, Dale. All the shoulda's in the world aren't going to change what happened." He tapped him on the back and sent him into the torn underbrush. With a new, nameless replacement beside him, Dale crept forward, sick at what he might find, fearful of how he would handle his own verdict.

Twenty meters before the LP they came across a dead NVA, his uniform a crimson pulp of beehive rounds. Dale signaled the cherry to stay there; he would see Jackson and Stensen alone.

Dale's heart was in his mouth, he ached and sweat profusely. His breath came in hot gasps. Then he saw the back of Stensen's head. As he crept closer he could see the hair torn away in little patches. There was no blood.

Now on top of the shallow pit, his eyes swept the backs of their fatigue shirts. His exhausted heart pounded with joy. "I didn't kill them!" he muttered. As the verdict registered, he lifted Stensen's head. The blond boy's throat gaped open, slit ear to ear.

68

AT 0730 ALPHA COMPANY WAS ALREADY MOVING TOWARD THE DAY'S MISSION in the Boi Loi Woods. The company commander had divided the company by platoon, each assigned to a different but simultaneous search-and-destroy mission.

Dale looked out at the hateful terrain, still trying to shake the night raid out of his soul. Unlike during the early parts of his tour, Alpha Company now wore steel pots and flak jackets.

Sitting on the moving track had once been exciting, even exhilarating. Now he was silent. A backlog of repressed images were gradually crawling forward in the dark tunnels of his mind, moving into the conscious gray of memory.

In the harsh light of a sadistic sun, Grubouski studied his friend from across the track. Dale's sleeveless fatigue shirt hung as if on a skeleton. On his arm a huge boil was building. Its bright red swelling stretched the skin in his forearm tight. Grubouski noticed how Dale sat there lost in his thoughts, nervously sucking air between his front teeth. His sergeant's eyes had the hollow look of an old man. The skin on his face, dark from the sun, barely covered the bones.

While the tracks ground forward, past large stands of trees and Rome-plowed mulch, Dale's thoughts went from gray to black. He pictured the gaping slit on Stensen's throat, but even more vivid was the shocked look on the dead boy's face.

It wasn't that he minded dying so much. Dying wouldn't be so bad. It simply would be over, he figured. He'd be hit, then the light would slowly fade to a pinpoint, and then darkness. It was the thought of being maimed. Of being sent home a cripple, some "thing" people felt sorry for. He didn't want that. His chest sagged under the flak jacket, his breathing already in the early stages of hyperventilation. It was as if the person inside of him had DEROSed and a replacement consciousness had been assigned to his body. The replacement was clearly very scared.

Standing on the deck of his APC, like a spit-and-polish cavalry officer, the temporary company commander, Captain Zonne, signaled to circle the wagons. In front was a steep riverbank, lined with thick jungle.

Grubouski nudged Dale, nodding toward the captain. "Does that real well, don't he!"

"Real well!" Dale forced a grin.

Zonne shouted, "Dis-mount!"

Lieutenant John McShane stood on the dry earth shaking his head like he knew better. He was new in country, but he realized the essence of the track platoon was to have them at the ready, to move up with the dismounts and repress the enemy with firepower. They had turned his platoon into grunts.

"This is fuckin incredible," Grubouski said under his breath. He snapped his flak jacket.

Dale stared into the trees across the river and shook his head. "Fuckin incredible." His voice shook.

He didn't care if Grubouski noticed. He thought a lot about Grubouski. Since that mistake on the fifty caliber two nights earlier, his friend seemed to act differently. He had always looked for Ed's respect, and now believing it was gone, he hated himself.

A pressure was building inside his chest, so real it almost had color and substance. It was building into a drive to say "fuck it!" and run. He only prayed that no one saw it. He had given up trying to push it away.

When his feet hit the cool water of the narrow river, his bladder revolted, compelling him to pee. He had barely reached midstream when he relieved himself.

Within seconds all twelve dismounts had assembled on the far bank. Lieutenant McShane motioned for Second Platoon to come on line. Dale's squad of four men would take point. Lieutenant Hodges did the same with First Platoon, heading his men off to the east.

The captain stayed in the protective circle of tracks with his two RTOs, the drivers, and fifty-caliber gunners.

Second Platoon moved west some 150 meters, then north. Upstream 300 meters, First Platoon, with its cherry Lieutenant Hodges in command, had crossed, turned north, then organized into a line assault of twelve men. They moved slowly forward into an area of low shrub and elephant grass. There was no one on point.

The jungle canopy above Second Platoon was shattered by warfare. In the sunny spots, heat bore down on the crouched men, creating a thirst worse than any Dale could remember.

Grubouski crept up beside him. "We ain't a fuckin leg unit! The man in charge has lost it. Humpin' through the jungle! What the fuck is this?"

Dale managed a faint smile and shrugged his shoulder. That was all Grubouski wanted; he fell back five meters, just ahead of Lieutenant McShane.

A piece of Dale's mind wondered if Grubouski had seen something different in him. He was sure the redhead had. There was a part of him that started to hate his friend. The man had always complained, so that couldn't be it. In the long moments as Second Platoon inched forward, Dale stumbled on the source of his hate. He had been cored like an apple somehow, emptied of his false notions of life and death and invulnerability. Stripped of his warrior identity. But Grubouski remained the same.

Ahead, the jungle grew thicker; the heat soared. This was no bunker system or a simple assault. They knew from intelligence that this was probably a staging area, an NVA base camp. The tracks lay one hundred meters back, hopelessly stranded on the other side of that creek. Dale's intestines cramped.

Crack, Crack, Crack. A nervous AK-47 opened up. The squad dropped to their chests. Denning, the M-60 gunner, signaled for his assistant. They belly-crawled out of sight. Dale motioned for Lieutenant McShane, his RTO, and the rest of the platoon to follow. Twenty meters ahead, Denning set the pods of his M-60 down. The assistant gunner snapped two belts together.

Denning looked back at Dale. Dale reswallowed breakfast, then nodded in the affirmative. The gunner dropped to his chest and opened up, *Dow-Dow-Dow!* The big gun tore into the green ahead. After three long volleys from the M-60, Dale was up and moving toward the front. Far to his right, he could hear the faint staccato of AK fire. Bullets tore the trees overhead. The ten M-16s from Second Platoon opened on automatic. Screams were heard from the trees beyond.

Seconds later the firing stopped, and so had the screams. Head pounding, breathing heavily, Dale signaled Lieutenant McShane to order the men to advance.

Through a clearing they could see four foxholes. In at least one sprawled a dead NVA.

A faint barrage of shots came from the distant First Platoon. In the well-dug VC foxholes, Dale's Second Platoon found two more dead and one living, very horrified Vietnamese boy cringing against the bottom. He seemed to be praying. Dale nudged the boy with his gun, and the Vietnamese rolled over mumbling. Tears ran down his small face. "He's probably a cook. These guys didn't know what they were doing. They're not line soldiers." Dale's voice came in short gasps, but it sounded familiarly efficient. "Search the area."

He signaled for McShane and the RTO to come up. McShane cleared his throat "We got three NVA KIA and one prisoner. We're conducting a search of the area. Will report back. Over." McShane's radio clicked twice.

Dale looked at his platoon. Three NVA dead and not a scratch, he thought, trying to build his confidence. But then he remembered his own words: "They're probably cooks."

Grubouski and Denning pulled the rifles from the fingers of the dead NVA. A fifth hole was found and Dale was signaled. "It's a tunnel. I need a volunteer to go down there." Ed Grubouski volunteered and smiled at Dale. Dale saw it as a victory sneer.

Out of the hole came bundles of food, clothing, and two Chicom grenades. Grubouski was breathing hard; sweat mixed with dirt dripped down his face. "You were right. This complex is not a defensive position; it's living quarters."

McShane radioed in the results of the search, but before he could make his request the transmission was interrupted.

Captain Zonne was excited. "First Platoon's been hit bad. I want you to pull back. We are going to move east, sweep their area, and pick up their wounded. Over." Back in the security of the track perimeter, Zonne made it sound easy enough.

When Second Platoon had finally traversed the 300 meters of ruined jungle and grass, they found what was left of First Platoon huddled in a narrow creek drainage.

Dale was frightened by what he saw. The platoon was down to five men standing. On the ground he saw one wounded and one wrapped in a bloody poncho liner. McShane walked up to one of the squad leaders. "Sergeant Esswein, what's the situation?"

The man looked scared, and confused. "We were fired at by a sniper. We took him out with no casualties . . . As we advanced, machine gun and AK fire got Lieutenant Hodges and his radioman. We pulled back . . . When we advanced to deal with the wounded, they hit us again with machine-gun and AK fire. That's when Stearns and Jacobs here got hit. The LT and RTO are still up there."

McShane's nose twitched. "Fu-uck!" he cursed the operation. He called for his RTO and grabbed for the headset. "Red Eagle One, this is Red Bird. We've got big trouble down here. We've got two wounded still in the kill zone, two more, one dead; the other wounded are ready for Charger dustoff. Should we call in arty? Over."

"That's negative, Red Bird. I want a rescue squad assembled and sent back in. I want that machine gun taken out. Is that clear. Over!"

Dale looked up, hating Captain Zonne. High above them the battalion commander's Loach seemed to float silently in the sky. He hated the Higher Higher man too.

Then he looked over at the shattered group of men that had been First Platoon. Good men when they had their tracks, they now sat on the ground demoralized, nervously smoking cigarettes.

McShane spoke to his platoon. "I want our platoon to move up and bring out the missing men." There was total silence. No one moved.

McShane signaled Dale to move closer. Dale spoke to the inexperienced lieutenant in hushed tones. "Sir, it's a suicide mission and for what? I'm afraid we're going to get some boys killed trying to bring out some bodies. Dying for dead men, sir, it doesn't make sense." Dale's voice almost pleaded.

"I know," McShane responded, "but we don't have a choice. One of the dead is an officer and the Higher Higher will not let that body be captured ... it's policy. I want you to organize Second Platoon for a rescue mission."

Cold sweat poured down Dale's back; his mouth tasted like shit, and his knees shook. "OK! Second Platoon up!" was all he said. Grubouski stood, followed by the M-60 gunner Denning, Smitz, Holland, and Private Stallings with the rest of the men. No one from First Platoon rose. They only looked at each other with whipped faces.

Dale's mind reeled. The black thoughts of the morning returned. He knew with certainty he would not see some of these faces again. He was asking them to sacrifice themselves for the dead, and he hated himself. Damn! He hated the war.

Balancing the building panic was this new sensation of icy-cold, bitter resentment. He hated with a blinding passion the insanity of what he was about to do.

He turned to Sergeant Esswein, the surviving NCO from First Platoon. "What the fuck does it look like up there?" He even hated the question.

"At the top of that hill, up about one hundred meters, there's a bunch of little grass- and brush-covered mounds. Some or all of them are bunkers. You, you can't see the fuckers." His voice seemed to beg for forgiveness.

All but ignoring his "pretend" lieutenant, Dale signaled his platoon to come around him. "I want you men to buddy up, get all the frag grenades you can carry and keep your fuckin heads down. This is bad enough! We don't need anybody else dead." When they had gathered all of First Platoon's grenades, Dale motioned them to move to the far bank of the narrow stream.

Running at a crouch, with Grubouski on point, thirteen men disappeared into the elephant grass. McShane and his RTO took the center. Fifty meters in, legs cramping, Second Platoon dropped to their stomachs. From here they could see nothing.

Long, agonizing moments later, Dale thought he could feel the eyes of the man in the machine-gun bunker searching the bush. He sensed the enemy's eyes on him! Crawling on their hands and knees for another five tense minutes, Second Platoon closed the gap. Lieutenant Hodges, eyes staring dull and blue in death, and the luckless radio operator were within grasp.

DuhDuhDuhDuh! The NVA machine gun banged to life. Denning crumpled onto his face, moaning loudly. White horror ripped through Dale's bowels. He hadn't seen a thing and already he'd had a casualty. "Fuckin madness," Dale choked. "Pull back!" he yelled. Grubouski pulled back the body of the dead lieutenant; Holland dragged the First Platoon RTO. Under sporadic machine-gun fire, Assistant Gunner Smitz dragged the unconscious Denning and his gun back.

Back at the bottom of the ravine, Lieutenant McShane radioed Zonne. "Red Eagle 1, two missing men were KIA. We need immediate medevac. Spec Four Denning needs an urgent evac."

Dale and Smitz had grabbed Denning and carried him down the hill. When he had caught his breath, Dale called to his lieutenant. "Sir, I think you should call in arty; we got the bodies."

McShane was standing with Sergeant Esswein from First Platoon, looking at the ground, shaking his head in disgust. He motioned for his sergeant. "Well, Dale, I got bad news. Seems Sergeant Fuck-up here can't count. Now he says there were four men down up there. There are two guys still up there."

Dale snapped. "Well, that's fine, John, you just take this fuck-up and go right back in there and get them. I'm having a smoke and a Coke. This is a death trap. I am not asking my men to go back in. Those men are probably dead." He heard his own voice, then thought of Stensen and Jackson out in the listening post, and cut short his tirade.

McShane got Captain Zonne on the radio. "Looks real bad here, Red Devil. There are still two men from First Platoon unaccounted for. I feel I should tell you things are bad down here. We're losing good men, sir. That nest can see us but we can't see him. Over"

The captain was irate. "I don't care! We are not going to leave dead or wounded in there. The Higher Higher is ordering in a smoke screen. When it's down I want you to rush that position. I don't want to hear from your sorry asses until you've taken out all of the missing men! We do not, I repeat do not, call in arty from Dau Tieng until then. Do you hear me? Over."

"Yes, sir. Out!" The lieutenant slammed the headset down.

The men of Second Platoon sat under the cover of the riverbank cursing the captain while they ate C-rations and drank warm pop.

Within minutes the steady drone of helicopters distracted them. McShane looked at the men from First Platoon. They weren't looking at him. "All right, I want Second Platoon back up the hill. As soon as the smoke screen is down, I want you men from First up and moving. There's two more bodies up there. I want you to retrieve them and get your asses out of there."

Grubouski and Dale were the first two up. The rest lingered, weighing the effects of disobeying orders.

From the southern horizon, one helicopter dropped in over the dustoff site; the other swung wide for a pass over the ambush site. The other men in Second Platoon stood and slowly climbed the deadly embankment.

On first pass, a weak screen of white smoke left the chopper. Dale's head pounded, he could hear his own heart, but he struggled with every fiber to stay in control. Barely managing to wave his arm, he signaled the men to wait for the second pass.

Past the ambush site the Cobra gunship turned west, then turned back over the area where the tracks were parked, then east for another pass over the kill zone.

Dropping low, smoke emerged from small canisters on the skids. The bird headed straight into the ambush site. The machine gun in the nest opened up. To the horror of the men on the ground the Huey wobbled, then lifted, circling back toward the west. The men of Second Platoon watched in helpless wonder as the helicopter began to slowly rotate on its axis, dropped, and impacted the soggy land not far from the waiting tracks.

Dale looked at McShane. The man was trembling, shaking his head, cursing the day he ever met the ROTC recruiter.

"Let's go!" Dale yelled. A barrage of moans and cursing came from the eleven men in the draw. They moved up the hill away from safety. At the crest of the hill they dove in unison for the ground, noses in the dirt.

Dale shouted. "Take turns, one throwing grenades, the other laying down suppressive fire." Inch by inch they crawled forward.

Back at the track perimeter, screaming and confusion broke out. Two hundred meters away the Cobra lay in a crumpled heap. "I want volunteers!" Captain Zonne shouted. "Someone's got to check on those men in the Cobra. I need volunteers for a medevac. You will be rewarded!"

After a long hesitation, two men from the track perimeter jumped off, moving in the direction of the dead Cobra.

Ten meters from the machine-gun nest, Dale finally saw it. He pointed, then signaled the men to move up. The bunker was low, made of heavy logs. The gun slit was small. From it protruded the fat barrel of a thirty-caliber machine gun. As if it had eyes, the black metal tube moved back and forth searching for a victim. To his right PFC Hancock rose up to toss a grenade. Holland laid down fire. The grenade fell two meters from the hole. Shrapnel flew back into the squad. Two men screamed as tiny fléchettes hit them.

This time, someone to the left of the line rose to his knees. Dale could not see who it was, but the machine gunner did, and Second Platoon suffered its next serious casualty of the day.

Dale turned to look for McShane, who was lying facedown in the dirt to his right. "John, this is crazy. We've got to get arty to soften this fucker up." McShane raised his head enough for Dale to see the wild fear in his eyes. The panicked lieutenant managed to shake in the affirmative, and Dale signaled his platoon to pull back.

Back in the narrow streambed the wounded were beginning to be loaded on a medevac. The dead were to be extracted to Graves Registration later.

Dale listened to McShane on the radio. "Red Devil, it's bad over here, real bad. We got to have an artillery strike. We can't get close. Every time we do, we take another casualty."

There was a pause, then the radio crackled. "I'll call Red Eagle and see what he says. Out." Grubouski pulled out a can of pork and beans and started to devour them, then shrugging, offered some to Dale. Dale smiled and declined. The radio crackled again. "Red Bird, I have just spoken with the Red Eagle One. He rejects your request, says we've got to get all of the men back before we call in arty. You've got your orders, follow them! Out."

Once again the lieutenant approached Dale. It was now obvious to all of the men who was in charge. "What the fuck are we going to do, Dale?"

Dale looked at the Huey lift off with Denning. "I don't know, sir, have lunch I guess."

The men from First Platoon still sat exactly where they had been before the last advance.

Moments later the crackling voice of Captain Zonne came on the radio again. "The man upstairs wants to know what the hell is going on. I told him you were ready for another assault. Over. Get your asses in there. Out." McShane started to pace and mumble to himself.

All of the men were filthy, covered with sweat and dirt. All were swearing and complaining. Then Holland stood. "With all respect, Dale, I'm not going back in there. You can all go to fuckin hell."

"I'm not going either!" another yelled. "Not until they call in a strike. I'm not dying for some dead asshole!" Soon all the men except Grubouski were up, standing, yelling at Dale and McShane. Dale looked at his lieutenant and whispered, "Have you ever heard the expression 'fragged'? Well, that's what's going to happen to you and me if we try going up there again without an artillery strike first. I think I can calm them down if they hear an artillery strike."

McShane motioned for the RTO, grabbed the headset, tried to calm himself, then spoke. "Red Devil, it's getting worse over here. These men have had it, sir. They won't move and First Platoon has not moved since the first ambush. Red Dog says we need an artillery strike. Over."

A stream of profanities came from the set. Then, "I'll try once more Red Bird, but Red Eagle is going to have your ass."

"He can have it!" McShane said, loud enough for Dale to hear.

Back at the tracks, Captain Zonne called the colonel. "Red Eagle One, we got a situation developing with the men on the ground. It seems they don't want to move up until they hear an artillery strike. Over"

There was a pause. Then, "Well, you tell those sorry sons of bitches that I'm coming down for a visit, and there will be court-martials! Out."

Zonne didn't bother to call McShane back. He jumped from the track and signaled the RTOs. "All hell is about to break loose. We better be over there when the colonel lands." The three men left the perimeter, heading toward the draw.

Grubouski was the first to hear the Loach descending to their position. He waved for Dale to look up. "Fuck! I don't believe it!" Dale muttered.

"I don't care if God himself comes down here; I'm not moving!" Holland looked straight at McShane, hatred glittering in his gray eyes. Trembling he pointed his rifle at McShane. Others stood and did the same. The colonel's Hughes Cayuse rattled the air to the south, then came in low, landing behind the swale.

By the time the battalion commander jumped from the bird, the men had lowered their guns. In three furious steps he was in McShane's face screaming. "Where's Zonne? Who's in charge here?"

One of the enlisted men said "No one!" A giggle went up.

McShane cleared his throat. "I am, sir."

"You look like you fucking are!" the colonel growled.

He turned to face the men. "What is wrong with you sorry sacks of dog shit? We got men out there, down, wounded, dying wondering when you fuckin chickenshits are going to rescue them, and here you sit! Well, I got something for you men that go up there and find the wounded. I've got the thanks of the United States Army. But I got something a lot less cordial for you fuck-ups that refuse, and that is a general court-martial. I'll have your sorry asses court-martialed!" he screamed.

Dale studied the man. Not since high school drama club had he seen a staged performance like this. The colonel had all the right moves, all the right words, his uniform was crisp, his face appropriately red with anger.

Just then Zonne emerged through the grass with the two radiomen. Sergeant Esswein stood up and moved near Zonne.

"Where the Sam Hill have you been, taking a group dump? I thought you were in charge here!"

"I am, sir," Zonne panted. Dale began to see that all of this was an act, staged for the purpose of intimidating frightened boys into dying only to make a point. Just what the point was, however, remained unclear.

"What I see here is a breakdown in command. I want this reported and I want anyone, I repeat, any sorry ass who is not on their feet and headed for the ambush site, court-martialed. I want those men to feel the full extent of military justice. Is that clear?"

"Yes, sir!" the captain saluted. The colonel waved him off and stomped back toward the bird. Dale almost clapped.

"You heard what the colonel said," the captain yelled. "Get moving!" No one moved.

Sergeant Esswein spoke up. "I'll organize what's left of First Platoon to support Second." The colonel spun at the door of the tiny helicopter. "Now that's the fuckin spirit. What's that man's name!"

"Esswein," the captain called out.

The colonel jotted something on a little pad, then jumped into the plastic bubble and signaled the warrant officer to take him back up.

When the bird's blades had spun to life, Grubouski turned to Dale. "What an asshole!" Dale didn't hear him. He was too busy hating Esswein.

"You heard the colonel . . . get your asses moving!" McShane yelled. After a long pause, without a word to his men, Dale stood up, followed by Grubouski, then McShane himself.

Climbing the small hill, Dale was sick with fear. With every movement he fought panic. His limbs were weak, exhausted, and shaking. His mind was almost incoherent with the bright, searing red of fear. "Oh God . . ." he muttered. "Oh my God." Only Grubouski heard him.

At the top of the knoll Dale stopped and stuttered. "I, ah, we're going to get this fucker. Work in teams. Try to get inside past his fire zone." He scribbled in the dirt. "Watch his barrel, and keep your fuckin heads down. If you stay down until you're ready to throw, that guy can't hit you."

With that said, the men slithered forward. Thirty meters from the bunker, Dale looked back for Sergeant Esswein and First Platoon. If they were back there, they were invisible.

Ten meters from the deadly barrel, Dale fought his own crazed thinking long enough to signal the men to keep their heads down and move in closer. He vaguely realized the gun couldn't shoot at the ground and that with each inch forward, the clearance above the men actually grew.

Six meters from the hole, Dale signaled a halt. He had forgotten entirely about McShane.

Pulling a frag grenade from his fatigue pants, he tried to calm himself. Grubouski nodded his head and Dale was up. The one-pound canister flew through the air tumbling, shining in the sun, and exploded on top of the enemy bunker. The gun roared to life, raking the air. Bullets struck the earth behind them.

Then it was Grubouski's turn. Up he went, on his knees while Dale fired at the opening in the bunker. *Crack-Crack-Crack.* Again a black can arced up over the grass straight for the hole, then dropped short. *Whoomph!*

Five other teams did the same. Grenades landed everywhere but in the tiny hole. The gun kept firing, unaffected by the blasts outside.

On Grubouski's fifth try, he pulled the pin, rose, tossed the grenade, then yelled, "I'm hit!" Grabbing at his chest, he fell in slow motion.

Dale's mind raced, He's not hit! But Grubouski lay there not moving. "Fucker thinks he's funny," Dale muttered desperately to himself. Thick grass blocking his view, he could not see a wound. His mind flashed to the night when he got shrapnel in his neck. He'd yelled the same thing. That's it! Ed's taken a little piece of shrapnel. What a dramatic fucker! Dale decided. Thinks he's John Wayne.

"Ed! How bad you hit?" No answer. Dale's panic became total. He slid over to his buddy, the only man who had gone the distance with him, and nudged him. There was no response. Dale knew he was teasing. Grub is always teasing. He wouldn't go out like this! Leave me alone up here! He grabbed the limp man's shirt and tugged him back until they were clear of the relentless gun.

"Grub?!" He shook his friend. "Ed, you bastard, come on!" he punched the man. He did not move. There was a perfectly round red hole in his shirt. Dale studied the face. It was peaceful. The eyes did not stare out, bulging in death's horror from the face. They were closed, sleeping. "Grub!" Dale was now crying, sobbing beside the man. "Fuckin Grub." He lay there sobbing for seconds that seemed like minutes. "Got to get you out of here, man."

He grabbed Grubouski's hand. Then crawled forward. "Holland, Grub's hit. Take him back."

Holland was thrilled at the order. "Sure thing!" He slithered toward Grubouski.

His throat salty, mud and tears streaking his haggard twenty-year-old face, Sergeant Dale Edward Nielsen couldn't think. Could not organize his thoughts. Still his toes pushed him forward. He hated his toes, he hated Grubouski. He despised himself and his bravado, his bullshit about death not being the worst. His mind had spun one hundred eighty degrees on that one.

Death was the worst thing, and he was going to die. He knew it. Right here in this patch of shrubs and red dirt. "I'm going to die!" he moaned. Still his body inched forward, while his nose dug a furrow in the dirt and decay of the jungle floor.

He began to mumble. "Shoulda stayed home. Shoulda stayed home . . .," over and over. He had killed himself and he knew it, just as if he had pulled the trigger himself. In his mind's eye, Dale could see the sun setting over the Black Hills. All he wanted now was to see that again. "Why did I do this?" he muttered.

Now the gun port was four meters away. Tilting his head, Dale could see the opening of the muzzle. His heart rose again. Nobody's been this close, he thought. Nobody. His ears pounded, but he was too weak to move. He could taste the dirt in his mouth, smell it in his nose. This is what it must be like to be dead, he thought. Terror pinned him to the ground, weakened him. He tried to rise, but he shook so badly nothing happened. Then he collapsed and wept openly. "Please, God, I want to go home!" he wailed. He dug his fingers into the wet loam wanting to get below the earth. "Please, God, get me out of here. God, I just want to go home." He hugged the narrow stock of the bush in front of him. He blubbered and prayed with the bitter tears of an atheist who hopes without hope that all his arguments about death and God are wrong.

Then he thought of Ed. Slowly the boy's sun-reddened face, his stupid smile, appeared to him. A slight calm overtook him. He would simply die and join Ed. Dale twisted to see the deadly muzzle: it laid down fire, first to the left of him, and then started to swing right. He pulled a grenade from his pants.

A steady stream of green tracers and bullets flew out. Chopped grass, shrubbery, and dirt filled the air only a few meters behind him. When the awful gun was directly at him, he inched up. Then when it sprayed to his right, he was on his knees pulling the pin. When it began its slow return, Dale threw. He knew it was impossible even before the grenade cleared his hand. His heart sank as he fell to the earth.

The tiny can spun end over end. In a low arc it floated downward into the tiny hole. A smile came at once to Dale's agonized lips. Then there was a blinding flash. The deadly barrel flew from the bunker. An arm landed at Dale's feet.

69

MATTHEW SAT IN FRONT OF THE OLD TRAILER ON HIS BROTHER'S BLOCKED-up Buick staring at the new station wagon. Its contact-paper wood shone in the late August sun. Then he looked at the new pickup, its white, metal fender already creased by a careless brush with the fence post at the turn. Finally his eyes came to rest on the tiny church.

It had been months since Billy's funeral, since music or prayer had come from inside. A loose clapboard had broken off, exposing the building's ribs. Under a peeling eaves hung an abandoned mud swallow's nest. A wasp hive clung to the other.

The cook shade had not been rebuilt since June. Its yellowed pine boughs, now sparse, had mixed a layer of needles into the gumbo dust. Trash and broken toys littered the once-neat churchyard.

It was past noon when they heard it. They'd heard it before, yet with each repetition the honk of the station wagon's horn became more alarming. Matthew stood, as did Clynda, and looked out through the glass in the door toward the Chevy. Like the five times before, there was no one in it.

About two o'clock, Bernice wrapped her head in a new scarf, and the new baby, Bobbie Jo, in a bright star blanket. She climbed into the green pickup beside Clayton and Verla; Carol and Julie climbed into the box. After starting the engine, Clayton called to Matthew. "Heading toward Martin, need anything?" Matthew shook his head.

By dusk they had not returned. Clynda and Matthew sat outside waiting for the August heat to leave the house. There had been little to eat. Peeling and frying potatoes together, they had made the best of it. Few words had passed between them.

Now the boy sat under the stars in silence, staring first at the church, then at the Chevy Bel Air.

"Something's really bothering you, isn't it?" Clynda sat on a block of wood looking at her volleyball. In the glow of the bare bulb by the door, its worn surface reflected moon blue. "It's the car, isn't it? You don't like it that Mom and Dad got a car with that money from Billy's GI insurance. Don't you think they should have something nice just once?"

"That's not it, Clynda; just leave me alone." His voice sounded resentful.

Clynda turned to face him. "You think I'm too young to understand? Well, I'll be fifteen soon, and I think that's old enough to understand a lot."

"Jeeze! Just pouty, aren't you?" Matthew pushed her on the shoulder like Billy used to. "That's partly it, the car. I guess there might have been a better way to remember Billy, but I'm not even sure what it is. All I know is that I'm leaving pretty soon.

"The other day Dad was drunk and he was looking at me. It was as if he hated me for being alive, like he wished it was me that got killed. And there's something else . . . I think Billy is out there somewhere." His arm indicated the hills near the house. "Like he's going to walk up the road and be here, that it was the wrong body in that casket, and that he's going to walk right up the road and just be here. In a way, I want to be here when he gets home, to stay here until he does."

She walked to the ball and picked it up. "That's not so hard to understand. I have all kinds of weird thoughts too."

Matthew went on. "But that's only part of it. Part of what I think. Why does the horn on that car beep by itself? Everyone calls that 'Billy's car.' Maybe it is. Maybe Billy is not coming back, maybe he's already back and he wants to be near us." A mild chill descended Clynda's long back. She tossed the ball at Matthew.

It was ten when the horn sounded again. Matthew jumped like a nervous cat. Clynda spilled her coffee.

• • •

Bernice and Clayton had come back late and slept in. It was noon and Matthew had already been to town, seen the bootlegger, and gotten himself worked up. He wobbled slightly as he walked into the yard. Before him, under a bright sky, stood the big station wagon with its keys hanging in the switch. Tossing a brown paper bag through the open driver's window, he pulled the door open.

The clear vinyl seat covers of the station wagon were hot under his legs. "I'll show her who can drive her fancy car," Matthew said to no one. The new tires skidded, spinning loudly on the hard ground, throwing dust toward the house. The same fence post that had scarred the pickup snapped against the large chrome bumper.

Bernice came running out of the little house. "Clayton! Clayton, that alcoholic son of yours is stealing the car!" Clayton stuck his head out the door, rubbing the sleep from his eyes.

The station wagon sped toward the main corner in Wounded Knee, then swung north to Porcupine. As he dropped below Porcupine Butte, Matt thought he felt someone in the car with him. Barbed wire and blacktop whizzing by, he said, "Take some and pass it back."

Just before he saw Porcupine, he again felt someone was sitting by the passenger door looking out. When he looked again there was no one, nothing but the bottle of cheap burgundy and the crumpled sack.

At Emma's house, he beeped the horn. She came out smiling as usual, but when she got close, her expression changed to worry. "What is it, Congo?"

Matthew slapped the seat. "Get in. I want to take you for a ride in Billy's shiny new Bel Air station wagon!"

"I can't," Emma said. "I would, but Mom and Dad wouldn't like it, besides . . . ," she laughed, "you've been drinking."

He grinned back. "A little." His head swung heavy on his shoulders. "I was thinking how highly everyone thinks of this new car with electric windows." He played the glass up and down. "And I was thinking of my best girl and, well, I thought I should take you for a ride to Scenic or Rapid." He pushed the passenger door open. "Get in!" This time his tone was adamant.

Emma tried to smile and pushed the door closed. "I can't, but maybe if you come back later, and I ask, and if you're sober, I could."

Five miles north of Porcupine, Matthew realized his passenger was back. He didn't remember when he had stopped for him, but he was there. He passed the last of the bottle over to him and said, "Feenish it!" The car squealed on the hot pavement.

"Pretty quiet, aren't you?" He looked over at his passenger. The smiling man looked familiar, but still he didn't answer. Near Twiss's Ranch, after a draw on the bottle, Matthew tried once more to engage his smiling friend into conversation. "Whatdoyou think of mywheels man?" he tried in English, then in Lakota. Still the man only grinned.

"Who the hell doyou thinkyouare?" Matthew was getting angry with his quiet passenger. "Riding in mycar and youwon't eventalk withme?"

Head nodding, brow creased, Matthew stared at his passenger. Except for the pale skin and quietness, it could have been . . . "Billy?"

The car flew past the critical point before Matthew noticed the curve. He wrenched violently on the wheel with a force that separated the right front tire from its rim. The car slid loudly off the narrow road and up against an embankment. In a thunderous rending of metal and glass it sailed up toward heaven, then landed flipping end over end. When it came to a stop, Matthew was lying on the vinyl ceiling.

• • •

The face was wet with a mixture of blood, wine, and vomit. The officer held the light on it for a moment. "It's Matthew Jealous. He doesn't look too good, better get the back board," he yelled toward the car.

When he was out of the smashed wagon, and strapped down to the back board, he opened his eyes, looked at the wrecked car, and said, "There wasaguy in there withme, youbetter help him." The tribal cop just shook his head and lifted the board.

Emma and her mother reached the hospital thirty minutes after the ambulance. Bernice took one look at them and burst into tears. Scared and confused, Emma asked, "Is Matthew in a coma? Is he dead!?" Bernice was clearly hysterical, and Clayton was not around.

Emma's mom went over and hugged the sobbing stepmother.

The woman wept so loudly that Emma became more panicked. Moments later, Bernice choked out a few words. "I hope they arrest him. That drunk wrecked my car!" Mrs. Eagle Bull looked shocked and let go of Bernice. Knowing Matthew was all right, Emma sagged into a chair.

"It's the car you're crying about? Matthew is OK, and you're crying about the car?! Aren't you glad he's OK?" Emma pleaded.

"Why sh-should I cry for him? He, st-stole my, my new car. The one we bought with, with Billy's money, and he wrecked it with his damn drinking! Oh, I feel faint!" she sobbed, leaning against the wall.

In the emergency room, Clayton stood by his son while the nurse cleaned his cuts. Every now and then Matthew let out a groan, but it was not until they'd stitched his head and the nurse had gone that he spoke. "God, I wrecked your car, Dad. I wrecked Billy's car, and somebody was with me, and the cops wouldn't even look for him!"

"There was nobody in the car but you. What are you talking about?" Clayton said angrily in Lakota.

"There was, and he looked like Billy." Matthew was sobering up.

"You saw Billy in the car?" Clayton's mouth fell open.

"He was just going along for the ride. It's like he knew that was his new car or something, Dad! You heard the car honk. It's like once I got in that car, it just kept going faster and Billy just kept smiling the same as he always did." Matthew's face relaxed. "Maybe he wanted me to go with him."

Clayton leaned against an empty gurney, tears in his tired eyes.

It was later in the ward when they spoke again. Matthew looked ashamed. "I'll bet Bernice is pretty upset, isn't she? She's mad about the car."

"Well, yes, she is mad about the car, but she's glad you're OK."

Matthew smiled. "No, she isn't. You don't need to say that, Dad. I know how she feels about me. How she always felt about me and Billy. Lately even you look at me as if you were missing Billy. And if you miss Billy so much, how come you didn't build that church you always wanted and name it after him? At least it would have been something, Dad."

Clayton turned and faced the door. "Well, the car's done with. I just got off the phone with the tribal police. When you get out of here, they're going to make you serve one week for drunk driving. By then Bernice will calm down a little. It'll work out," he said weakly.

"No, it won't, Dad. I wish I could bring Billy back. I miss him real bad too."

"It's tough son, real tough. I just stay drunk because I can't stand to be here on this earth anymore. I try, son, but I'm all gone inside." Standing beside the hospital bed, Clayton looked small, exhausted.

"Right now, I'm just making things worse. So when I get out of jail, I'm gonna hit the road. Bernice can have a break for a while." Matthew tried to smile.

Clayton's lower lip quivered, but he kept his silence.

70

DALE NIELSEN WALKED THROUGH A RAGGED, BOMB-CRATERED JUNGLE. THE sun was bright, but for once it wasn't hot. He could hear the singing of birds, something he hadn't heard much in Vietnam. These craters were the biggest he had ever seen, and he marveled at their perfect shape, wondering what type of bomb had caused them. It was then he felt the eyes. Spinning, he dropped to the ground and pointed his M-16 in the direction of the sensation. There, in a tree, was a Vietnamese sniper with his weapon trained directly on him. Why doesn't he shoot? Dale thought. He had the chance, he had me!

As platoon leader for the last three weeks, Dale had not pulled guard or had to walk once, and it was a relief. His weight had dropped to one hundred thirty and the damn boil on his arm was coming back. In a feverish sweat he slept, caught in the sights of his phantom sniper till he was wakened.

At breakfast, Dale found some beef slices and drifted over toward John Evans, the commander of a flame track recently assigned to reinforce his beleaguered platoon. He noticed that the man usually ate by himself. This had him curious. Besides, since Grubouski had been killed, Dale had felt profoundly alone. "Mind if I join you?" he asked.

"No, no, not at all," Evans replied.

"I noticed you like to hang by yourself, and sometimes people who like to be alone are just that way."

"Well, actually I don't really like to be alone. It's just that people don't know what to make of me. It's that well . . . I don't fit." Now Evans grinned. "It's because I'm not itchin' to get home and I'm not a lifer. In fact, at this point, I've kinda had my fill. This is my third tour, and I guess the single-tour guys find that weird, like I'm a mad-dog killer. In fact I've been saddled with the nickname Spook; it kind of stuck."

"Well, Spooky, three years driving a flame track isn't exactly mild-mannered work." Dale put a piece of C-4 under his coffee. "And I must tell you, John, you're the first guy I've met who's been here for three tours. I think one is plenty long."

Sergeant Evans opened a pack of dried fruit. "It's not quite as weird as I put on. I made the stupid mistake of joining for four years when I enlisted. Instead of going to Germany like they promised, I get sent here. After being in this man's army for about five fuckin minutes, I realized it wasn't for me, the military bullshit and all.

"But this way, assigned to units like yours way out in the fuckin boonies, I can get through it without going nuts. You know, I think you're the first person that really heard me out or even asked. When I go home this time, I get out. And, I haven't had to salute an officer in two and a half years!" He laughed, and then grew serious. "Besides, I guess I'm good at it . . . still alive. That's more than I can say for a lot of guys I've served with."

71

SEPTEMBER FOUND THE SECOND OF THE 22ND MECHANIZED CAVALRY STILL playing bait and capture with the enemy. To the newer men in Second Platoon it was obvious a professional bond had formed between Sergeants Nielsen and Evans. A price had been paid to get this far, and they trusted one another.

Captain Zonne had departed a week earlier, leaving Alpha Company in the hands of inexperienced lieutenants. But the older veterans' caution and experience seemed to help the newer men get through each day.

In the growing daylight, the two sat out of sight on the far edge of the perimeter, exchanging a joint, listening to the growing sound of an approaching C&C Huey.

"Wonder who we'll be stuck with now?" Dale passed the joint back to Evans.

"I don't know, but the way things been going, I'm sure he'll be a winner."

The bird settled down into the dust storm it had created; the giant rotors began to slow. Dale peeked around the side of his track.

Boxes of C-rations, ammunition, tins of fuel were thrown from the open bay. A man in new fatigues appeared at the door, frowned briefly, and jumped lightly to the ground.

In full uniform the two platoon lieutenants from First and Third stood by. The new captain said, "Relax, boys," then introduced himself.

Dale stayed where he was for a moment, passing the joint back to Evans. Then he stood and sauntered over to the new arrival and lieutenants. He did not salute.

"Captain Charles Olinger. Glad to meet you." The man extended his hand.

"You can call me Chuck."

"Staff Sergeant Dale Nielsen here. You can call me short."

The man looked confused for a moment, then grinned. "So you're the sergeant that's a platoon leader?"

"Yes, sir, Second Platoon." Dale stood, arms crossed, hand on his chin.

Olinger was being studied and he knew it. "I hear you do a pretty good job out there," he indicated the tree line.

"Just trying to keep the men alive, Chuck."

"I know there's been an absence of leadership, sergeant, but I plan to give you guys a hand. I served my first tour here and know the area pretty well. Served with a track outfit too." Olinger again extended his hand.

Dale brightened and stuck out his hand. "That's a real plus Chuck, because Battalion Command thinks we're foot soldiers. We've suffered a lot of casualties because of that." The last comment seemed to make an impression.

"I'm going to make my rounds, son, then I want to have a chitchat with you." Olinger slapped Dale on the shoulder and moved with the platoon lieutenants toward the command tent.

Sergeants Nielsen and Evans watched the officer all day. He moved comfortably from man to man, casually engaging them in conversation, taking notes, and inspecting the tracks. At 1600 he flagged Dale to his tent.

When he walked in, Olinger handed him a beer and smiled broadly. "I guess you're senior man here; I've heard good things about you all day, Nielsen. That's good. Now I want to hear from the horse's mouth, as it were, what your assessment of the company is."

Dale liked the man's attitude, and relaxed a bit. "Well, sir, things aren't good and the men know it. We've been taking a lot of casualties. I think there's a reason for that."

"And what's that?" the captain asked.

"Like I was saying earlier, we're not infantry. They've got us crawling up on NVA bunkers, out of visual or organic support from our tracks. Our job as a track company is to find the enemy, come up on line guns blazing, and blow the shit out of the bunker." Dale waited to see if he'd been too blunt.

Captain Olinger looked thoughtful. "There may be another reason you're not aware of for your increase in casualties. Intelligence says the NVA are out to get Alpha. That's a backhanded compliment if I ever heard one. I don't want that to leave this tent." He stood, indicating the conference was over. "Well, I'll see what I can do about that, and thank you for your assessment. I'll check in with you after chow."

Evans waved Dale over when he left the command tent. "So what do you think?"

"I'm fairly impressed. He's sharp, in good shape, and he listens. He might do some good." Dale's tone was ambivalent; he was thinking about what the captain had shared with him.

At 1900 Olinger approached Dale's track. "Nielsen, I've been giving some thought to what you said, and maybe I can help a little."

"That's good," Dale said, his supply of enthusiasm all but run out.

"Well, I got to thinking back on my first tour, and I couldn't put it together at first. Then it hit me. I didn't see a ninety millimeter all day." He shook his head slowly.

Dale was incredulous. "Recoilless rifles?"

"That's what I said." The captain went on. "We used them all the time. They're deadly when used right, and they help to confuse the enemy. You got one?" he asked, pointing toward the track.

Dale was confused. "Ee-yah, I believe so." He didn't move.

"Can I see it?" Olinger insisted.

"Yeah, sure," Dale crawled into the rear hatch of the track. In the near dark, he moved boxes of ammo, personal gear, C-rations, beer, and spare parts. He found it rusting under the driver's seat.

"This thing?" Dale's voice made no attempt at masking his skepticism.

"That's the one," Captain Olinger responded. "I want every track in the company to have theirs cleaned and ready for inspection at oh-seven-hundred. They'll see some fireworks tomorrow!" The captain turned and walked back toward the center of the perimeter.

At dawn, the new CO called the platoon leaders together. "Battalion Command wants us to move against a bunker system here. They think it's heavily fortified. We're to rendezvous with an ARVN company here at ten-hundred and move forward in a V formation. Then we'll dismount and assault that system. First Platoon takes center with me, Third Platoon takes middle, and Nielsen's Second Platoon takes right flank. Let's move out! Oh, one more thing. I want nineties and ammo on every deck. Let's get them little bastards!"

By noon they had found their "little bastards." With twenty-four tracks on line, Olinger figured the enemy should have fled—should have but hadn't. Machine-gun fire from the trees spread out from bunkers spanning fifty meters along an abandoned rice paddy. It was constant and Olinger was looking worried. He ordered a salvo of recoilless rifle fire that exploded uselessly into the trees, and then two more with the same effect.

Seconds later, thirty-caliber bullets with their green tracers left the trees in a steady stream, a few pinging off aluminum, most just tearing up earth.

A wide, dry ditch broke the ground in the front of the bunker system. Dale didn't like it. He turned to Evans on the flame track and shook his head. Then over the radio came the command, "Dismount!" Dale punched himself violently in the head. Evans stood by helpless on his track.

It was like fishing in a barrel—only Alpha was to be the catch of the day, and each man on the ground was bait. Dale remembered Olinger's line about the NVA out to get Alpha, and here they were walking into it. A gnawing fear crawled up from his gut, his forehead wrinkled. "And so goddamned short!" he swore into the din.

To his surprise, Olinger jumped off his track to lead the assault. Dale almost rubbed his eyes to see if they were working. Not since Crocker had a captain moved in line, risking his life with the men.

It worked. The men almost sprang forward. Dale smiled. He was finally convinced they had a new CO.

By 1300 things had gotten bad. Already six men were down, three dead, one close. Dale lay on his stomach in a thicket and prayed for the Higher Higher to wake up and send in arty.

He radioed his concern to Olinger, who replied, "I want you to increase your forward progress and sweep through their position. We've got a chance to teach these NVA troops something! Now let's do it!"

Olinger repeated the command to the platoon leaders. Dale slammed the handset into the RTO's palm.

One hundred meters back, the tracks stood in a circle, motors idling, useless.

AK fire opened to Dale's right. My worst nightmares weren't a thing like this! he thought. He turned to his platoon and ordered them to suppress the flanking action of the NVA. Sporadic gunfire erupted again, this time further to his right. "They're moving!" he screamed, trying to control his growing panic.

His mind racing, he signaled the squad sergeant. "Have your men move back with the fire, then hold position. If they get in behind us, it's going to get rough."

Dale was thinking ahead, trying to meet the flanking action of the NVA company. Trying to buy precious time. "I'll be right back! Stay with them," he said.

He belly crawled twenty-five meters, and found Olinger trying to organize an assault in the center of the fire.

"What you doing here?" Olinger shouted.

"It's bad, sir!" Dale shouted, face in the dirt. "They're flanking us. If we get them up our back door, they'll be between the tracks and us. Then we're in big fuckin trouble, and believe me, they're moving!"

"Fuck!" Olinger said in desperation. "About all you can do is tell your men to defend their positions," he panted.

"That's not my plan, sir. We can cross that ditch with the tracks. Repulse that flank assault. It'll confuse them and it will save some lives."

"But we got orders." Olinger pointed up, then forced a grin. "Go for it!"

In a half-run, half-crawl, Dale pulled his platoon back toward the tracks out of the range of the bunkers. Meanwhile the tracks pulled across the ditch, meeting the running dismounts at the tree line.

The four tracks, Evans's flamethrower blazing, repulsed the flanking action.

• • •

It was chow time when the final dustoffs had lifted toward Cu Chi. Air strikes and artillery had leveled the bunkers. Only four enemy bodies were found.

Filthy from the fight, exhausted and hungry, Dale sat warming dinner on a heat tab. Evans strolled over. His face was grim. "So what do you think?" He squatted next to Dale.

"I think we were damn lucky," Dale said, opening a can.

"No, about Olinger." Evans searched Dale's face.

"I think he at least gets in there and fights with the men. I'll give him that, and he's not afraid of them." Dale pointed up, grinning slightly.

"You haven't heard?"

"Heard what?" Dale placed the pork over the heat.

Evans looked down. "He's dead, man. He was shot in the head . . . died on the way to Cu Chi."

72

ON A MOONLESS NIGHT, DALE SAT ALONE ON THE PERIMETER OF THE FIRE-base. He had offered to pull guard even though it wasn't the duty of a platoon leader. He had told the men he was proud of the way they had performed the day before and he meant it. Pulling guard was just his small way of showing it. Besides, the boil on his arm was getting larger, and it hurt so bad he hadn't slept well the night before.

His thoughts drifted while his ears strained to hear into the jungle. One thought was recurrent: Alpha was targeted for destruction, and he wanted out. Ten months into his tour, and he had thirty days left in the field.

He thought of Olinger's one-day tour, and of the futility of his death. Now we've got a new company commander and I'll bet he reeks of aftershave and rear area.

When Captain Edison Muller stepped off the helicopter at 1600, he looked strangely foreign. His boots sparkled; the man's fatigues were crisp camouflage, something the men in the field had only heard of. On his blouse it said "Capt. E. Muller." He had metal bars pinned on his helmet cover. After eyeing the scruffy company, he didn't even attempt to make the rounds. He sat by the command track, looking for all his new gear like a pathetic lost Boy Scout. A small roll of fat crested his belt. The captain's face was pale from lack of sun, his fingernails clean.

The more Dale studied the man, the more of a tragic clown Captain Muller appeared. He sat there hating the army all the more. They had sent Alpha Company this cruel joke when they desperately needed a leader.

It seemed to Dale that the very idea of being in the field scared this officer. He had seen Muller's eyes darting around when he spoke, as if a sapper in black pajamas might catch him off guard.

Later that afternoon Dale commented to Evans: "It's as if he's been dropped head first into a war he's only heard about, and wants no fuckin part of it. And guess what, he's the asshole that's been signing our orders in Tay Ninh!"

Evans snuffed his cigarette. "They must be scraping bottom, or he fucked up and the colonel found Muller trying out his chair."

At chow, Evans nodded toward Dale, grinned, and walked over to the new captain. "Sir, I don't want to seem rude, but I'd take those bars off your helmet. The NVA have a way of targeting officers."

Muller's eyes snapped up. He snatched the helmet from his head and yelled at Evans. "Soldier! You're not telling me something I don't know. And as for being rude I'd say you're skating on insubordination. I'll have you know this is my second tour!" Evans faked an apology, saluted, and said, "I was just trying to be helpful, sir!" then went behind his track nearly doubled up with laughter.

Sitting alone in the darkness, Dale wondered, Why, if the United States Army can come up with so many men to be killed and wounded, can't they come up with a few officers who know what end their assholes are on? The question fed on his own guilt for turning down Officers Candidate School.

At 2200, the new CO stopped at Dale's guard post on the track. "Soldier, is everything secure here?"

Nobody had ever asked him that, and Dale's arm throbbed so badly he was not in the mood for small talk. "Why yes, sir, I believe so." He tried to be polite.

"God, it's dark out there." Captain Muller peered out.

"Yes, it is, sir."

"Son, do you have your starlight scope handy?"

"No, sir, I don't. We don't use them."

"Don't use them! What the hell do you think they're issued for?"

"Damned if I know, sir."

"Soldier, how long you been here?"

"Ten months, sir."

That seemed to startle the pudgy officer, "Well, ah, where is your scope? I want to check things out for myself."

Remembering Olinger's short-lived recoilless rifle fetish, Dale grinned into the darkness.

Moments later he handed Captain Muller the dusty scope. "Here's the scope, sir; you can have it if you want."

Muller held the scope up and looked beyond the perimeter. "What the fuck is wrong with this thing?" He lowered it and felt inside the eyepiece with his index finger. "There's some leaves or debris in here, soldier. Is this how you take care of equipment?"

Dale did not answer. He was trying to control a building urge to laugh.

"Some kind of fuckin leaves in here or something." In the dark the captain tore something from each of the eyepieces. "That's better," he said, holding the scope up.

"No, it's not, sir," Dale said flatly.

"What do you mean, addressing me that way, soldier? I don't like your fucking attitude."

"It's not my attitude, sir—it's the scope. Those things you tore out are back light shields. Even with them, the scopes make two bright green targets . . . without them they're practically neon. Excellent targets, sir."

"Fuck!" Muller croaked. Tossing the scope toward Dale, he stomped back toward the command area.

Soon Dale could hear the man speaking in agitated tones on the radio, but could not make out what he was saying.

He was asleep when the chopper came to take Muller back to Tay Ninh.

73

FOR THE MEN AT FIREBASE HUBERT HUMPHREY, THE DAY BEGAN WITH A BLAST of tropical humidity. During chow that morning, the company first sergeant made a strange announcement to the men of Alpha. "I want the men on this list to appear in clean fatigues at 1600 for an awards ceremony. Anyone whose name is listed must appear, but I'd like all the men of Alpha to be there. Wear your best fatigues. The battalion commander's coming down to make the presentations."

As the morning drifted by, between repairs and resupply, the men in Alpha casually wandered by to check the list. Dale tightened the last bolt on a new drive sprocket at 1200, then sauntered over toward the white page that had posted. He squinted at the bright paper. "To: Company Commander, Alpha Co. 2nd of 22nd. The following soldiers are to be decorated for the events which took place August 21, 1969."

He scanned down the list, his eyes coming to rest on the line that read "Grubowski, Edward, Spec 4." Either it was the faded copy or the hot light of the sun, but the name seemed to float on the paper. When he spotted the next name, he shook his head angrily, muttered "Fuck," and walked off.

The company buzzed with rumors about who was to get what. Some even said the list was wrong. At chow, Dale thought of Ed and the list, and how awards for the dead were a strange idea. He did not get dressed for the ceremony.

A small group formed in the center of the firebase just before 1600. The rest of Alpha sat on bunkers bullshitting about the list or slept in a shady spot, ignoring the whole thing.

Dale, now a veteran of the catnap, woke when the C&C chopper landed. Blasting the firebase with a shower of red sand and gravel, the big blades slowly came to a stop. The Higher Higher, who looked to be in his mid-thirties, face tanned, uniform starched, jumped from the bay. That in itself was worth the show.

The colonel walked from the chopper toward the assembled group. An aide jumped off, scurrying after him carrying a flat black box.

"'Tention!" the first sergeant commanded. This modern reenactment of an ancient ritual was beginning to intrigue even the most cynical men, who now craned their necks for a view.

Dale pulled himself on top of the sandbags and sat next to Dickerson. "You were here when I got here. Right?" he asked quietly.

"Yeah, you got that right." Dickerson's voice was tense.

"You ever seen anything like this before?"

Dickerson flipped three cigarettes from a full civilian pack and held it out for Dale to pull one. "No, never." He slid the pack back in his shirt, then lit one. "I know a lot of guys who should have gotten some kind of mention." He took a drag on his Pall Mall. "I'll tell you something weird. Some of the heroes are gone home, some of them are dead, and some of them are here, but none of them are standing out there." His voice dropped. Then his face brightened into a grin. "But, fuck, my man, don't mean nuthin', 'cause I'm out of here!"

The commander's aide read the citation. "On 21 August 1969 at approximately ten hundred hours Second Platoon of Alpha Company did engage a heavily entrenched NVA force, resulting in stranded casualties. After repeated valiant attempts under intensive hostile fire, they were successful in eliminating the enemy machine-gun emplacement and in recovering all of the missing men. For bravery above and beyond the call of duty, the following roll is called."

The first sergeant stood beside the colonel holding the box. Caught up in the drama, the tiny band of dusty men seemed to straighten.

"Specialist Fourth Class, Ansen, Carl. Posthumous: A Bronze Star."

"E-Five, Cavanaugh, Frederick. Posthumous: A Bronze Star."

"Specialist Fourth Class, Grubowski, Edward. Posthumous: A Bronze Star."

Pressure built up in Dale's chest when that name was read. He turned to hide the wetness in his eyes.

When the fuzzy-cheeked corporal had finished listing the honored dead, the medals were held up for the inspection of the living troopers, who saluted them. These were set aside for shipment to their families.

One by one, the standing men were called forward. A medal was pinned on the chest of each one by the commander. With a curt salute, they returned to formation. When a Silver Star was announced for Esswein, a low grumble came from the bunker tops.

• • •

After darkness fell on the compound, Dale and Dickerson sat on their bunker in silence, drinking warm beer. Evans pulled himself up and sat down next to the black man. "What are you two looking so excited about?" he taunted.

"Oh, don't mean nothing," Dickerson said, saluting Evans with his beer.

"Well, I got something from a Mama-san that will cheer you up."

"Unless it's her daughter-san, I don't want it," Dickerson chuckled, poking Dale in the ribs.

"You'll want this." He produced a fat misshapen joint from his sleeveless shirt and lit it with his Zippo. Evans sucked in deeply and handed it to Dickerson, who in turn took a deep hit and then passed it to Dale. When it had been reduced to ashes, the men sat in silence, staring out across the tracks on perimeter and the listening posts into the blackness of the trees.

"It's truly fucked, man," Dickerson said. "The whole thing was fucked."

"What was fucked?" Evans asked.

"I'll tell you what's fucked." Dale's voice was bitter. "That Sergeant Esswein from First Platoon gets a Silver Star for crawling away from a firefight and leaving his men, and Ed who gave his life gets a Bronze Star. That's fucked!"

"As usual, I think you're missing the point, Nielsen my man," Dickerson laughed. "Sometimes for a smart man, you're real stupid!"

"Yeah, and what's that?" Dale winced as he touched the painful, bulging boil on his forearm.

"It's not whether Ed gets the bronze. It's you that should have gotten the Silver Star. Everyone knows who took that machine gun out! Whoever wrote up that report was writing fiction. Sure was nice to see the Higher looking so official when he pinned the medal on old Sweinhundt." Dickerson broke out in an extended snicker.

"You know what's funnier yet?" Evans interrupted. "That asshole will walk around the rest of his life, explaining something that never happened, or living with the lie that he's a hero." They all laughed at that.

74

THE HUGE RED BOIL PREVENTED DALE FROM SLEEPING AT ALL. MORNING found him feverish, and even the grin on Evans's face could not shake him from his dark mood. At 1000 hours, Second Platoon crept out of the perimeter on a search-and-destroy mission. C&C was sure a large unit of NVA was rebuilding its forces in the area.

As the track bounced forward, Dale mentally counted his days. 29, 30, 31. Except for Evans, it seemed he was surrounded by cherries. Their scared faces always turned toward him for reassurance, but he had none left to give. He acknowledged that he was losing his grip. He hated himself.

The damn pussy lump that had become his arm and the army's relentless procurement of young men to die drained his soul. Now it all seemed pointles.

At lunch, fifteen klicks from the firebase, Staff Sergeant Nielsen called a halt and told the men to take ten. The two short-timers sat on Evans's track having lunch; this time it was ham slices for Dale and spaghetti and meatballs for Evans.

"You know," said Dale, "I don't even care if we find this complex we're looking for. I just want to go home in one piece. I used to think we were here for something, but anymore I think my job is just to keep these boys in one piece. So their moms won't get the fuckin visit from the recruiter. I stay popular with a lot of women that way."

"Shit! You're crazy, Dale!" Evans laughed. "Know what you mean, though. Probably aged my mom ten years, me being over here so long and all." He looked off into the jungle and fell silent.

Dale continued. "I used to think I knew a lot about a lot of things. Come real far on that one though. I've had a lot of friends die here." Dale thought of Crocker, and then Frank for the first time since R&R. "I used to think only the scared ones or the dumb ones died, and that's kinda stupid when a fella thinks about it!" He laughed, and then he too fell silent.

Spec Four Frederick Dunbar on the lead track waved his arms frantically, pointed to his ears and then to the trees. The platoon froze. Dale signaled the man to come over, then whispered, "What is it, Fred?"

The man was excited. "It's gooks, man! Over there in the trees . . . could hear them talking. Are we going to see some action?"

"Calm down my man. Thanks, I'll get back to you on that." Dale signaled the men to get into positions. Some of the men looked excited, others scared. Dale moved back toward Evans. Now the whole platoon could plainly hear voices.

Evans studied the terrain. "Holy shit, will you take a look at that?" he whispered, pointing into the thick trees. "We just found your missing complex."

Dale looked where Evans pointed. There was a distinct grassy mound, beside it another. As he adjusted his thinking, he could clearly see six bunkers on the small ridge. Searching his mind for options, he could feel his heart start to pound. Whatever happened next, he would have to live with it. At twenty years old, he was in charge now.

"What do you think, John? You're the most experienced one here. We could attack them and have a real battle on our hands. We could fry the suckers and hope we hit them all, or we could call in an air strike."

John thought for a moment, then grinned. "There is one more option." His voice was even lower. "We could just back on out of here. We call in an air strike, and we're going to have to come back in here and mop up. This is a pretty big complex. If we had the whole company that would be one thing, but with four tracks?"

Dale thought for a moment, then he too smiled. "This bunker system is probably tied in with others. It could turn into a real hornets' nest. I'm for backing out and hoping the NVA like our plan."

Dale signaled the squad leaders to back out. The engines ground noisily to life. The look on Dale's face was tense. If there was going to be a fight, it would likely be in the next thirty seconds. In unison, the four tracks backed up. Fifty meters out, they swung around and headed back toward Fire Base Hubert Humphrey.

On the command track at the rear of the little column, a smile spread across the thin face of the platoon leader. He'd made his decision in more ways than one. He felt relieved, lightheaded, and almost giddy. Dale reached into his ammo can and pulled out a perfect apple. Ahead in the flame track, Evans broke out in an identical grin.

75

THE RED BOIL HAD GROWN TO AMAZING PROPORTIONS, STRETCHING THE skin into an ugly volcano of flesh that now doubled the size of Dale's forearm. He had not slept or eaten well in a week. His weight had dropped to 125 pounds on a six-foot frame. His blue eyes were sunken, their gaze becoming more distant by the day.

A fever, both physical and spiritual, left him confused. Should I go into Tay Ninh and deal with this arm, he thought, or should I stay and try to save a few men from stupidity?

At 0700 Dale stood before the small command tent in the middle of the firebase. "Sir, I want to speak with you."

"Yes, Sergeant, may I help you with something?" Lieutenant Froiland, the new company commander, glowered at him from inside.

"It's my arm, sir." Dale bent to enter the little shelter. "It's pretty badly infected." He displayed the grotesque mound for the first lieutenant.

"Fuck! How long have you had that thing?" The man looked like he might get ill.

"About a month, sir. I had one before, but I got it to clear up. This one's even bigger; I think it started with a saw grass cut."

"Do you think Lieutenant Douglas is ready to take over your platoon?" The question seemed odd coming from a man who had been in the field only three days.

"Ah, no, sir, with all respect, I don't."

"Why not?"

"He doesn't learn very fast, and I haven't had much time to show him. He's too gung ho. I think he'll get men killed, sir. He doesn't seem to take what I have to say very seriously."

The first lieutenant looked angry. "Well, soldier, there may be a reason for that. There's a rumor floating around the command post that you could have engaged the enemy on Monday but didn't. Maybe Lieutenant Douglas doesn't want that to happen again."

Dale's ears burned at the company commander's naïveté, but he remained silent.

"I'm only temporarily in charge; we need you here, soldier. You know we're short of men. Have one of the medics look at it." The clean-shaven man looked down, indicating the discussion was over.

"I beg your pardon, sir, but I already did. He sent me to you, said I better go to Tay Ninh, that it was a real bad staph, sir."

"Staph? Fuck. Isn't that contagious?" The lieutenant pushed his canvas stool against the back wall of the tent.

• • •

By the time Dale was evacuated to Tay Ninh, he was suffering the onset of delirium. The doctor looked at the arm and shook his head. "Jeeze, son, what did you wait so long for?" He smiled at Dale, eyebrows arched.

When he lanced the goitrous infection, yellowish pus shot across the bunker. Dale winced, laughed stupidly out loud; eyes glassy, he collapsed to the wooden floor.

"Son, I think two cups is a new record. Let's have a little talk." He pulled Dale up and steered him toward a cot. "How long you been in the field, son?"

"Ten terrific months." Dale felt light-headed. "I'm supposed to get out early and go back to Ames. I mean college, sir, next month, so I've got about three or four weeks left, sir."

The captain looked at him, his voice lowered. "Why did you wait so long to come in? This is real bad; it's obvious you have an incredible staph infection boiling in your blood. You were really playing games with your future, Sergeant." The captain reached for some gauze and a brown glass bottle.

"Well, sir, things are real bad in my outfit right now, and I thought I might do some good if I stayed."

"That's real fine, son, but it's going to be a week, maybe longer, before the antibiotics run their course and I'll let you go back. Do you want to go back?"

Dale sat for a long time watching the doctor debride the edges of the crater, fascinated by the size of the opening and how loose his skin looked. "I, ah, I'm not sure on that one. I'd like to go home right now, I guess, but . . ." He winced as the doctor poured on some disinfectant. "I guess I feel like a lot of boys are going to get hurt if I leave." His head spun.

"Well, you've got to leave sometime, and sadly, more boys are going to die whether you go or stay. Look, this thing is bad. I could use it to your advantage. I'll tell you what, you've got a week to make up your mind." He wrapped the offending arm with a thick pad of fresh gauze and then reached for some pills. "Take these and come back tomorrow."

• • •

Two weeks passed, the arm healed, and Dale had gained back seven pounds. It preyed on him that he still hadn't returned to the front. He now had to admit to himself that he was skating, slacking, something he had never done in his life.

He was lying on his cot, hating himself, when Spec Four Greenway poked his head in the door of the bunker and squinted. "Sarge, you in here?"

"Yeah, I'm here. What's up, Greeney?"

"Nothing much. Caught a little shrapnel last night. Heard from the doc you were here, so I just thought I'd drop by. What you been up to, Sarge?" Dale hesitated, so the soldier went on. "Some of the guys say you're coming back; some say you'd be crazy."

Dale wanted to ask about the shrapnel but didn't. "Oh, I was in charge of the NCO club last week and then some club scandal broke out in Germany. Some rip-off or something and they closed it. Then I organized perimeter guard. But mostly I've been hanging out trying to be invisible."

The boy's mood changed. "So you're not coming back?"

"I don't know what to do, to be honest." He pointed to the bandages on the man's shoulder and face. How'd that happen?" He sat up, hating the question.

"Last night Lieutenant Douglas really fucked up. Four guys got killed.

Including me, there were four wounded, but I got off easy, I guess . . . I'm going back."

Dale's stomach became queasy.

"What exactly happened? Sit down." He reached for the bulb dangling from the ceiling.

"Our platoon went out on patrol last night, crashing down the road through a village. We were only supposed to go out ten klicks. Instead Douglas had us go out twenty, and then he had us come back the same way we went out. On the way back, just past a little set of hootches, we snagged a wire, or maybe a command detonator, and the whole squad got hit with fragments from a howitzer shell. Pretty fucked, huh!"

"Shit! That smart-ass bastard; I suppose he's fine."

"Fuck yeah! Nobody on his track got hit. We lost our track too. I know if you were there to stop him, those guys would be here now." His head dropped to hide his tears. "It's really bad, man." His voice cracked, and he stopped talking.

Greenway had said it all. Dale sat there absorbing his nightmare turned reality.

• • •

It was eight o'clock the next morning, and Dale hadn't slept all night. On the floor was a wrinkled paper with the names of the boys in his platoon that had been killed.

Even two weeks might prevent another massacre, he thought. Maybe Douglas would listen now . . . maybe I'll be killed trying. That thought crippled him with what he took to be cowardice and indecision.

After morning mess hall, he had decided he should go back. He stood in the dim light of his tent looking at the death list, shaking his head, hating everything and everyone.

There was a knock on the plank door. "Staff Sergeant Dale Nielsen?" A precisely dressed MP stood silhouetted in the narrow entrance.

"Yes?" Dale's heart sank. Someone had turned him in for loafing, and now he was in big trouble.

"Captain Muller requests you report to Battalion Command immediately. I'm here to escort you."

The Command Bunker was a heavily timbered and sandbagged complex of subterranean offices. It had permanent concrete steps and air-conditioning. Fat sandbags lined the entrance. Inside the cool office was a maze of desks and rear-area clerks pounding on typewriters. The MP did not follow him in.

"Excuse me, do you know where I might find Captain Muller?" The small, pale man at the desk squinted at Dale. "You going in to see him looking like that?" A small ripple of laughter moved through the room.

Dale had never thought of it: he felt the stubble on his face, felt the cold air against his bare legs and arms. "He's down in the office to the right, the one that says Battalion Executive Officer."

A large room opened to his left. On the wall was a huge map of III Corps. Impersonal-looking pins and flags indicated units of the 22nd Battalion. Ahead was a desk where a male secretary sat behind a stack of reports. "Sergeant Nielsen here to see Captain Muller," Dale said crisply.

The man picked up a phone. "Sergeant Nielsen here to see you, sir . . . Yes, sir."

On the desk in the well-constructed office was a brand new steel pot, its captain's bars crisp against the camouflage. Behind the desk sat the same man who had lasted one night in the field, who had torn the light shields from the night scope and ran, tail between chubby legs, back to headquarters. On the slab wood wall was a photo of General Westmoreland and Richard Nixon shaking hands. Under it hung a holstered, chrome-plated forty-five.

Dale saluted. "Sergeant Nielsen, sir, reporting as requested." A chill of apprehension and resentment shot up his torso.

Muller looked up as if surprised. "Well, what the living hell do we have here?" He glowered at Dale, obviously not recognizing him. "Sergeant No Name, is this how you report to a commanding officer, in rags?" The man's face reddened, his voice grew shrill. "Sergeant, just the sight of you is sickening. Is this how you show your respect for the battalion?"

"No, sir."

"No, Captain Muller, sir! You stupid son of a bitch!" the captain yelled.

"No, Captain Muller, sir!" Dale struggled to control his growing rage.

The pudgy captain picked up a file. "I've been in the field, son," he pointed to the revolver. "I know your type, soldier; you're a wise ass, aren't you? Think you're too good for the uniform of the United States Army! Well, I've got something special for you, since you hate the military so much."

His voice dropped. "The commander of American forces in Vietnam, General Creighton Abrams, is coming into Cu Chi to review the troops and you, Sergeant No Rank, No Name, are going to represent the battalion. You're going to get your skinny ass over to Company Supply and get yourself looking like a staff sergeant and then you're going to Cu Chi and play tin soldier for the general. Here are your orders." He shoved some papers across the desk.

"Now get your disheveled ass out of my sight."

"But, sir, I was going to go back, sir. I, ah, was thinking I—"

"Soldier, when in God's name were you asked to think?" Muller stood, tiny sweat beading up on his forehead. Realizing he was shorter than Dale, he sat. "Get out of here." Muller waved Dale off like a bothersome fly.

As Dale moved past the clerks with their brand-new camouflage fatigues, clacking typewriters, and whirling fans, his heart pounded with joy. A thin smile spread across his face. It broke into a broad grin as he thought of Brer Rabbit and Brer Fox.

Sergeant Dale Edward Nielsen bounded up the stairs, almost dancing into the hot sun. "Please don't trow me into da briar patch!" he yelled as he threw a salute toward the gawking MP.

76

DALE STOOD IN THE TEMPORARY ASSIGNMENT BARRACKS GRINNING AT himself in a shower room mirror. Before him stood a perfect soldier, all military spit and polish—as if uniforms had anything to do with a man's courage in a fight. He thought of Muller's steel pot and straining shirt buttons and then thought about his own internal changes.

In his mind, he visited briefly with Miller, Grubouski, and all the boys who had died. His thoughts came to rest for a moment on Crocker's occasional grin.

Standing in this antiseptic barracks in the Republic of Vietnam, it seemed to him that this awful war was already fading into his past. For all the bad memories, he had escaped from this hell on earth with few regrets, and fat boy Muller had helped with that. He grinned at the thought.

Cu Chi, with all its apparent permanence, once so impressive to him, was now only a means of salvation. The same day as his fortunate meeting with the good captain, he had picked up new fatigues and proper insignia and arrived back where his journey to hell had begun.

Standing there before the glass, he looked burnt, creased, thinner, older, remarkably unlike the cherry kid he remembered from eleven months earlier. He saluted himself, spun on his heel, and headed to the mess hall for a rear-area sit-down lunch.

At 1300 hours, he stood in the center of the massive base beside the parade ground, absorbing the pointless hustle and bustle of the post. Airplanes landed, bringing endless lines of wide-eyed kids to "summer camp." Civilian aircraft left, taking the worn-out, wounded, and dead men back to the States.

Overhead, cargo transports roared in, then rolled toward supply areas to disgorge tons of munitions and Coca-Cola on the tarmac. Thousands of men scrambled with trained efficiency, as if there was a war to win. Dale slowly shook his head.

Alone on the green parade ground, in his crisp uniform and flashing boots, he felt almost giddy. Even the grass looked strange to him. In time he was joined by other men, some weary and distant, some as fresh as the San Francisco sunrise they had left only the day before.

They represented supply units, clerk/typists, cook specialists, motor pool —every manner of rear-area MOS. They were all assigned this day to learn how to look like an enthusiastic battalion for *Stars and Stripes* or *Newsweek*.

Here and there a couple of fresh-faced boys were talking in whispers. The few combat veterans, mostly short-timers, stood solitary, looking distant and detached from their current mission, from life itself.

By 1500 they had been organized into positions. Empty wooden staffs had been handed out to those representing combat and combat-support battalions. The military band had been through its routine. The assembled men had marched to a proud drumbeat onto the field. Here they held a mock review, marched off the field and back on. At 1700 the Officer of the Day commanded, "See you here tomorrow at twelve-hundred. Diss-smissed."

That night Dale ate a relaxed meal of shrimp and steak, then took in *The Graduate* at the PX. After the show he walked around the base lost in his thoughts, slowly filing into mental drawers his days in the military. By 2000 hours he was back in the air-conditioned barracks, sleeping like the dead between cool cotton sheets.

The next day, under a sky as blue as God permits, men sparkled in military splendor. Gold braids hung from their shoulders. III Corps battalion flags snapped softly above the straight, green rows of men. Fluttering their history into the tropical breeze, campaign ribbons lined the wooden flagstaffs. Some battalions had tattered colors dating back to the Civil War, Indian fights, the Spanish-American War, World War I, World War II, and Korea.

At 1200 the men were standing in formation, then marched to the center of the field. Like human hedgerows, they stood for an hour under the broiling sun.

During that long, still hour, Dale's mind continued its slow reverie, examining his participation in a war he now had serious doubts about. He briefly replayed specific scenes, jurying his own actions. The scenes did not appear in any order, but tumbled from the dark, backward and forward, as if the subconscious had reordered them by psychic shock value.

He never saw Abrams. He heard the band, saw the cars and the officers get out, saw the Press Corps men shooting pictures. Through the lines of men, he could not honestly say he'd gotten a look at him.

His mind wandered forward: he could see his grandchildren spread out on the carpet before him, and he would have to tell them he almost saw the general. He smiled at the thought: At least it looks like I'll have grandchildren.

Next he thought of Grubouski, and the others, their fogged pupils, frozen in sudden death. The grim thought removed his smile.

While they marched off the field, before the Sergeant of the Guard commanded for the last time, "Dis-smissed!" Dale calculated his next few days. If I do this right, I could return to Tay Ninh tomorrow evening, report in the next day. Say at noon. And that would give me four days to be sent back to Cu Chi, and processed out to San Francisco.

As the sergeant's command faded in his ears, Dale Nielsen drifted away, wandering slowly across Cu Chi, toward the barracks and his rendezvous with the Freedom Bird.

77

OCTOBER WIND HAD TORN CLAPBOARD LOOSE FROM THE TINY CHURCH. IT now banged constantly against the structure. The green pine of the summer shade had shifted to brown, leaving the frosted ground littered with dead needles. Gray tumbleweeds choked the fences.

It was eight when Clayton woke from a dreamless sleep. He had stopped dreaming when Frank died. Now he dreamed while he was awake, awful dreams made bearable only by the countless wine bottles that had come and gone.

This day he awoke with purpose. He grabbed the half-full bottle and swept past the little ones. It was not that he wanted to keep his wine for himself, although Bernice would likely accuse him of that; it was for something more powerful. He had discovered that in this precarious state, brought on by the Muscatel, he could see another place. It was a mysterious place where life and death could meet and interact.

Without buttoning his shirt or tucking it in his pants, he set off to ask a question he asked himself over and over. "You'll have to answer me this time. I've got you now!" he chuckled in Lakota.

Today it hit him. He would ask the question directly, but would need the sacred wine to do it. He cradled the bottle, feeling its roundness. He would have to be careful on this journey, or with the last swallow, like so many times before, it would end before he had his answer.

. . .

After a brief visit with his parents, Dale found himself standing in a little apartment in Ames, Iowa amid a humble array of bundles and taped boxes. Only imagining what a man in this strange setting was supposed to do, he kissed Gail good-bye and walked out toward the campus.

At first there was no focus to his thoughts, only a mild panic that he would not remember things that he should, that his late return to school would be difficult.

There was a vague fear that his history might be visible on his clothes, that people passing by would smell the rot, see the death—that he would not fit in. He almost feared someone would say, "He's a foreigner, the devil, a killer, he's been over there." He feared that perhaps his cautious gait or his eyes would betray him. In the mirror that Monday morning he could see clearly that his eyes were not the same as theirs.

. . .

Unnoticed, because repetition makes men invisible, Clayton walked at a determined speed down the narrow lane, turning north past the busy store in Wounded Knee, toward Porcupine. He wasn't sad because today would be the day. Somehow he had known it since his eyes had opened. Clayton Jealous Of Him moved with the speed of a younger man.

He stopped only with guarded infrequency, each time carefully sampling, and fearfully eyeing, his dwindling supply of holy red medicine. He reminded himself out loud, "*Wana ecani ewahuni kte,* I'll be there soon."

. . .

It was in microbiology class, a month after his return, that Dale first observed a clarity that seemed to connect his ears and his brain in a manner he had never noticed before. It seemed that the professor spoke precisely, in a way that was remarkable. While he drank in the words, absorbing the concepts directly, he noticed the students around him taking notes at furious speed.

It was a wonder to him. What had been confusing only twenty-four months before was now so simple. Can't these people see this requires only a small amount of attention? he thought.

Moments later the class was over. Pushing themselves up from the tables with their arms, Dale thought his fellow students looked exhausted. He felt refreshed.

The ex-killer crossed the October-browned campus commons looking at the faces, noticing mostly how adolescent, almost childlike they looked. More out of a sense of wonder than resentment, he sometimes stared at the hairless faces of boys and the rosy complexions of girls, whose skin radiated life. Their smiles and gleeful greetings were like strange, sweet music. It was as if the plane to Vietnam had been a time machine squeezing precious years out, aging him at a phenomenal rate. This same machine had just transported his reality from an insufferable place, where innocence did not exist, to a simple campus green where it abounded.

More than anything, he sensed the soft, steady fall of large snowflakes drifting in swirling patterns toward the ground. This early, miraculous autumn snow softly swept over his shoes, cushioning the earth, cooling mildewed flesh that five weeks before had stood in a distant and horrible land. It was the snow that first began the healing.

Lingering on that commons with its gauze of white snow, drinking in the strange and familiar world he had left behind so long ago, flooded the ex-soldier with an unseen, unnoticed joy in the truth of life itself. It seemed he had been granted a gift of vision: to see the world and all its concerns as clearly as an X ray.

He equated life to the red- and yellow-leafed oak trees that lined the campus. *The things in the center of the tree of life are the essentials of human happiness. The outlying branches produce the temporary concerns and greedy preoccupations that, like falling leaves, only clutter the ground and people's lives.*

While he swam in the flood of thoughts and feelings, his feet were headed for the choir room. By the time he moved up the stone steps, energy seemed to well up in his legs. Inside he smelled the old wood, and he heard the sound!

• • •

Clayton prepared himself for the meeting by calling out "Bil-ly! Bil-ly!" only to have the wind defeat him, throwing his voice back toward Wounded Knee. Tears of joy ran down his cheeks, mixing with the wine taste in his mouth. "Bil-ly," he repeated, like some ancient spirit-calling song. "Bil-ly." He smiled, calling blindly ahead. He was now on the final leg of his journey.

• • •

"Ahn-yoos deh-ee, kwee tohl-ees peh-kah-tah moon-dee." In perfect harmony, the Latin ascended upward from sixty voices, pulling Dale down the broad wooden stairs. He moved quickly now, toward the harmony. At the glass door, he hesitated for a minute, almost afraid the beautiful noise might sense the changes and run from him. He pushed the door open and stepped inside.

· · ·

In front of Clayton was the bronze plaque. It was fixed on plywood before the humble earthen mound. Clayton's memory hated this place, but his heart pulled him here often. "Bil-ly," the gray-haired man croaked, but the metal plate didn't have the name Billy on it. This had never fooled the man, and it would not fool him today. Bernice and the kids could think Billy was out there in the world of the living, somewhere, that he would come back. Unlike them Clayton had been a man of God, and God presents to some men an understanding.

That's why only out loud could Clayton wonder if Billy might not come home one day. Inside he knew Billy lay under that mound, beneath the cold metal plaque with all the dates and numbers.

"Billy?" Clayton's voice suddenly brightened. "Billy, *Wayunk cihi*, I came to see you." It seemed to Clayton that Billy only sat there smiling, leaning his elbow on the marker. "Billy. I came to see you, and to ask you something." Clayton staggered a little, then set the empty bottle down.

· · ·

The rich sound intensified. The practiced blend of male and female, falsetto and bass, vibrated the air, then ceased. Dr. Pritchard tapped the thick manuscript. "Not bad . . . not bad at all, and don't forget we do have practice tomorrow night and it is mandatory." He grinned up at the tiers. "See you then!" he said, saluting them with his hand.

While they gathered their coats, he collected the music before him and turned to descend from his podium. It was then that he noticed the thin man with the mustache standing near the door.

The choirmaster's brow wrinkled, then lifted in recognition. "Nielsen!" He pointed with his baton. "Dale Nielsen." He charged down the steps. "My goodness! You made it!" Tears came to the musician's eyes. He dropped the wand on the floor and hugged his former student, squeezing him hard, right in front of the other students, and Dale let him.

"My God, it's good to see you! That day you walked out of here, I knew what you were going to do. I was actually in awe of your idealism and your naïveté, but I knew you would go." He stood back now, looking at the tired man, and dabbed tears quickly from his eyes. "Well, how are you?" Pritchard chuckled, now embarrassed by his lack of composure.

"Not bad, Doc, not bad all in all. Seen a lot. Seen an awful lot." He managed a weak smile.

The professor quickly gathered up his notes. "Walk with me to my Choral Conducting class." He grabbed Dale's elbow and pulled him along. "So tell me, my fine friend, did you learn any great truths from all this?" His arm arched vaguely outward.

Dale thought for a moment. "You know I respect you, sir, and I would like to say something profound, or philosophical." A grin came to his face as Pritchard turned to look at him. But as he spoke, the smile faded. "I, ah, if I learned one thing, it's just that some men are born lucky, some are not."

• • •

In the sharp wind Clayton wobbled, his arms outstretched. "Billy, I don't want to stay here," he screamed in Lakota. "I want you to take me with you. I know you can hear me." He saw Billy smile gently; then his beloved son's face was replaced by a swirl of dust. "Bil-ly!" Clayton's legs caved in and he collapsed to the earth. He sat there and wept.

EPILOGUE

ON FRIDAY, JUNE 13, 1969, FOUR DAYS AFTER FRANK JEALOUS OF HIM WAS killed and Albert Farinelli seriously wounded, their former company was overrun and wiped out. Fifty-five men were killed or wounded. Albert Farinelli told the author, "I would have been killed if not for the wound I received trying to reach Frank." Albert has had a career as an engineer/accountant. He and his wife, Beth, live in Florida where they have raised two children.

Ron Gilbert still lives in Hitchcock, South Dakota on a farm where he and his wife, Mary, raised two children. He returned from a full tour to finish a four-year degree in agriculture. In Vietnam he served daily with Garfford High Pipe. Ron and Mary were helpful in every aspect of this book, believing deeply in the importance of recognizing the sacrifices of South Dakota's Indian people in Vietnam.

Garfford High Pipe, son of Eli High Pipe and Salina At The Street-High Pipe, true to his prediction, came back to the Rosebud Reservation from Vietnam. He then returned to Vietnam to serve a second tour with the 173rd Airborne.

While on his second tour he received the Bronze Star for leading a charge with a sixty-caliber machine gun against a fortified enemy position. He was promoted to staff sergeant and contracted malaria during his second tour and came back to the States. He died in his car during a blizzard near Cody, Nebraska, December 30, 1976. Ron Gilbert said, "Garfford and I became closer than brothers, and stayed in touch until his death. When he died it was like losing a piece of myself."

Dale Nielsen (name changed) came home to finish an undergraduate degree in zoology and complete medical school. He and his wife had two children and eventually divorced. The two children are now young adults. Dale is remarried and has a ten-year-old son. He continues to farm, ranch, and practice medicine in rural South Dakota where he is a beloved healer.

Matthew Jealous Of Him married Emma Eagle Bull. They have five children and five grandchildren. Emma teaches the Lakota language on the reservation.

Clayton Jealous Of Him still lives in Wounded Knee and has never recovered from Billy's death. Bernice passed away in 1998.

POSTSCRIPT

THE ESTABLISHMENT OF THE VIETNAM VETERANS MEMORIAL IN WASH-
ington, D.C. in 1982 was the emotional and triumphant culmination of years
of effort to recognize the valiant service of American youth in the nationally
divisive, failed attempt to prevent South Vietnam from falling to the Communists. The selection jury for the memorial reviewed over 1,400 submissions;
their unanimous choice was Maya Ying Lin's design of a black granite
V-shaped wall. Then in 1984, a bronze statue—Frederick Hart's *Three Fighting
Men*—was dedicated at the site, resulting from demands by conservatives that
a more heroic, representational memorial be added to Lin's "black gash of
shame." The inclusion of the bronze likenesses of an African American, an
Anglo-American, and a Hispanic-looking combat soldier seemingly intended
to cover all the racial and ethnic bases.

When Hart's statue was unveiled, most of America cheered, feeling rightly
that this was an important step in the healing process. Others, however, like
the women and Asian Americans who had also served, were angered; Indian
Country fairly burned. Still unrecognized, many Native American veterans
returned home from the war to the same grinding poverty, racial prejudice,
and lack of opportunity they had left a few years earlier.

Lakota Indian veterans I spoke with on the Sioux reservations were
outraged and hurt that a nation that had taken so much from them had now
slighted by exclusion the sacrifices they had made. America had not paused
to consider the Indian reality that killing child-sized people who looked more
like them than their non-Indian comrades would have severe and permanent
effects. Extreme psychological reactions, resulting in joblessness, homeless-
ness, alcoholism, drug abuse, suicide, and early death were once again the
rewards for their service to America. Indian veterans organizations, which
keep the growing tally of their war casualties, know all too well the grim and
mounting toll that is the truthful measure of Indian sacrifice.

As a young Indian Studies instructor at the University of South Dakota, I was well aware of the fact that Native Americans had fought valiantly for the United States in every war, including the American Revolution. On that morning when the bronze memorial's design was announced, I felt angered by the hurt it caused Indian veterans and their families.

I knew that since the Spanish-American War, Native Americans had volunteered in numbers that had placed them in battle in a higher proportion to their population than any other ethnic group.

Unchanneled anger is useless. On that day I made a quiet vow to write something that might in some way honor their sacrifice. To spend eighteen years working on any project, as all writers know, requires a passionate dedication.

I have found it is often those who have seen and endured most who are least likely to talk about their experiences. During an eight-year friendship with a white Vietnam veteran, he never spoke to me of the war except to acknowledge he was there. For three years fate placed us in close proximity, and late at night he occasionally responded to my naive questions about a soldier's experiences in Vietnam. As a struggling writer, I at least knew a good story when I heard one, and I was convinced that these private conversations might lead to a book. Dale Nielsen, as he is called here to protect his privacy, reluctantly indulged my curiosity until the recollections necessary to verbalize his experiences began to seriously affect him, resulting in awful flashbacks bordering on hallucination. We had to stop, and for three years we did.

However, a casual comment about an Indian enlistee, Frank Jealous Of Him, Dale's "bunk mate" during basic training, caught my attention. Dale had once told me, "I always wondered why, when Frank and I were at the top in everything in Basic, the military presented us with two very different futures. Frank was sent to jump school. I was sent to Non-Commissioned Officers School. I have to think that his being a full-blood Indian had something to do with it."

Dale progressed enough in the resolution of his pain to believe that finishing the book might complete his own healing. The potential addition of the second story line (Frank's) reawakened his enthusiasm for this book. "If my story will aid in the telling of Frank's story, I'll do it gladly," he said.

From that point on, everyone I asked to help in the project did so enthusiastically, with the exception of the U.S. Army. Webster Poor Bear, a friend and Indian veterans activist, encouraged me, trying to allay my fear that a nonveteran simply could not write this story.

Dale helped me track down another man who shared the same basic and advanced infantry training: Ron Gilbert from Hitchcock, South Dakota, whose photographs, sharp memory, and old letters home proved invaluable. Ron's wife, Mary, supplied addresses of veterans groups and suggested I contact the Military Records Center at Suitland, Maryland, a branch of the Smithsonian Institution. The director, a Vietnam veteran named Richard Boylen, answered my call. His help also proved essential and eventually led to Professor James Reckner's help in the editing process. Another person who helped with initial editing was Miriam Todoroff, who donated her efforts because she believed deeply in the importance of the project. In Maryland Dr. Thomas Venum graciously loaned us his home for two weeks while I completed the research for the manuscript.

In 1992 I received a National Endowment for the Arts fellowship in creative nonfiction for my book *Madonna Swan: A Lakota Woman's Story*. The money allowed me to go to Suitland in order to pore through a mountain of records. My wife, Tilda Long Soldier-St. Pierre, an Oglala Lakota from Pine Ridge Reservation, helped me search and photocopy. She has willingly been first proofreader, cultural adviser, companion, driver, and sounding board for every step of this journey. This project would not have been completed without her.

Many interviews were conducted on the Pine Ridge Reservation, and without them this story could not have been told. Indian veterans, friends such as Adolph Hollow Horn, and family members of Indian veterans revived painful memories because they too wished to proclaim the story of the Native Americans in Vietnam. I am especially grateful for the assistance and support given by the Jealous Of Him family—sister Clynda and dad, Clayton, and especially brother Matthew and his wife, Emma, without whose help Frank's story would not have been told. There are many more individuals who deserve mention here. Hal Noyes, a Korean War veteran, and John Ross, a World War II veteran, both read and commented on early drafts as well as provided support for me and my family in a variety of critical ways. Other early proofreaders included Robert W. Tenney, Frank Marshall (Oglala Sioux Tribe Veterans Affairs), Larry Bush and Lamoine Pulliam, Vietnam veterans, civilians Julie Beekman, Mary Scouts Enemy, Jan Mangelsen, Amanda Takes War Bonnet, Reverend John Klinger, SCJ, and *Kola* Jim Carlin. My warmest appreciation goes to Albert and Beth Farinelli without whose painful sharing the book could not have been completed. This book would not exist without the attention of John Drayton, director, and Charles Rankin, editor-in-chief, at the University of Oklahoma Press. A *wopila tonka* (great thanks) to Daniel Simon, who saw the value of the book as literature and fought hard for it at every level. Warm thanks to John Mulvihill, whose close editing improved my story immeasurably. I'd also like to thank Marian Stewart, Karen Wieder, and Yvonne Evans at the Press, who answered so many questions always with great humor and spirit, and Jennifer Cunningham, who fell in love with the project and saw it through to its long awaited birth.

In telling this story, I had to pick and choose dramatic elements and evolve a story line from a vast collection of taped, transcribed stories, to which I added settings and dialogue. The names of some participants were changed, either at their request to protect their privacy or when the name could simply not be remembered. Although the thematic choices are mine, this is a true story. It is my sincere hope that all who served in Vietnam, or who know someone who did, will appreciate this effort and the greater effort of the almost forgotten Native American veterans.

Mark St. Pierre
Kyle, South Dakota
March 2002

GLOSSARY

AERIAL OBSERVATION   Intelligence gathered through the use of various helicopters and fixed-wing aircraft.

AIR STRIKE   Generally, a bombing or strafing run at close quarters. It is used in this book to refer to raids called in to drive the enemy NVA/VC from a specifically identified position, and/or kill the enemy in entrenched or fortified positions.

AIT   Advanced infantry training, eight weeks in duration, for infantry soldiers who will be assigned to combat-related military occupational specialties. *See* MOS.

AK-47   Soviet-built Kalishnikov 7.62 mm automatic weapon. Common rifle of North Vietnamese soldier.

APC   M113 armored personnel carrier. Tracked aluminum vehicle, also referred to as armored cavalry assault vehicle, outfitted with one or two side-mounted M-60s (7.2 mm machine guns) and a 50 mm gun with armored shield.

ARTILLERY BATTALION   Refers to four companies of artillery using various types of equipment usually located so as to provide fire support for all infantry operations in a large locale. Infantry battalions were located so that overlapping zones provided cover to a very large area.

ARTY   Slang for artillery strike.

BASE COMMANDER   Ranking on-site officer.

BASIC TRAINING   Eight weeks of training and conditioning required of all army recruits or draftees.

BEEHIVE ROUNDS   22 mm cadmium darts packed into large artillery shells. They were capable of penetrating steel helmets or armored jackets at

500 yards. Methods were used that could fire 3,000 rounds per minute, instantly carpeting an area the size of a football field.

BERM   An area built to raise rural structures above the wet ground level but more often to create dams that held rice paddies. Defensive positions also had berms around them to provide some protection for troops within that perimeter.

BIA   Bureau of Indian Affairs, branch of the Department of Interior, whose duty it is to administer various tribal resources, land holdings, social welfare, health, and educational programs.

BUNKER   A usually semisubterranean building, reinforced with a roof and sandbags. These bunkers could be one-room affairs or a complex of relatively permanent offices.

C-4   Plastic explosives. Used for many purposes: as an explosive, as a source of fire, to burn down vegetation, or in tiny pieces to heat a can of C-rations.

CAMOUFLAGE CLOTHES   Cotton combat fatigues printed with a jungle-leaf pattern. These much-desired fatigues were generally only available to rear-area officers.

C&C   Command and control.

CANOPY   The coming together of the upper leafy tree limbs to form a ceiling in a jungle area. Some jungle had three separate layers of intact canopy. These conditions would affect light, sound, heat, humidity, and visibility.

CHARGER DUSTOFF   Coded call for an emergency medical evacuation for Company Air Evac.

CHARLIE   Slang term for the enemy, including Vietcong and North Vietnamese Army regulars.

CHERRY   An enlisted man very new to Vietnam, a "virgin."

CHICOM   Chinese Communist-manufactured grenades, rockets, rifles.

CHIEU HOI   Former North Vietnamese soldiers or Vietcong, who then worked for the South to teach U.S. personnel Vietcong politics and military tactics.

CLIP   Holds rounds of ammunition for a rifle. There were eighteen rounds to a clip in an M-16; each man carried seven to fourteen clips at all times.

COMMAND BUNKER   A semipermanent earth-bermed and sandbagged sub-terranean area, ranging from one room at an LZ or firebase to a whole complex of offices at a large rear-area base.

COMMAND POST   An area set up in the middle of a temporary defensive position (also called here a night laager) where the officer in command and radiomen could be found. It might also refer to a more permanent site such as a bunker.

COMPANY A   company at full manpower comprised four platoons each with four squads of ten people plus attendant officers, for a total of 160. The informants for this book recalled that never did they operate with a full contingent; most squads had six men.

CONCERTINA WIRE   Spiral whirls of razor-sharp barbed wire set up around a defensive perimeter.

C-RATS   C-rations.

DEROSed   From DERO, Date Expected Return (from) Overseas.

DI DI MAU   Vietnamese expression adapted by U.S. GIs to mean "Run!"

DRAG   "On drag"—behind main maneuver element.

DUSTOFF   Picking up dead or wounded by a medical evacuation helicopter. A Charger dustoff refers to C Company Evac team.

FATIGUES   OD (Olive Drab) cotton uniforms used either in part or in whole by combat troops in the field.

FIFTY   Fifty-caliber machine gun used extensively in South Vietnam, mounted on APCs or on a tripod by crews of two in field infantry units. According to the veterans interviewed for this book, the average lifespan of a fifty-caliber gunner in Vietnam was the shortest of any MOS.

FIREBASE   Home of an artillery company or battalion. A place where infantry or APC companies would rotate in, to provide defensive support and to have a stand-down area where showers and warm meals would be available. These areas were equipped with permanent bunkers inside a well-developed defensive perimeter usually including a raised berm, outlying listening posts, and remote-controlled Claymore mines. The purpose of these firebases was to provide support to all infantry companies in an area, and they were set up to overlap so that all soldiers could call in artillery support regardless of their position.

FIRE ZONE   Generally refers to an area in which accurate deadly fire could be applied either from a fixed position such as a night position or ambush.

FLARES   There were three uses for flares made of burning phosphorus: first, in the perimeter as trip flares that would fire if the enemy disturbed a trip wire; second, as routine illumination over a given area by mortar and artillery companies; third, to provide continuous illumination in the event of an enemy attack at night. These night flares would be fired into the air by artillery to drop suspended from a tiny parachute.

FLÉCHETTE   Small, dart-shaped projectile.

FOO-GAS   Sticky petroleum by-product stored in drums at the top of a slope on the edge of a defensive perimeter. Once lit it was spilled downhill to kill or frighten the enemy in hopes of preventing them from getting in the perimeter and overrunning the firebase.

FRAGGING   The killing of an unpopular officer by his own troops; the term refers to killing with a fragmentation grenade.

FREEDOM BIRD   A military plane or private contractor that took U.S. military personnel home after their tour of duty in Vietnam.

FREE-FIRE ZONE   An area that as defined by the Geneva Convention is to be free of civilian noncombatants. Anyone within that area without proper identification can be considered the enemy.

FRIENDLY FIRE   Rockets, bombs, howitzer, mortar, or rifle fire aimed mistakenly at U.S. troops by U.S. forces or the army of the Republic of (South) Vietnam, ARVN.

GRUNTS   Derogatory term for infantry soldiers who stayed in the field while on lengthy patrols. They carried all necessary supplies in a heavy rucksack.

H&I FIRE   Harassment and interdictory fire, generally used at night to discourage enemy troop movements in the vicinity of a rear area, LZ, or a firebase.

HEAT TAB   The size of a quarter, it was lit with a match and used to heat C-rations.

HIGHER HIGHER   Battalion commander, generally a colonel or lieutenant colonel, or executive officer, generally a major.

HOOTCH   Simple grass and bamboo huts used by rural Vietnamese. The term might also refer to "private" huts used by U.S. military personnel while assigned to a rear area.

HOWITZER   Each firebase would have six to eight 105 mm artillery pieces.

HUEY   UH-series helicopter. This versatile light helicopter was equipped to serve as a gunship, a standard assault aircraft, resupply vehicle, or an air ambulance. They are credited with saving the lives of thousands of U.S. casualties as air ambulances.

INTELLIGENCE   Information on enemy troop deployment, movements, construction locations, or supply routes gathered from any source.

KILL ZONE   A narrow area of extremely deadly firepower either inside a perimeter or as part of an ambush site.

KIT CARSON SCOUT   A South Vietnamese soldier assigned to a U.S. platoon or company to act as a scout and interpreter. Comes from a term for the Navajo men hired by Kit Carson to track down and round up fellow Navajos. These scouts were often considered a security risk and were credited with supplying both the enemy and black-market merchants information about U.S. troop movements. Interviewees said, "We were constantly amazed at how civilians would be waiting at precise places on a patrol to sell us whatever we wanted."

KLICK   Slang for kilometer.

LAAGER   Refers to a temporary defensive position. Platoons would move from one night laager to another—in Frank Jealous Of Him's case, for up to thirty nights in a row. The laager would also serve as a resupply drop site.

LOACH   Hughes OH-6 Cayuse helicopter, used for finding the enemy and directing the movement of U.S. ground forces.

LURP RATIONS   Dried food, including fruit, that could be eaten raw or reconstituted. (*Lurp,* or *LRP,* stands for "long-range reconnaissance patrol.")

LZ   Landing zone; a permanent, semipermanent, or temporary area cleared from the jungle to allow helicopters to land.

M-16 Plastic-stocked automatic rifle; fired a 5.56 mm round and was the standard rifle carried by all U.S. Army infantry.

MACV Military Assistance Command, Vietnam, which controlled the war in Vietnam. MACVs were U.S. personnel working directly for MACV in civilian pacification, in medical, farming, language, and educational services. They were the original U.S. advisers in Vietnam and also served to collect intelligence.

MAMA-SAN Refers to older Vietnamese women who often followed or caught up with U.S. GIs to sell black-market goods. These goods ranged from cold Coca-Cola to women and drugs. It is said a company would come to a public road after a long "secret" mission and the Mama-sans would be waiting there for them. This made U.S. GIs very nervous about Kit Carson Scouts and *chieu hois.*

MEDEVAC Medical evacuation of wounded U.S. personnel, usually by Huey helicopter; also called a dustoff.

MINI-GUN Water-cooled, multibarreled, rotating automatic canon used to fire thousands of 5.56 rounds per minute. These guns were mounted on large helicopters and fixed-wing aircraft.

MORTAR PLATOON In a combat field company it fired 105 mm shells. When part of a track company it fired 4.2-inch rounds.

MOS Military occupational specialty.

NCO SCHOOL Non-Commissioned Officers School produced buck sergeants (E-6) for combat leadership. Lowest ranking non-commissioned officer in the chain of command.

NVA Soldiers serving in the regular North Vietnamese army.

OCS Officers Candidate School. Used for producing second lieutenants, sometimes referred to as "shake-and-bake" lieutenants.

OD Officer of the Day.

OD Standard Olive Drab.

PLATOON At full force comprised four squads of ten. Platoons in Vietnam seldom held a full contingent of men.

PONCHO   Standard-issue rain gear also used as tents by leg units. APC companies did not carry them.

PONCHO LINER   Taken out of the poncho and used as a blanket. Also used to cover the dead.

POINT MAN   Man out in front of a moving group of soldiers. Usually a volunteer position and would be rotated or fall to someone good at detecting disturbances in the ground or foliage. American Indian veterans speak often of "inheriting" this position because they were Indians, becoming the willing or unwilling victims of ethnic and racial stereotyping. A few veterans told me that if you had good eyes and ears, it might be better to be on point because the enemy set up for ambush would often let the point man pass so they could hit the middle of the patrol.

POINT OF POINT   Point man of point squad of point platoon in a company-sized maneuver.

PUFF THE MAGIC DRAGON   A modified C-47 aircraft set up as a gunship equipped with multiple mini-guns; it was capable of dispersing 3,000–6,000 beehive rounds per minute, carpeting a large area in a tight pattern so that all life was eliminated.

REAR AREA   Command and control headquarters in areas generally theoretically removed from threat of regular enemy attack. Men in the field generally distrusted rear-area personnel.

RIF   Reconnaissance in force. A company-sized operation on a sweep through a given area looking for whatever would be found. Different from a squad- or platoon-sized reconnaissance mission in which the men would move very quietly through an area.

ROAD PATROL   Refers to regular mine sweep and surveillance patrols on main and secondary arteries for resupply and troop movement. Roads were perpetually mined and booby-trapped by the Vietcong and thus required surveillance preceding each convoy. Even with these patrols, convoy casualties were high.

ROME PLOW   Defoliating chain attached to heavy armored Caterpillars, built in Rome, New York. The actual device looked like a large ship's anchor chain with short pieces of train rail welded to it.

RPG   Rocket-propelled grenade; generally refers to Russian-made RPG-7 rounds fired from handheld launchers.

RPG SCREEN   Carried rolled up on each track, it resembled a tall chain-link fence. It was placed directly in front of the track to cause premature detonation of incoming RPG-7 fire.

RTO   Radio transmission operator.

SAPPER   Usually a Vietcong soldier who (on a suicide mission) would tape explosives to his body and under cover of darkness try to infiltrate American defensive perimeters with the goal of reaching and destroying the command post and its personnel.

SAW GRASS   A tall grass with sharp serrated edges that can grow six to eight feet in height.

SEARCH-AND-DESTROY MISSIONS   Another term for RIF operations in which soldiers look for enemy resistance or supplies.

SHIT PILLS   Literally, Halazone pills added to water to prevent serious diarrhea, a very real problem in Vietnam. For the field infantry, infected saw grass cuts, funguses, diarrhea, and constipation were common health problems. Figuratively or jokingly, they were pills to help you "keep your shit together," to stay cool under fire.

SHORT, SHORT-TIMER   Refers to time left in country. Tours were generally twelve months in duration. Superstition and tradition dictated pulling the men out of dangerous assignments after eleven months. A short-timer being killed was also bad for morale.

SIXTY   An M-60 machine gun firing a 7.62 mm round.

SNIFFER MISSIONS   Missions to find active trails, bunkers, and tunnel systems, utilizing trained dogs.

SQUAD   At full capacity, ten men.

TOPO   Topographical map.

TRACERS, RED, GREEN   Every fifth round of automatic weapons fire is a tracer made of burning phosphorus. These tracers make possible the sighting in of automatic weapons fire. Americans used red; the NVA used green.

TUNNEL SYSTEMS   Tunnels, some quite permanent and extensive, used in guerilla warfare to hide, house, equip, and feed soldiers. They were also used as command posts and hospitals.

UTILITY PACKS   Foil packets containing candy, cigarettes, toilet paper, shaving supplies, and soap.

VIETCONG   Members of the insurgency loyal to the Communist north; acted in various capacities, including intelligence gathering, farming, rubber harvesting, soldiering, and guerrilla warfare.

VIETNAMESE   A citizen of the Republic of (South) Vietnam. These civilians often wore black silk clothing, and although popular films have insinuated this was the uniform of the Vietcong, in fact it was more common than blue jeans are to American youth.

WATER BLADDER   Plastic multiquart water bottle.

WEB BELT, GEAR   In basic training, equipped with suspenders, used to carry a one-quart canteen, first-aid pack, a light backpack with poncho, and possibly C-rations. In the field men carried bandolier straps and clipped to these grenades, a one-quart canteen, and cloth pockets that contained seven of the fourteen to twenty-one loaded M-16 clips each man was to carry. Frank Jealous Of Him's infantry company also carried external frame rucksacks.

FRANK W JEA

OUR NATION HONORS THE COURAGE
SACRIFICE AND DEVOTION TO DUTY AND
COUNTRY OF ITS VIETNAM VETERANS.
THIS MEMORIAL WAS BUILT WITH
PRIVATE CONTRIBUTIONS FROM
THE AMERICAN PEOPLE.
NOVEMBER 11, 1982

1975

1959

IN HONOR OF THE MEN AND WOMEN OF THE ARMED FORCES OF THE UNITED STATES WHO SERVED IN THE VIETNAM WAR. THE NAMES OF THOSE WHO GAVE THEIR LIVES AND OF THOSE WHO REMAIN MISSING ARE INSCRIBED IN THE ORDER THEY WERE TAKEN FROM US.

LOUS·OF·HIM

Rubbing from the Vietnam Veterans Memorial in Washington, D.C.
Frank Jealous Of Him was killed in action June 9, 1969.

IN HONOR OF T
WOMEN OF THE
OF THE UNITED
SERVED IN THE
THE NAMES OF
GAVE THEIR LIV
THOSE WHO RE
ARE INSCRIBED

E MEN AND

ARMED FORCES

STATES WHO

IETNAM WAR.

HOSE WHO

S AND OF

IAIN MISSING

. .

U.S. MILITARY PERSONNEL
KILLED OR MISSING OR CAPTURED
IN THE VIETNAM WAR, 1957-1984

AMERICAN INDIANS

NAME	RANK	BRANCH	HOME OF RECORD
Acosta, John Michael	PFC	Army	Sacramento
Adikai, Alvin, Jr.	PFC	Army	Window Rock
Alberts, Roger Duane	PFC	Army	Ft. Totten
Aleck, John Ira	PFC	Marines	Reno
Anderson, Dennis William	SSGT	Army	Norfolk
Antonio, Johnnie, Jr.	LCPL	Marines	Crown Point
Arkie, Vallance Galen	CPL	Marines	Parker
Arlentino, Dudney Nelson	SP4	Army	Coolidge
Armstrong, Dean Edward	GSGT	Marines	Atoka
Arthur, Johnny	SP5	Army	Fruitland
Arviso, Herbert	SGT	Army	Farmington
Atole, Floyd Samuel	SGT	Army	Dulce
Austin, William Eugene	SGT	Army	Lenoir
Baker, Elwood	LCPL	Marines	Battiest
Baltezar, Theodore	SP4	Army	Gregory
Barnett, Paul Wayne	SP4	Army	Dustin
Barney, Luther	SP5	Army	Mexican Springs
Barr, Edward Nasuesak	SN	Navy	Brevig Mission
Barr, Thomas M.	SP5	Army	Anchorage
Barrios, James Patrick	SP4	Army	Lemoore
Battiest, Andrew	CPL	Army	Calipatria
Bear, Donald Earl	SFC	Army	Mountain View
Beaulieu, Leo Vernon	PFC	Marines	Lengby

STATE	DATE OF CASUALTY	COUNTRY OF CASUALTY	CATEGORY OF CASUALTY
CA	21 Jan 1968	S. Vietnam	Hostile, Died - Wounds
AZ	14 Mar 1971	S. Vietnam	Hostile, Killed
ND	5 Feb 1968	S. Vietnam	Hostile, Killed
NV	7 Mar 1969	S. Vietnam	Hostile, Killed
NE	11 Dec 1966	S. Vietnam	Non Hostile, Died - Other
NM	27 Dec 1967	S. Vietnam	Hostile, Killed
AZ	3 Sep 1967	S. Vietnam	Hostile, Killed
AZ	7 Dec 1967	S. Vietnam	Hostile, Killed
OK	13 May 1967	S. Vietnam	Hostile, Killed
NM	10 Jun 1971	S. Vietnam	Hostile, Killed
NM	26 Oct 1969	S. Vietnam	Hostile, Killed
NM	21 Feb 1969	S. Vietnam	Hostile, Killed
NC	31 Jul 1970	S. Vietnam	Hostile, Killed
OK	24 Jun 1967	S. Vietnam	Non-Hostile, Died - Other
SD	20 Jun 1979	S. Vietnam	Hostile, Killed
OK	3 Jan 1969	S. Vietnam	Hostile, Killed
NM	21 Dec 1971	S. Vietnam	Non-Hostile, Died - Ill/Injury
AK	3 May 1969	S. Vietnam	Non-Hostile, Died - Other
AK	12 May 1969	S. Vietnam	Hostile, Killed
CA	12 Jan 1969	S. Vietnam	Hostile, Killed
CA	25 Jun 1968	S. Vietnam	Hostile, Killed
OK	8 Jul 1968	S. Vietnam	Hostile, Killed
MN	16 May 1966	S. Vietnam	Hostile, Killed

NAME	RANK	BRANCH	HOME OF RECORD
Begaye, Eddie Charles	CPL	Marines	Ramah
Begaye, Felix Dohaltahe	PFC	Marines	Little Water
Begody, Harold L.	SP4	Army	Tuba City
Bellanger, John George	LCPL	Marines	Minneapolis
Bernard, Vincent	LCPL	Marines	Dorchester
Bettleyoun, Percy	CPL	Marines	Rapid City
Bigtree, James Victor	CPL	Marines	Syracuse
Billie, Larry Rogers	PFC	Marines	Chinle
Blackfox, Robert Lee	PFC	Marines	Tahlequah
Blackwater, Dwight Thomas	1LT	Army	Phoenix
Boswell, David Henry	HN	Navy	Buffalo
Briseno, Johnny Charles	PFC	Marines	Waynoka
Brown, Randolph, Jr.	LCPL	Marines	North Highlands
Bruner, David	SP4	Army	Sapulpa
Butler, Lawrence Joseph	SP4	Army	Hayward
Campbell, Eugene Charles	LCPL	Marines	Redwood Valley
Cano, Jose Ramon	SP4	Army	Austin
Carney, Joshua Eli	SSGT	Army	McAlester
Charlie, Peter	LCPL	Marines	Farmington
Chester, Alvin	LCPL	Marines	Window Rock
Chino, Gerald Gregory	SP4	Army	Cubero
Chopper, Franklin Delano	PFC	Army	Brockton
Christjohn, Paul Emerson	PFC	Army	Oneida
Christy, Gilmore Wilson	SP4	Army	Tulsa
Claw, Peter Yazzie	PFC	Army	Kayenta
Cloud, Ronald Myron	SGT	Army	Ponemah
Corbiere, Austin Morris	LCPL	Marines	Canada
Crook, Elliott	SP5	Army	Phoenix
Cruz, Frank Bryan	PFC	Army	Detroit

STATE	DATE OF CASUALTY	COUNTRY OF CASUALTY	CATEGORY OF CASUALTY
NM	25 May 1967	S. Vietnam	Hostile, Killed
NM	10 Dec 1967	S. Vietnam	Non-Hostile, Died - Other
AZ	14 Feb 1968	S. Vietnam	Hostile, Killed
MN	14 Feb 1968	S. Vietnam	Hostile, Killed
MA	21 Sep 1968	S. Vietnam	Hostile, Killed
SD	28 May 1968	S. Vietnam	Hostile, Killed
NY	11 Jan 1966	S. Vietnam	Hostile, Died - Wounds
AZ	11 Oct 1966	S. Vietnam	Hostile, Killed
OK	17 Feb 1970	S. Vietnam	Hostile, Killed
AZ	19 Jun 1971	S. Vietnam	Non-Hostile, Died - Other
NY	6 Mar 1968	S. Vietnam	Hostile, Killed
OK	18 Jun 1970	S. Vietnam	Hostile, Died - Wounds
CA	12 Feb 1969	S. Vietnam	Hostile, Killed
OK	14 May 1969	S. Vietnam	Hostile, Killed
WI	4 Apr 1969	S. Vietnam	Hostile, Died - Wounds
CA	27 Aug 1967	S. Vietnam	Non-Hostile, Died - Ill/Injury
TX	15 Jan 1969	S. Vietnam	Hostile, Killed
OK	12 Feb 1971	S. Vietnam	Hostile, Killed
NM	8 Aug 1970	S. Vietnam	Hostile, Killed
AZ	5 Jul 1965	S. Vietnam	Non-Hostile, Died - Other
NM	24 Mar 1968	S. Vietnam	Hostile, Killed
MT	13 Jun 1967	S. Vietnam	Hostile, Killed
WI	9 Sep 1968	S. Vietnam	Non-Hostile, Died -Ill/Injury
OK	6 Feb 1967	S. Vietnam	Hostile, Killed
AZ	5 Apr 1968	S. Vietnam	Hostile, Killed
MN	4 Jul 1968	S. Vietnam	Hostile, Killed
	9 May 1966	S. Vietnam	Non-Hostile, Died - Other
AZ	17 May 1972	S. Vietnam	Hostile, Died - Missing BNR
MI	27 Jul 1967	S. Vietnam	Hostile, Killed

NAME	RANK	BRANCH	HOME OF RECORD
Cuch, Wilbert Wayne	LCPL	Marines	Springville
Curley, Albert Allen	PFC	Marines	Cubero
Dale, Bennie	SP4	Army	Wide Ruins
Davis, Christopher Wilmer	SP4	Army	Belcourt
Daw, Jerry Lorenzo	CPL	Army	Tonalea
De Vaney, James Price	CPL	Army	Goldsboro
Deer, Terry Louis	PFC	Army	Wewoka
Deere, Charles Kenneth	PFC	Army	Okemah
Deerinwater, Bruce Edward	SSGT	Army	McAlester
Dempsey, Warren Leigh	CPL	Marines	Church Rock
Denipah, Daniel Dee	LCPL	Marines	Tuba City
Dewey, Eric Melvin	PFC	Marines	Bishop
Doctor, Gary Dean	LCPL	Marines	Basom
Dunsing, Dennis Paul	PFC	Army	Ukiah
Durant, Forbis Pipkin, Jr.	LCPL	Marines	Atoka
Eisenberger, George Joe BU	SGT	Army	Pawhuska
Elisovsky, David Henry	SGT	Army	Cordova
Etsitty, Van	CPL	Army	Gallup
Fisher, William John	LCPL	Marines	Arlee
Flying Horse, Conrad Lee	LCPL	Marines	McIntosh
Fragua, George Leonard	PFC	Army	Jemez Pueblo
Francisco, Patrick Phillip	LCPL	Marines	Stanfield
Fraser, Thomas Edwin	PVT	Marines	Detroit
Fredenberg, Ralph	SP4	Army	Shawano
Frenier, Irving F.		Army	Sisseton
Gamble, Charles F., Jr.	SP4	Army	Juneau
General, Leslie Neil	CPL	Marines	Niagara Falls
Ghahate, Luther Anderson	SP4	Army	Zuni
Going, Wallace	BM2	Navy	Watson

STATE	DATE OF CASUALTY	COUNTRY OF CASUALTY	CATEGORY OF CASUALTY
UT	26 May 1968	S. Vietnam	Hostile, Killed
NM	30 Mar 1967	S. Vietnam	Hostile, Killed
AZ	12 May 1968	S. Vietnam	Hostile, Killed
ND	18 Mar 1967	S. Vietnam	Non-Hostile, Died - Ill/Injury
AZ	8 Jun 1967	S. Vietnam	Hostile, Killed
NC	28 Feb 1970	S. Vietnam	Hostile, Killed
OK	5 Oct 1970	S. Vietnam	Non-Hostile, Died - Other
OK	5 May 1968	S. Vietnam	Hostile, Killed
OK	25 Jan 1969	S. Vietnam	Hostile, Killed
NM	3 Dec 1965	S. Vietnam	Hostile, Killed
AZ	28 Dec 1967	S. Vietnam	Hostile, Killed
CA	29 Jul 1967	S. Vietnam	Hostile, Killed
NY	7 Oct 1966	S. Vietnam	Hostile, Killed
CA	6 May 1968	S. Vietnam	Hostile, Killed
OK	10 Mar 1968	S. Vietnam	Hostile, Died - Wounds
OK	5 Dec 1965	S. Vietnam	Hostile, Died - Missing BNR
AK	23 Jan 1966	S. Vietnam	Hostile, Killed
NM	1 Jun 1968	S. Vietnam	Hostile, Killed
MT	22 Sep 1966	S. Vietnam	Non-Hostile, Died -Ill/Injury
SD	31 Aug 1970	S. Vietnam	Hostile, Died - Wounds
NM	25 Dec 1966	S. Vietnam	Non-Hostile, Died - Other
AZ	26 Apr 1967	S. Vietnam	Hostile, Killed
MI	4 Apr 1970	S. Vietnam	Non-Hostile, Died - Ill/Injury
WI	24 Apr 1968	S. Vietnam	Hostile, Died - Missing
SD		S. Vietnam	Hostile, Killed
AK	28 Oct 1969	S. Vietnam	Non-Hostile, Died - Other
NY	1 May 1968	S. Vietnam	Hostile, Killed
NM	21 Oct 1968	S. Vietnam	Hostile, Killed
OK	23 Dec 1968	S. Vietnam	Hostile, Killed

NAME	RANK	BRANCH	HOME OF RECORD
Goodiron, Ronald Christy	PFC	Marines	Shields
Green, Larry	PFC	Marines	Niagara Falls
Gritts, William Archie	CPL	Army	Hulbert
Hale, Victor	LCPL	Marines	Topeka
Harjo, Kenneth DeWayne	SP4	Army	Seminole
Harris, Carl E.	SGT	Army	Rock Hill
Hatle, Theodore Magnus	CPL	Army	Sisseton
Hawthorne, Gene	SSGT	Army	Lupton
Hayes, Thomas	SGT	Army	Shiprock
Healy, Louis Glenn	PVT	Marines	Dodson
Henry, Robert Gregory	PVT	Army	San Diego
Henshaw, Larry Roy	SGT	Army	Sapulpa
Hicks, Donald	SP4	Army	Tonalea
Hickson, Leonard Martin	SGT	Army	Ft. Defiance
Howard, Charles Vincent	SGT	Army	Brimley
Hummingbird, Ferrell	LCPL	Marines	Oakland
Huskon, Benny Leo	SP4	Army	Leupp
Incashola, Jean Baptiste	PFC	Army	St. Ignatius
Ingram, John Lee	PFC	Marines	Weleetka
Ivey, Sam	PFC	Army	McGrath
Jackson, Lloyd Wilner	SGT	Army	Austin
Jackson, Michael Meredith	PFC	Army	Waubay
Jackson, Ralford John	PFC	Marines	Tuba City
Jamerson, Kenneth Robert	LCPL	Marines	Little Eagle
James, Billie	SP4	Army	Farmington
Jealous-of-Him, Frank W.	SP4	Army	Wounded Knee
Johnson, Clifford Curtis	CWO	Army	Fairfax
Johnson, Zane Everett	LCPL	Marines	Fruitland
Jones, Michael Bruce	PFC	Army	Mohave

STATE	DATE OF CASUALTY	COUNTRY OF CASUALTY	CATEGORY OF CASUALTY
ND	28 Feb 1968	S. Vietnam	Hostile, Killed
NY	9 Jan 1969	S. Vietnam	Hostile, Killed
OK	13 Jun 1968	S. Vietnam	Hostile, Killed
KS	8 Dec 1968	S. Vietnam	Hostile, Killed
OK	18 Nov 1969	S. Vietnam	Hostile, Killed
SC	15 Nov 1965	S. Vietnam	Hostile, Killed
SD	23 Jun 1969	S. Vietnam	Hostile, Killed
AZ	4 May 1966	S. Vietnam	Non-Hostile, Died - Missing
NM	27 Dec 1968	S. Vietnam	Hostile, Killed
MT	5 Jul 1968	S. Vietnam	Hostile, Killed
CA	25 Jun 1968	S. Vietnam	Hostile, Killed
OK	1 May 1970	S. Vietnam	Hostile, Killed
AZ	30 Jun 1968	S. Vietnam	Hostile, Killed
AZ	18 May 1969	S. Vietnam	Hostile, Killed
MI	2 Jul 1966	S. Vietnam	Hostile, Killed
CA	14 Jan 1967	S. Vietnam	Hostile, Killed
AZ	7 Jun 1968	S. Vietnam	Non-Hostile, Died - Other
MT	23 Nov 1966	S. Vietnam	Non-Hostile, Died - Other
OK	7 Apr 1968	S. Vietnam	Hostile, Killed
AK	16 Sep 1965	S. Vietnam	Non-Hostile, Died - Other
NV	7 May 1970	S. Vietnam	Hostile, Killed
SD	24 Mar 1966	S. Vietnam	Hostile, Died - Wounds
AZ	22 May 1969	S. Vietnam	Hostile, Killed
SD	5 Apr 1967	S. Vietnam	Hostile, Died - Wounds
NM	15 Apr 1968	S. Vietnam	Hostile, Killed
SD	9 Jun 1969	S. Vietnam	Hostile, Killed
OK	29 Jan 1966	S. Vietnam	Hostile, Killed
NM	27 Mar 1969	S. Vietnam	Non-Hostile, Died - Other
AZ	12 May 1968	S. Vietnam	Hostile, Killed

NAME	RANK	BRANCH	HOME OF RECORD
Kanosh, Wilbert Dwayne	CPL	Marines	Vernal
Kee, Wilson Begay	SP4	Army	Chinle
Kilbuck, George Gregory	PFC	Army	Bethal
Kipp, Raymond Sidney	SP4	Army	Oklahoma City
Lara, Chevo Garcia	SP4	Army	North Sacramento
Largo, Calvin David	SP4	Army	Shiprock
LeBeau, Andrew Ernest, Jr.	SSGT	Air Force	Sparks
LeBeaux, Loren	SP4	Army	Wakpala
LaPointe, Larry			Rosebud
LeClair, Prentice Dale	SP4	Army	Tulsa
Levings, James M.	SGT	Army	New Town
Little Sun, Thomas Lee	PFC	Marines	Pawnee
Locklear, Jimmy	SP4	Army	Maxton
Mackey, Talton Lee	SGT	Army	Red Oak
Malone, Robert Gary	CPL	Marines	Wichita
Maloney, Oscar	SP5	Army	Tuba City
Manselle, Eugene L., III	PVT	Army	Hartford
Marietta, Harold Joseph	SGT	Army	Sacaton
Marrufo, Rodney Elmer, Jr.	SP4	Army	Stewarts Point
Martin, Emerson	PFC	Marines	Churchrock
Martinez, Bobby Joe	SGT	Army	Ft. Wingate
Martinez, Manuel	BM1	Navy	Taos Pueblo
Matthews, Gilbert Lewis, Jr.	CAPT	Army	Pine Ridge
McClelland, Myron	PFC	Army	Downieville
McCosar, Winford	LCPL	Marines	Bell
McDowell, John Clark	CPL	Army	Corsica
McPherson, Dennis	PFC	Army	Gregory
Mermejo, Joseph Michael	PFC	Marines	Stockton
Meshigaud, Andrew Harry	SSGT	Army	Dallas

STATE	DATE OF CASUALTY	COUNTRY OF CASUALTY	CATEGORY OF CASUALTY
UT	30 Jan 1969	S. Vietnam	Non-Hostile, Died - Other
AZ	17 Jun 1970	S. Vietnam	Hostile, Killed
AK	27 Aug 1965	S. Vietnam	Hostile, Died - Missing
OK	17 Mar 1970	S. Vietnam	Hostile, Killed
CA	10 Aug 1966	S. Vietnam	Hostile, Killed
NM	19 Sep 1968	S. Vietnam	Hostile, Killed
NV	11 Feb 1968	S. Vietnam	Hostile, Killed
SD	Feb 1971	S. Vietnam	Hostile, Killed
SD	April 1968	S. Vietnam	Hostile, Killed
OK	9 Aug 1967	S. Vietnam	Hostile, Killed
ND	23 May 1968	S. Vietnam	Non-Hostile, Died - Ill/Injury
OK	16 Feb 1968	S. Vietnam	Hostile, Killed
NC	4 Sep 1968	S. Vietnam	Hostile, Died - Wounds
OK	9 Dec 1968	S. Vietnam	Hostile, Killed
KS	28 Jul 1966	S. Vietnam	Hostile, Killed
AZ	2 Nov 1970	S. Vietnam	Non-Hostile, Died - Other
CN	19 Jun 1968	S. Vietnam	Hostile, Killed
AZ	7 Feb 1966	S. Vietnam	Hostile, Killed
CA	23 May 1968	S. Vietnam	Hostile, Died - Wounds
NM	29 May 1969	S. Vietnam	Hostile, Killed
NM	11 May 1968	S. Vietnam	Hostile, Killed
NM	27 Feb 1969	S. Vietnam	Hostile, Killed
SD	24 Jun 1971	S. Vietnam	Non-Hostile, Died - Other
CA	20 Feb 1966	S. Vietnam	Hostile, Killed
CA	6 Mar 1968	S. Vietnam	Hostile, Killed
SD	9 Jan 1968	S. Vietnam	Hostile, Died - Wounds
SD	11 Nov 1967	S. Vietnam	Hostile, Killed
UT	29 Mar 1969	S. Vietnam	Hostile, Killed
TX	17 Dec 1971	S. Vietnam	Hostile, Killed

NAME	RANK	BRANCH	HOME OF RECORD
Mike, Steven	PFC	Army	Gallup
Miller, Charles Daniel	LCPL	Marines	Wewoka
Mills, Arthur Lee	LCPL	Marines	Rapid City
Molino, Eddie, Jr.	CAPT	Army	Fallon
Montoya, Joe Ned	CPL	Army	San Juan Pueblo
Moss, Weldon Dale	PFC	Marines	Ethete
Muller, Harold Bradley	SGT	Army	McKinleyville
Muncey, Jay Allan	SP4	Army	Battle Mountain
Muniz, Daniel Harold	PVT	Army	Dulce
Muskett, Wayne	LCPL	Marines	Shiprock
Nadal, Baldomero Arturo	CPL	Army	Delano
Noah, Josh Cain	SGT	Army	Hugo
Noah, Marvin Tidwell	LCPL	Marines	Broken Bow
Okemah, John	SFC	Army	Harrah
Ortiz, Randall Isaac-Jed	LCPL	Marines	Denver
Pahcheka, Robert Carlos	PFC	Marines	Indianhoma
Pamonicutt, Martin James	PFC	Marines	Neopit
Pappin, John Patrick	CR	Navy	Pawhuska
Parker, Larry	SSGT	Army	Winnemucca
Parkhurst, Vincent Bertram	SFC	Army	Chicago
Pashano, Jack Poola	SP4	Army	Polacca
Patten, Jimmie	SGT	Army	San Carlos
Paulsen, Warren	BM3	Navy	Valdes
Peina, Ernest Delbert	SP4	Army	Zuni
Perkins, David Drake	PFC	Army	Coolidge
Pesewonit, Russel Eugene	PFC	Marines	Lawton
Pete, Franklin Danny, Jr.	SP4	Army	Sacaton
Pinole, Babe	LCPL	Marines	Santa Rosa
Platero, Raymond	PFC	Army	Canoncito

STATE	DATE OF CASUALTY	COUNTRY OF CASUALTY	CATEGORY OF CASUALTY
NM	6 Jan 1971	S. Vietnam	Non-Hostile, Died - Other
OK	31 Mar 1968	S. Vietnam	Hostile, Killed
SD	12 Apr 1968	S. Vietnam	Hostile, Killed
NV	10 May 1970	Cambodia	Non-Hostile, Died - Missing
NM	1 Aug 1967	S. Vietnam	Non-Hostile, Died - Ill/Injury
WY	2 Apr 1966	S. Vietnam	Hostile, Killed
CA	13 Mar 1968	S. Vietnam	Hostile, Killed
NV	28 Aug 1970	S. Vietnam	Hostile, Killed
NM	17 May 1970	S. Vietnam	Non-Hostile, Died - Other
NM	26 Aug 1969	S. Vietnam	Hostile, Died - Wounds
CA	15 Apr 1967	S. Vietnam	Hostile, Killed
OK	20 Nov 1967	S. Vietnam	Hostile, Died - Missing
OK	24 Mar 1967	S. Vietnam	Hostile, Killed
OK	13 Apr 1968	S. Vietnam	Hostile, Died - Wounds
CO	20 Aug 1969	S. Vietnam	Hostile, Killed
OK	22 Oct 1968	S. Vietnam	Hostile, Killed
WI	23 Jun 1969	S. Vietnam	Hostile, Killed
OK	12 Mar 1970	S. Vietnam	Non-Hostile, Died - Other
NV	21 Mar 1970	S. Vietnam	Hostile, Killed
IL	20 Feb 1968	S. Vietnam	Hostile, Killed
AZ	19 Aug 1968	S. Vietnam	Hostile, Killed
AZ	31 Jan 1968	S. Vietnam	Hostile, Killed
AK	23 Jun 1969	S. Vietnam	Hostile, Killed
NM	13 Sep 1968	S. Vietnam	Hostile, Killed
AZ	11 Oct 1966	S. Vietnam	Hostile, Killed
OK	22 Jul 1966	S. Vietnam	Hostile, Killed
AZ	27 May 1968	S. Vietnam	Hostile, Killed
CA	7 Dec 1968	S. Vietnam	Hostile, Killed
NM	26 Jan 1970	S. Vietnam	Hostile, Killed

NAME	RANK	BRANCH	HOME OF RECORD
Pokerjim, Joseph Louis	PVT	Army	St. Ignatius
Poolaw, Pascal Cleatus, Sr.	FSGT	Army	Apache
Rader, Gary Philip	SP4	Army	Sacramento
Rainwater, Jewel Lee	PFC	Army	Van Buren
Ray, Darwin Esker	CPL	Army	East Highlands
Red Hawk, Jesse Milton	PVT	Army	Pine Ridge
Renville, Arden Keith	SP4	Army	Sisseton
Ridge, Jesse Lee	PFC	Army	Park Hill
Roach, Orlando Silas	SP4	Army	Eagle Butte
Roberson, Arthur Paul	SP4	Army	Banning
Roberts, Terry	PFC	Marines	Ottumwa
Robinson, Marvin Ray	SP5	Army	Livingston
Romero, Michael Andrew	LCPL	Marines	Sells
Rose, Leonard Dale	PFC	Marines	Herlong
Rowe, William Edwin	SSGT	Army	Costa Mesa
Roy, Russell	LCPL	Marines	Mission
Ruiz, Peter George	PFC	Marines	Ajo
Sam, Wilfred Gerald	PFC	Marines	Elko
Sampson, Gerald Hilbert	CAPT	Marines	Williamsport
Sawney, Jackie Lee	SP4	Army	Tulsa
Schmidt, Frederick Charles	PFC	Army	Parkville
Shay, Lawrence William, Jr.	LCPL	Marines	Portland
Simbola, Jose Scotty	PVT	Army	Penasco
Simmers, Garold Ray	PFC	Marines	Rock Hill
Siow, Gale Robert	ATN3	Navy	Huntington Park
Slim, Jimmie Farrell	PVT	Marines	Cow Springs
Smith, Gus, Jr.	SP4	Army	Oso
Smith, Preston Lee	1LT	Army	Essexville
Snow, Milton, Jr.	PFC	Army	East Aurora

STATE	DATE OF CASUALTY	COUNTRY OF CASUALTY	CATEGORY OF CASUALTY
MT	12 Oct 1967	S. Vietnam	Hostile, Killed
OK	7 Nov 1967	S. Vietnam	Hostile, Killed
CA	7 May 1970	S. Vietnam	Non-Hostile, Died - Other
AR	2 Apr 1968	S. Vietnam	Hostile, Killed
CA	3 Jan 1968	S. Vietnam	Hostile, Died - Missing
SD	10 Nov 1968	S. Vietnam	Non-Hostile, Died - Other
SD	24 Apr 1968	S. Vietnam	Hostile, Killed
OK	9 Jun 1969	S. Vietnam	Non-Hostile, Died - Ill/Injury
SD	27 Oct 1966	S. Vietnam	Non-Hostile, Died - Other
CA	19 Jun 1971	S. Vietnam	Hostile, Killed
IA	20 Dec 1967	S. Vietnam	Hostile, Died - Wounds
TX	11 Sep 1969	S. Vietnam	Non-Hostile, Died - Other
AZ	15 Mar 1970	S. Vietnam	Hostile, Killed
CA	23 Jan 1969	S. Vietnam	Hostile, Killed
CA	21 Mar 1969	S. Vietnam	Hostile, Killed
SD	13 Jul 1971	S. Vietnam	Hostile, Killed
AZ	29 Jun 1968	S. Vietnam	Hostile, Died - Wounds
NV	7 Apr 1969	S. Vietnam	Hostile, Killed
PA	28 Aug 1969	S. Vietnam	Hostile, Killed
OK	10 Jan 1971	S. Vietnam	Hostile, Killed
MO	23 Apr 1967	S. Vietnam	Non-Hostile, Died - Missing
ME	15 Jun 1966	S. Vietnam	Hostile, Killed
NM	17 Jun 1966	S. Vietnam	Hostile, Killed
SC	24 Feb 1969	S. Vietnam	Hostile, Killed
CA	11 Jan 1968	Laos	Hostile, Killed- Missing BNR
AZ	4 Jul 1970	S. Vietnam	Non-Hostile, Died - Other
WA	25 Apr 1970	S. Vietnam	Hostile, Died - Missing
MI	5 Sep 1970	S. Vietnam	Non-Hostile, Died - Other
NY	11 Oct 1967	S. Vietnam	Hostile, Killed

NAME	RANK	BRANCH	HOME OF RECORD
Snyder, Roy Jasper	CPL	Army	Ft. Washakie
Sota, Bravie	SGT	Army	Somerton
Spider, Alvin Richard	PFC	Army	Ft. Thompson
Stands, Daniel Gilbert, Jr.	PFC	Army	Phoenix
Starkey, Henry Morgan	PFC	Army	Auburn
Sterling, John Charles	CPL	Army	Concord
Sutton, Larry Ivan	SP4	Army	Danbury
Tafoya, Frank	PFC	Army	Jemez Pueblo
Tarbell, Clifford Lawrence	SP4	Army	Bombay
Tarbell, William M.	PVT	Army	Syracuse
Taylor, Ernest Vernon	PFC	Marines	Dallas
Teeth, Austin	PFC	Marines	Lame Deer
Thompson, Otha Theander	CPL	Marines	Fort Worth
Thompson, Turner L., Jr.	CPL	Army	Talihina
Toledo, Thomas Ambrose	SP4	Army	Jemez Pueblo
Tosa, Antonio Tony	PVT	Army	Jemez Pueblo
Tousey, Gearwin Phillip	PFC	Army	Green Bay
Tsosie, Albert	LCPL	Marines	Chinle
Tsosie, Lee Dino	CPL	Army	Cross Canyon
Two Crow, Blair William	PFC	Army	Kyle
Twoeagle, Gabriel Lawrence	PVT	Army	Parmelee
Tyler, Edward	PFC	Army	Oklahoma City
Vetter, Ernest, Jr.	PFC	Army	Oklahoma City
Walsh, Truman J.	SP4	Army	Dodson
White Mause, Joseph Lewis	PFC	Army	Ft. Thompson
Williams, James Alec	LCPL	Marines	Bishop
Willis, Harold Eugene	PFC	Army	Bishop
Wilson, Adam	WO	Army	San Diego
Wilson, Juan Jay	LCPL	Marines	Thoreau

STATE	DATE OF CASUALTY	COUNTRY OF CASUALTY	CATEGORY OF CASUALTY
WY	25 May 1970	Cambodia	Hostile, Killed
AZ	5 Sep 1967	S. Vietnam	Hostile, Killed
SD	18 May 1967	S. Vietnam	Hostile, Killed
AZ	18 Mar 1966	S. Vietnam	Hostile, Killed
CA	14 Feb 1966	S. Vietnam	Hostile, Killed
CA	5 Sep 1969	S. Vietnam	Hostile, Died - Wounds
WI	23 Jul 1967	S. Vietnam	Hostile, Killed
NM	15 May 1967	S. Vietnam	Hostile, Died – Wounds
NY	11 Apr 1970	S. Vietnam	Hostile, Killed
NY	26 Feb 1966	S. Vietnam	Hostile, Killed
TX	5 Feb 1968	S. Vietnam	Hostile, Killed
MT	28 Apr 1969	S. Vietnam	Non-Hostile, Died - Other
TX	24 Aug 1965	S. Vietnam	Non-Hostile, Died - Other
OK	19 Jul 1966	S. Vietnam	Hostile, Died - Missing
NM	6 Mar 1971	S. Vietnam	Hostile, Killed
NM	17 Aug 1971	S. Vietnam	Non-Hostile, Died - Other
WI	25 Feb 1968	S. Vietnam	Hostile, Killed
AZ	10 Jul 1970	S. Vietnam	Hostile, Killed
AZ	25 Jul 1968	S. Vietnam	Non-Hostile, Died - Missing
SD	4 Dec 1968	S. Vietnam	Hostile, Died - Wounds
SD	18 Apr 1971	S. Vietnam	Non-Hostile, Died - Other
OK	9 May 1968	S. Vietnam	Hostile, Killed
OK	18 Apr 1968	S. Vietnam	Hostile, Killed
MT	25 Feb 1969	S. Vietnam	Hostile, Killed
SD	8 Apr 1971	S. Vietnam	Non-Hostile, Died - Other
CA	1 Jul 1968	S. Vietnam	Hostile, Killed
CA	25 Jan 1966	S. Vietnam	Non-Hostile, Died - Missing
CA	15 Nov 1969	S. Vietnam	Hostile, Killed
NM	14 Feb 1969	S. Vietnam	Hostile, Killed

NAME	RANK	BRANCH	HOME OF RECORD
Winkempleck, George Harold	PFC	Army	Porterville
Wolfe, Mathew	PFC	Army	Macy
Yazzie, Dan	SP4	Army	Continental Divide
Yazzie, Jones Lee	LCPL	Marines	Tohatchi
Yazzie, Leonard Lee	PFC	Marines	Pinon
Yazzie, Raymond	CPL	Marines	Church Rock
Yellow Elk, Carlos Nichola	PFC	Army	Milesville
Youngbear, Richard Clive	SGT	Army	Tama
Zeigler, Thomas	SP4	Army	Ft. Thompson

(TOTAL OF 235 PERSONS)

- Of the 58,013 persons in the combat area casualty file there are 216 for whom race was not reported.
- For persons who died while missing, the date is the date died or declared dead, not the date declared missing.
- BNR indicates that the body has not been recovered.

For a complete listing, see United States National Archives and Records Administration, "State-Level Casualty Lists for the Vietnam Conflict, Sorted Alphabetically by Last Name," *NARA Research Room*, <www.archives.gov/research_room/research_topics/vietnam_war_casualty_lists/state_level_index_alphabetical.html>, (August 23, 2002).

STATE	DATE OF CASUALTY	COUNTRY OF CASUALTY	CATEGORY OF CASUALTY
CA	10 Oct 1967	S. Vietnam	Hostile, Died - Missing
NE	1 Feb 1968	S. Vietnam	Hostile, Killed
NM	15 May 1969	S. Vietnam	Non-Hostile, Died - Other
NM	4 Aug 1968	S. Vietnam	Hostile, Killed
AZ	28 May 1968	S. Vietnam	Hostile, Killed
NM	26 Feb 1969	S. Vietnam	Hostile, Killed
SD	29 Aug 1968	S. Vietnam	Hostile, Killed
IA	3 Feb 1966	S. Vietnam	Hostile, Killed
SD	8 Apr 1971	S. Vietnam	Hostile, Killed

OUR NATION H

COURAGE SACR

DEVOTION TO

COUNTRY OF IT

VETERANS.

NORS THE

FICE AND

UTY AND

VIETNAM